Get stuch In

Simma

I would like to dedicate this book to
Michel Roux O.B.E.

Michel Roux was not only one of the world's
great chefs but a man with a big heart. He
supported many organisations, including the
Beyond Food Foundation. Michel passed away
this year. He is sadly missed by the whole
hospitality industry and, in particular, the many
chefs he inspired through his cooking.

Simon Boyle

Serves Many

I can dig and plant and pull and pick

And wash and peel and chop.

You can slice and dice and boil and blanch

And mind to stir the pot.

He can oil, salt and season

And sit the pan upon the heat.

She can bake and toast and braise and roast

And baste and turn the meat.

But when we set the table

Fetch an extra seat

For not everyone can cook

But everyone must eat.

by David Baksh

Foreword by Michel Roux Jr

Beyond Food and Brigade provide a robust yet inspiring set of programmes for those more vulnerable than most of us.

My experience of Beyond Food's Feast with purpose was meeting Simon a few years ago at Le Gavroche. At the time, I had no idea of the amazing work of the Beyond Food Foundation, but we went on to work together on a monthly dining event and I was happy to put together a typically French menu for this.

I spent the day in the kitchen at Brigade on Tooley Street alongside Simon and his apprentices. We cooked for 90 socially hungry customers. The apprentices were completely focused on preparing my dishes the way I wanted them to look and taste. It was a really enjoyable and enlightening experience for me. So enjoyable in fact, that I encouraged my daughter Emily to host her own Feast with purpose a few months later. I've been amazed and impressed by how those who have experienced homelessness have gone on to become professional chefs.

During this time of Covid-19 taking the idea of Feast for Purpose and transforming it into a recipe book with ideas from such a wide range of chefs is brilliant and inspirational. I think Simon and the Beyond Food team take on an important but challenging responsibility to help support our hospitality industry at this difficult time. So, it's only right that we chefs help Simon and Beyond Food in their campaign.

I am also proud to see that Simon has dedicated this book to my uncle and grand chef, Michel Roux, who very sadly left us this year. I know that Michel inspired Simon in his earlier years as a chef and then much later in his charitable work.

I hope the collection of Chefs recipes inspires its readers to carry on cooking.

Simon Boyle

"I am a chef first and foremost. But I have taken my passion for food and used it in the most impactful way that I feel I can. I believe that food can be transformative in people's lives - not just for diners in our restaurants and the corporate world at large, but also for the vulnerable, hungry and socially excluded."

It's why I always prefer to take the route that, as I see it, will make the most difference. I believe that we need to learn and act every day to make a fairer society, that some of the world's biggest issues are simplified if we just get up in the morning and see the day as an open door.

I am so proud of our work at Beyond Food Foundation and our social enterprise restaurant Brigade, near London Bridge. My team are awesome, and the collaborators, chefs and donors behind this book are an extension of our family - all pulling together to support those that need it most.

That's really where 'Feast with Purpose' came from. Our monthly supper clubs at Brigade Bar + Kitchen are attended by some 80 people each month. We often chew on life's big issues. While I host and cook, I invite guest chefs and friends to bring their food and stories to inspire our apprentices and diners. It has become an extraordinary event with charitable intent and includes some amazing and inspiring food. It becomes a feast with a purpose.

Previously we've been privileged to work with the likes of Chris King (The Langham), Michel Roux Jr (Le Gavroche), Nigel Haworth (Northcote Manor), Lesley Waters (Lesley Waters Cookery School) and Ping Coombes ('Masterchef' winner of 2014).

As with those supper clubs, all proceeds from this book will go towards the funding of our training programmes at Beyond Food Foundation - and in particular our desire to help those in the hospitality industry adversely affected by COVID-19.

How this Book Came About

Pre-COVID-19, Beyond Food Foundation's priority was to use the hospitality industry to help homeless people. Now I started to think that, post COVID-19, Beyond Food needed to help the hospitality industry prevent its workforces from becoming homeless. We gratefully received a grant from the WSH Foundation. I asked if we could use this grant in order to produce a valuable reward for a crowd funding project.

Then came a conversation with Peter Marshall, publisher of Yes Chef! Magazine, who had commissioned an article about my work at Beyond Food during the pandemic. Peter was thinking about publishing a book to inspire chefs in the industry at this difficult time. Very quickly we collaborated and started to work on this book, 'Feast with Purpose'.

"I am very pleased," said Peter "to have worked with Simon to publish this recipe book. The amazing support from all the chefs has been humbling, especially at a time when many chefs are facing a very unknown future as we all grapple with the pandemic."

"Personally I feel very proud to support The Beyond Food Foundation and expect that all the proceeds from Feast for Purpose will help a lot of chefs struggling through the effects of coronavirus."

It was Shakespeare who said that "adversity brings out the best in man."

It is certainly words that could have been written about Simon Boyle, who seems to rise to any challenge and combines his considerable skill as a chef with an equal talent to care for others.

As the man behind Beyond Food, a London-based social enterprise he set up to help the vulnerable, the homeless and those just down-on-their-luck get a chance in life, it's not surprising that he was one of the first to rally when Covid-19 struck.

He immediately set up a support line, appealing to anyone with skills as a mental health counsellor to offer their help, asking people to volunteer to talk to the lonely and vulnerable at what has become the biggest challenge in everyone's life.

Amidst all of the doom and gloom however Simon has cause to feel very proud – thanks to some of his former apprentices who were among the first to contact him.

"Two of the people that have been through the Beyond Food Foundation got in touch to see what they could do," he revealed. "These were two guys who had really hard lives, they'd been to prison both through circumstances not of their own making and came to us and learned to become really good cooks.

"They managed to get great jobs and have done exactly what we set out to do – break the cycle of homelessness and get a chance in life.

"They had both been put on furlough so immediately they got in touch with me to see how they could help other people."

The coronavirus situation saw Simon spring into action almost immediately – initially using the restaurant to feed vulnerable people, creating around 3500 meals in just a matter of days.

When it became apparent for the need to socially distance Simon looked at other ways to help – including using his vast array of contacts to ensure that any unused food went to charities and organisations supporting the vulnerable.

Doing something practical to help seems to be a way of life for Simon, who headed out to Sri LAnka in the aftermath of the tsunami in 2004 to help feed the thousands of displaced people who were victims of this terrible natural disaster.

Prior to that Simon's career had seen him work everywhere from The Savoy to luxury cruise ships, but the experience of being part of the humanitarian efforts in Asia was the catalyst for a change.

He set up Beyond Food and his social enterprise restaurant,

"Two of the people that have been through the Beyond Food Foundation got in touch to see what they could do"

Brigade, with the vision of helping who he calls "the unknown vulnerable" to get a chance in life.

"There are so many people who are suffering from mental health issues, financial hardship and homelessness who just need some support," he said.

"When I went to Sri Lanka it made me realise the power of food and how I could use it as a catalyst for change.

"I went out there and came back ten weeks later a changed man, It made me think about what I was doing and that perhaps I could use my experience to make a difference."

The concept of Beyond Food on paper is a simple one – giving vulnerable people and the homeless – the opportunity to learn real skills which can help them get work and change their lives. In reality however it takes someone with a huge amount of tenacity, perseverance and sheer bloodymindedness to make it

happen – and that's what Simon did.

He secured a huge amount of funding to run programme at Brigade, which although currently closed, will undoubtedly open again when the Covid-19 crisis is over.

He has won a mind-boggling amount of awards and is now much in demand with companies wanting to build their social agenda, but his ambitions for Beyond Food still continue to grow.

Coronavirus has also put – temporarily – on hold plans to launch Me and You, a scheme to help prevent youth homelessness and to look after "those for whom education is not a fit and who have fallen through the cracks."

This piece started with a quote, so let's end with one – Simon Boyle is a living example of the fact that "not all superheroes wear capes."

Peter and I have worked night and day to get our chef network to contribute to the book by donating a recipe. Getting hold of chefs at this time was difficult enough, then asking them to supply a recipe with quality images was a further challenge. Some chose to take a picture from home during lockdown and some sent a recipe that was already part of their profile at their place of work. Josh Simms has been editing at speed.

Whatever and however, we have put this book together in less than a month, and with it starring no less than 140 chefs - some with Michelin stars and some at the start of their careers.

Funds from this Book

We have decided to create a new programme for people working in the hospitality industry - to inspire them to re-imagine their careers after the COVID-19 fallout has settled. Called Made Again, this programme will be open to anyone in the hospitality sector, no matter what their level, or what job they do, if they have been laid off or their working circumstances have become untenable due to COVID-19 business closure, restructuring of working hours, pay or their personal circumstances.

www.beyondfood.org.uk

Made Again will help raise aspirations, increase motivation, provide alternative business awareness, re-define job capabilities, readiness and provide new world-class skills development. Participants will gain greater confidence in themselves to find something that they are truly passionate about within the wide-ranging hospitality sector, which will. I believe, and despite opinions to the contrary, be robust once again, no matter how long it may take. A new culture is already being created, one with a strong sense of resolve and with good business opportunities for people with amazing attitude, a hard working ethic, and who are prepared to do something different within the sector.

Made Again will be one of our most important programmes, with an ambition of helping thousands of people get back on their feet. It will provide new skills for hospitality workers whose current jobs may never come back. There are already businesses thinking of new ways of doing things in this sector. We will be looking to partner with them to help grow a newly-inspired workforce.

Beyond Food

Over the last 10 years, we have built a successful charity for the homeless, uniquely based around hospitality and our social enterprise restaurant Brigade Bar + Kitchen.

Our mission is to inspire people who are at risk of, or who have experienced homelessness towards gaining meaningful employment. That's lived out in the reality of the proactive programmes that we run. Homelessness is a blight. The more people find themselves homeless, cut off from modern society's prosperity, the greater the need for Beyond Food and projects akin to it.

Most people are fortunate enough never to experience homelessness. But for those that do it's extremely traumatic. It's very hard to escape the toll it brings - physically and mentally. But homelessness causes a cycle of vulnerability with significant cost not just to the individual, but to their friends and family, to the taxpayer and to society at large. That understanding has fired our determination to find a way to help those unfortunate individuals get back standing on their own two feet - because we've seen how the benefits don't come just to them.

We aim to give them something real and tangible to get stuck into into, something they can commit to and grow through. In large part that's found in a sustainable role out there in the hospitality world. But we also go beyond that when needed - we have a dedicated team of supporting progression experts that counsel, coach, mentor, challenge and cajole, who know how important it is to sometimes assist in separating participants from the self-defeating behaviours and chemical crutches that hold them back. It's an arm around the shoulder - with the occasional poke in the ribs...

All of our team build relationships with participants at each stage of the programme - it means we can really support people during the tough times. Participants often come back informally after leaving, perhaps to ask for a little extra help, perhaps to volunteer to help the new intake.

Our outreach programmes have extended to hostels, job centres, prisons, housing associations and charity partners.

We have now supported over 3,500 people. We've reached yet more people through interactive workshops. We've trained over 1200 people with a range of professional workshops that provide the vital skills needed to get and keep a meaningful job. And we've employed 134 apprentices ourselves, each receiving a two-year, full-time hospitality service or production chef apprenticeship. Year one equips them with the skills and work experience; year two sees them in a full-time position a world-class employer in the hospitality sector. Having that level of security is typically life-changing for them.

Our Response to Covid-19

Beyond Food's response to Covid-19 has made me truly proud. In March 2020, when we started to hear about the virus, it soon became apparent that restaurants would close and some never reopen. As a social enterprise we knew we needed to play a different role in our community.

We decided to close earlier than others in order to utilise our food, our staff and our know-how in order to feed some of our beneficiary organisations. This moved to utilising other hospitality businesses' lockdown food waste - companies such as BaxterStorey and Searcys. We prepared 3500 meals in five days. Then we turned to manufacturers the likes of Unilever to help them distribute their food stock. In all we helped move 12,500 meals over the first fortnight of lockdown.

Soon after we decided to social distance ourselves and create the Beyond Food Reachout support line to connect isolating and vulnerable people. We enlisted the help of volunteers, including qualified professionals in their field, to build our Support Service, and we are noW helping over 100 people every day to overcome the impact that COVID-19 is having on them.

In addition, we continue to support all of our beneficiaries - our apprentices, for example, are all receiving regular calls, food boxes and financial hardship grants as required.

It's been down to the generosity of many donors and grant providers that we have been able to support so many vulnerable people. We are eternally grateful to all the individuals and organisations that support our work.

In April, during the peak, we could envisage the effects on the economy and in particular the hospitality industry. We could see that people were going to at best lose some valuable income and at worst their jobs, livelihoods and their homes.So, we partnered with Shout to set up as 24/7 text crisis support line.

And then came along the idea of this book. How can we continue to inspire people about our work and our Covid-19 response, create awareness of the potential for a 'hospitality homelessness' and, of course, of our support services - all while continuing to raise vital funds so we can keep on reaching out?

I contacted some of my friends - ones who just happen to be inspirational chefs. They share our need to support the hospitality sector's people at this time more than ever. And they've supplied the fantastic recipes found inside these covers. A big thanks to them.

All funds from this book will help go towards this support service and hopefully in preventing hospitality workers from joining the downward spiral of homelessness. So thanks too to those people who have given us their money, in order to help us help others.

You are amazing and we are very grateful.

Good Food Doing Good

Beyond Food has been working alongside Brigade Bar + Kitchen for eight years now. It's at the coal face of the industry open to hard work and talent - you can start from the bottom and reach the very top with just the right attitude, working ethic and sometimes minimal qualifications. Our amazing staff not only have a desire to cook and serve outstanding food but also to help bring on vulnerable people in a working environment.

A unique collaboration with PwC, BaxterStorey and the Beyond food Foundation. In 2018 our space was completely refurbished. During that time we refocussed our business around buying 80% of our produce directly from farmers, fishermen and food producers, and, where possible, also supporting other social enterprises.All of our profits from Brigade go into training our apprentices. By enjoying yourself at Brigade you're helping to put into full-time employment many fantastic people who have faced the kind of challenges most of us, thankfully, never will.

STATE OF THE ART

Beyond Food is charity which works on two fronts – to help the hospitality industry and to support those dealing with homelessness. It has been supported by PwC and BaxterStorey for many years and together these three organisations have made a great difference. Throughout the Covid-19 pandemic we have seen people really pull out all the stops to highlight others and we would particularly like to help one project which has helped feed our NHS staff during this crisis. We all know how they went completely above and beyond the call of duty often putting their lives at risk.

Andy Aston is a chef with BaxterStorey and a member of the recently formed London Food Team, Andy's role sees him supporting the London teams and clients with individual and specific bespoke projects.

Food plays a big part in Andy's role, as does the wellbeing of his teams and through community workshops they deliver various health and food experiences that create awareness of a variety of wellness topics. They also serve to bring the teams closer together to create shared experiences that help build individual confidence and inspire future collaboration and openness.

> **Throughout this time the hospitality industry has reacted and collaborated in supporting the communities around them and our brilliant NHS frontline teams.**
>
> Andy Aston, BaxterStorey

NHS -2020

In the weeks during the COVID-19 lockdown, Andy supported Kingston Hospital with meal kits which created vegan takeaway dishes, all cooked from his own kitchen at home. This project has kept Andy busy and mentally focussed, and he feels blessed to have been able to play a small part in supporting our brilliant NHS during these times. None of this would have been possible without donated ingredients and products that he received from a number of BaxterStorey's fantastic producers, they have been incredible, and to date the London Food Team have delivered more than 11,500 meals to hospitals in Surrey, Essex & London.

Throughout this time the hospitality industry has reacted and collaborated in supporting the communities around them and our brilliant NHS frontline teams. It has also continued to cook in our care homes. It's a community spirited industry and it will now need our help as the after effects of the pandemic start to hit.

Hospitality is a world, a community, a team and a family
We can help people that have lost the thread of life, a
job, pay, confidence and their dignity.
Hospitality is an incredible industry. From the bottom
you can reach the top. You just need the right attitude
and inspiration from others.

Simon Boyle

Beatrice Sharp

Before joining the apprenticeship at Brigade & Beyond Food, I had been out of work for over five years. I suffered from severe anxiety and depression, isolated from family and friends and felt completely alone. Through the completion of my apprenticeship at Brigade I am now in full time employment as a Commis Chef.

Along with this, I now have the support and the tools I need to deal with and manage my mental health. They helped me to find myself again, be strong again and be confident again, when I thought it was too late. Now I have a stable and loving home, with my family and friends back in my life supporting me.

This is all due to the amazing work and support from everyone at Beyond Food who have helped me get my life and family back.

I will be forever grateful, thank you! Xx

Chorizo empanadillas

Stuff you'll need

375g ready made puff pastry - thawed if frozen
2 tablespoons vegetable oil
1 white onion, finely-chopped
1 pepper, finely-chopped
2 garlic cloves, finely-chopped
225g cooking chorizo, outer casing removed and finely-chopped
4 tablespoons tomato purée
2 teaspoons sugar
½ teaspoon salt
½ cup of boiling water (approx.)
1 egg beaten for glazing
2 tablespoons plain flour for dusting
Smoked paprika for dusting

Get stuck in

Heat the oil in a frying pan over a medium heat.
Add the onion, pepper and chorizo and fry, stirring regularly until soft and the chorizo is sealed and a slightly darker colour.
This should take around 7-8 minutes.
Add the garlic and stir this through for no longer than a minute until aromatic.
Add the tomato purée, sugar and salt along with a generous splash of boiling water.
Simmer on a low heat until the filling has a rich and thick consistency.
Set aside to cool. Pre-heat the oven to 200°C.
Line a baking tray with greaseproof paper.
On a lightly-floured surface thinly roll out the puff pastry.
Using a plain round cutter cut the pastry into circles.
Place about 1 ½ teaspoons of the filling in the

centre of the pastry circles.

Dampen the edges of the pastry with a little bit of water and fold them in half so that the filling is completely covered and the edges meet.

Seal the edges gently with your fingers and then with the end of a fork press against the edges to seal them and create a decorative finish. With the tip of a sharp knife, make two small slits in the top of the pastry to allow the steam to be released when cooking.

Place the finished empanadillas onto the greaseproof lined baking tray and brush lightly with the beaten egg.

Bake for 12 - 15 minutes until the pastry is golden brown

and has puffed up.

Finally, once out of the oven, place the finished empanadillas

on a cooling rack and dust lightly with the paprika.

Serve with a salsa made from chopped spring onion, tomato,

garlic and seasoning.

Enjoyed either whilst still warm or once they have cooled down.

Ben joined the Army in 1995, working his way up through his local infantry battalion (Kings Own Royal Border Regiment), doing various deployments to the Former Republic of Yugoslavia, before transferring to the Royal Army Medical Corps as a combat medic.

His role primarily involved "dealing with the worst trauma that war can bring", as he puts it. "I found myself in many psychologically and physically difficult moments."
He was awarded a force commander's commendation for rescuing a civilian with life changing injuries from a mine field. But it was something much smaller that would prove more problematic for him.

Fast forward to 2008, Ben was bitten by a tick in Afghanistan, which led to Lyme's Disease, at the time so prevalent in the region that it was labelled Helmand Fever. "It destroyed my body and in time my mental health," says Ben. "But in time I met the Beyond Food team and was accepted onto the apprenticeship scheme. I am not going to lie, it was tough leaving hospital and doing this course."

But since qualifying he has worked at the Conduit Club, spent some time in France and Norway, worked with Simon Boyle on client events and, more recently, with Supporting Wounded Veterans in devising and delivering a 'resilience' training package.

"Change is inevitable," Ben tells himself. "Be mindful and kind to yourself."

Stuff you'll need

4 rashers home cured streak bacon
2 slices Haighs famous Doreen's Black Pudding
4 brown-cap portabello mushrooms
12-16 plum tomatoes from the vine, room temperature
6 teaspoon olive oil
2 slices sourdough bread
2 Philip Warren Old Cornish Sausages, rubbed with sage and parsley
2 free-range, rich eggs, room temperature
15g butter
Bubble and squeak, cold crushed boiled potatoes, butter, onion, cabbage

Get stuck in

Lay the bacon, black pudding, mushrooms and tomatoes onto a tray. Brush the tops of the mushrooms with 3 teaspoon of the oil and both sides of the bread with the remaining oil. Set aside. Heat the grill to very hot. Lay the sausages on a small foil-lined tray (best not to prick good-quality sausages or they may lose moisture). Grill for about 10 mins until cooked, turning occasionally.

In a hot frying pan add the butter and panfry the bubble and squeak until golden on both sides.

Meanwhile heat a griddle pan to very hot. Place the tomatoes, bacon, black pudding and mushrooms under the grill for 3-4 mins without turning. At the same time, lay the bread on the griddle pan, cook until crisp, about 1 min each side. Drain everything on kitchen paper.

In a small non-stick pan heat the oil but not hot enough to fry. Crack the egg onto a small plate or saucer (don't crack it straight into the pan in case some shell ends up in there as well). Slide it off the saucer into the pan. You want to poach for 3 minutes in the oil not necessarily fry. Check the white is set, season with salt and pepper.

Arrange on a plate, serve with a big mug of tea and fresh orange juice

23

Amani Garcea

Sticky wings, with a pickle peach dipping sauce, steamed plantain arancini

I trained at Brigade as an apprentice for a year and it was exciting, challenging and helped me to rebuild my life.

I've always been passionate about food but never considered training as a chef. I was previously self-employed as a photographer but juggling work as a single mum was not easy. I had no support network; I was struggling financially and with my mental health. I had to take a step back from work, to focus on myself and sought professional help. My support worker recommended Beyond Food and it felt like a stroke of luck.

Starting at square one was not easy, but I wanted to rebuild my life and career, and the hard work has been absolutely worthwhile. I now have a new job placement in a major international company, cooking for the senior team, alongside the Head Chef.

Brigade was an inspiring place to be and I feel like I'm now in a position again to harness my creative energy and my new culinary skills. I've created a food vlog and I am developing my cooking style. I'm doing photography again and I want to build a business.

One step at a time but I'll get there.

Stuff you'll need

12–16 chicken wings
2 lemons (quartered)
1 tablespoon browning sauce
1 tablespoon all-purpose seasoning
2 teaspoons Japanese 7 spice
1 teaspoon fresh minced ginger
1 teaspoon ground cinnamon
2 teaspoons crushed garlic
1 teaspoon chili flakes
1 teapsoon mixed dried herbs
1 teaspoon Himalayan fine salt
1 teapsoon cracked black pepper
Sesame and olive oils for frying the chicken
Steamed plantain arancini
350g risotto rice
½ teaspoon mixed dried herbs
½ teaspoon Japanese seven spice (optional)
30g butter
Salt and pepper to taste
1 ripe yellow plantain, diced cm
2 eggs beaten
Bread crumbs
Pickle peach sauce
1 can of tinned peaches, syrup drained
150ml tomato ketchup
100ml of white vinegar
3 tablespoons clear honey
2 tablespoons mild/ Dijon mustard
2 tablespoons mayonnaise
1 tablespoon chili powder
½ tablespoon chili flakes

Get stuck in

When you are ready to cook the chicken, pre-heat the oven to 200°C Lightly shallow fry the chicken wings in a little sesame oil and olive oil over high heat, only to brown. Cook each side until brown, approx. 3 minutes. Remove and drain on kitchen paper.

Meanwhile, fry the risotto rice with the butter, herbs, salt and pepper. Stir in 750ml water, 250ml at a time, stirring well between each addition. Add more water if needed while cooking to ensure it doesn't dry out. Cook for 20 mins, until the rice is cooked.

Meanwhile, make the pickle peach sauce. Put all of the sauce ingredients into a blender and mix until creamy and smooth. Simmer over a medium heat, stirring often, until it starts to bubble, approx. 10 minutes.

Place the browned wings on a baking tray and coat them in the peach sauce. Bake in the oven for 10 minutes until they're a rich deep brown colour and sticky in texture.

Steam your diced plantain until slightly opaque. Let it cool down, and then mix into the cooked risotto rice.

Have the beaten eggs ready in a bowl, and the breadcrumbs on a plate. Roll the rice mix into even, bite size balls. Roll in the beaten eggs, and cover them evenly with breadcrumbs.

Deep or shallow fry the arancini until golden. If you are shallow frying, ensure you turn regularly so they are the same in colour all over.

To serve, plate the chicken, with the salad on the side.

Pour the sauce into dipping ramekins and serve.

Carlos Barbosa

Training to become a chef has changed the narrative for me – it has given me hope, focus and the support to help me address my problems.

I was caught up in drug addiction and heavy drinking.

Life was unbearable and, at times, unimaginable. I had no vision, no goals and nothing to look forward to, but a chance encounter with Simon Boyle changed everything.

Whilst working as a kitchen porter at an event at Brigade, Simon approached me and asked if I wanted to be a chef. I've never looked back.

My focus shifted from drugs and alcohol, to learning new skills, making new friends, and getting a new perspective on life. I could build a better relationship with my wife and son.

I was supported unconditionally by the team at Brigade and I can't thank them enough. This process has taught me so much, and to be able to say that I'm a qualified chef, with a full-time job, is something I am genuinely proud of.

Stuff you'll need

500g salted cod (bacalhau),
soaked in water for 24 hours
6 evenly-sized potatoes, peeled
100ml extra virgin olive oil
2 onions, thinly-sliced
3 cloves of garlic, crushed
200ml double cream
200ml milk
30g butter
½ teaspoon grated nutmeg
White cheese
100g of breadcrumbs
Black pepper
Sea salt
Chopped parsley

Get stuck in

Preheat the oven to 200°C
Cook the soaked cod for 10 minutes.
If it flakes easily it is ready.
Break the cod into pieces and remove the skin
and bones.
Meanwhile, cook the potatoes in salted water for
15 minutes until just cooked.
They will cook a little more in the oven.
Meanwhile, in a frying pan cook the onion in 50g
of the olive oil over medium high heat for 10
minutes.
Add the garlic.
Stir the onion and garlic into the cod,
and season well.
Stir in the milk, cream, butter and nutmeg
and cook to thicken the sauce. It should hold
together when spooned.
Remove from heat.
Strain the potatoes and cut into cubes.
Add into the cod mixture and stir well.
Spoon into a baking dish or individual baking
dishes. Mix the remaining olive oil with the
breadcrumbs, salt, pepper and chopped parsley
scatter on top and bake for 20 minutes in the
pre-heated oven, until the top is browned.
Serve piping hot.

Beyond Food Foundation at Brigade Bar + kitchen

27

Jamila Hussain

I left my home country of Eritrea when I was 15 years old, travelling via Sudan to Saudi Arabia to escape war and search for a better life. Working as an in-house domestic worker, I came to the UK in 2009 with a family educating their children in London. Yet despite working 24/7, I lost my job when they moved back to Saudi Arabia and was left in the UK alone and with nothing, unable even to speak the language. Even now, when I think about that time, it's difficult not to become emotional.

After becoming homeless, I found refuge in a hostel in Marylebone and began volunteering in relief kitchens. I'd always loved cooking and, as someone who had spent a lot of time working in kitchens, I knew this was something I could do well.

That's when I knew what I wanted to do with my life! My key worker introduced me to Beyond Food and the rest is history.

The year at Brigade was extremely hard work but I'm so happy to have completed it. I'm now a qualified chef working in the kitchen at a major international law firm with an honest, friendly and supportive team. I feel very lucky.

Serves 4

Stuff you'll need

Teff injara
200g teff flour
450ml water
1/2 teaspoon baking powder
50g Coconut oil
Salt

Ajibo
1 litre buttermilk

Zigne
50ml olive oil
1 onion, chopped
1 teaspoon chilli powder, or more to taste
4 fresh tomatoes, chopped
3 garlic cloves, chopped
5cm fresh ginger, grated
Pinch ground nutmeg
400g fresh boneless chicken, diced 5 cm
Seasoning
4 soft boiled eggs

Salad
Cucumber
4 tomatoes, halved
2 tbsp fresh lemon juice
2 tablespoons olive oil
Chopped fresh green chillies, to garnish

This is a traditional Eritrean dish, which we serve at parties and family gatherings.
Teff is a type of millet, and is the main grain that is used in Eritrea. It is gluten free. The injara bread is delicious, a chewy and substantial texture. The Zigne is a spicy tomato-based sauce, served with any protein that you like. I have used chicken here.
You can also add a vegetable or keep it simple.

Get stuck in

Teff injara

Mix together the flour and water, until it is smooth and well blended. Transfer to a clean bowl, cover and set aside to allow the mixture to make a "sponge".
NB The dough can be cooked straight away, it will not be as Flavoursome sour. If you prefer the full, malty sour flavour, leave it for 24 hours.

Ajibo

Put the buttermilk in a pan and simmer for 45 minutes, until it separates. Ensure that it is not boiling when it separates. Sieve the curds and whey through a sieve, and allow the ajibo to cool in the sieve. Set aside in a serving dish.

Zigne

Heat the olive oil over a medium heat in a pan and fry the onions until golden. Add the chili powder. Stir in the tomatoes. Then add the garlic and ginger. Add the ground nutmeg if using. Stir

in the chicken. Season well, and simmer for 20 minutes on a low heat.
Peel the boiled eggs, add to the stew. Simmer for a further 10 minutes.
Meanwhile, prepare the salad. Peel and dice the cucumber, and add to the tomatoes. Spoon over the lemon juice and olive oil.

For the teff injara

Mix in the baking powder. This will make the mixture go flat.
Heat up a large frying pan. Put some coconut oil on a piece of kitchen paper, and immediately wipe all over the base of the pan. Reduce the heat to medium low.
Pour on one quarter of the batter, tilting the pan as you go to get an even spread across the base. Cover the pan with a baking sheet or lid, and allow to cook for 5 minutes. Check occasionally, and if it is burning on the base, reduce the heat.
Bubbles will form on the surface, and when the surface is dry, the bread is cooked. Set aside on a piece of baking paper, to avoid the breads sticking together.
Repeat with the coconut oil, and cook the remainder of the batter, storing each one between baking paper sheets. Serve the Zigne with the Ajibo, salad, green chillies, and Injera flat bread.

Two years ago, I was homeless, now I'm a fully trained chef, with a job, and I've worked alongside some of the leading cooks in our industry.

I came to the UK from France after the death of my sister, mother and father within the space of two years. Arriving in London, I was looking for a fresh start, work and opportunity, but fell upon hard times and, with no one to turn to, ended up homeless. Some nights, if I was lucky, I might spend the night in a hostel, other nights I would sleep on the streets.

I came across Beyond Food Foundation at a demonstration at drop in centre for vulnerable and marginalised adults in Earls Court. From never having cooked before, I found myself undertaking a fully qualified, two-year apprenticeship scheme at Brigade Bar + Kitchen. Training across a number of different sections — the larder, fish, meat, vegetables, front of house — and working alongside some of the UK's best chefs (including John Campbell, Chris King and others) was such an inspiring experience. I now have a job and a home. Life is looking up!

Stuff You'll Need

2 aubergines, halved and flesh scored
80ml olive oil
4 teaspoons dried thyme
1 medium leeks, diced 1cm
1 carrot, diced 1cm
1 medium potato, diced 1cm
1 onion, sliced
2 cloves of garlic, crushed
1 chili pepper, chopped
50ml double cream
1 egg yolk
Flesh of 1 ripe avocado
Juice of fresh lemon
1 red onion, chopped
1 green chili pepper, chopped

Plating

Chili flakes
Chopped fresh parsley
Pomegranate seeds
Grilled hazelnuts, chopped
Greek yogurt
Sea salt
Black pepper

Get stuck in

First make the aubergine caviar. Pre-heat the oven to 180/200°C. Drizzle over half of the olive oil and add thyme on the top. Season.
Bake the aubergines for 30 minutes. Remove the flesh and add 2 teapsoons of dried thyme. Grill the aubergine skins, until browned.
Meanwhile, boil the leek, potato and carrot in salted water for 5 minutes. Drain.
Sauté the carrot, leek and potato, onions, garlic and chili peppers in olive oil over medium heat for 10 minutes. Mash together with the double cream, egg yolk and remaining dried thyme. Season. Set aside the purée.
For the guacamole, blend the avocado flesh with the lemon, red onion, green chili pepper in a blender. Season.

Add the aubergine caviar, and stir in the vegetable puree. Season.

Plating

Fill half of the aubergine skins and garnish with fresh parsley and chili flakes.
On a plate, swipe some Greek yogurt.
Put the half aubergine on the Greek yogurt.
Garnish the plate with pomegranate seeds, grilled hazelnuts and olive oil.

Fawzia Mirza

Aloo tikki chaat

Stuff you'll need

Aloo tikki

1kg potatoes, diced 2cm
4 spring onions, thinly-sliced
1 green chili, thinly-sliced
Pinch chili powder
1 teapsoon anardana powder

For the dipping sauce

5 heaped tablespoons gram flour
½ teaspoon ajwan seeds
½ teaspoon chilli powder

For the mint sauce

250g natural yoghurt
Handful mint leaves, finely-chopped
1 green chili, finely-chopped

For the tamarind sauce

250g dried tamarind pulp
1ltr water
1 level tablespoon of sugar

For the chaat

250g natural yoghurt
150g canned chickpeas
½ teapsoon chili powder
2 spring onions, thinly-sliced
½ tomato, finely-diced
1 green chili, finely-sliced
1 teaspoon chaat masala

To garnish

Fresh pomegranate seeds
Sev (crisp Indian noodle for chaats)
Fresh mint leaves

When I first walked through the door at Brigade, never in my wildest dreams could I have imagined what was ahead of me. Now I'm working in the kitchen at one of London's best-known hotels and I'm so grateful for the support that I received.

Before finding Beyond Food Foundation, I had been homeless and penniless, with three small children, having escaped a suppressive, and at times violent, marriage. Having moved with my husband and children to Pakistan over a decade before, my life fell apart when I decided to flee the country, and my marriage, in search for a better life back home in the UK. Yet, arriving in Manchester with nothing to my name was a wholly different challenge.

My journey saw me returning to London, struggling to find a place of my own, taking solace in alcohol and eventually finding a support group that would help me identify my passion for cooking and put me in touch with Beyond Food.

I could begin to rebuild a life for myself and my family and four years on my ties with Beyond Food remain strong. I receive calls regularly from the team and I really feel like part of a family. I've gone on to secure jobs in kitchens such as in Harrods and The Dorchester Hotel.

Get stuck in

For the aloo tiki

Boil the potatoes in salted boiling water until cooked through. Drain. When they are cool enough to handle, break up with a fork, and add the aloo tikki ingredients. Divide the mix evenly into 12-16 portions, and shape into round patties.

For the dipping sauce

In a bowl, put the gram flour, ajwain and chili powder. Season with salt. Mix and add water slowly to make into a paste, not too thick, that will nicely cover the back of a spoon.
In a wok or deep fryer, put in oil to a depth of 5cm. Heat the oil, and when it's hot, cook the patties one by one. Dip the aloo tikki patties in the dipping sauce to coat, and deep-fry until a nice golden colour. Remove with a slotted spoon,

and drain on kitchen paper.

For the mint sauce

Blend together the yoghurt, mint and green chili. Season with salt.

For the tamarind sauce

Set a pot over medium heat, and add 1l water, and the tamarind pulp. Simmer and reduce to a nice, syrupy consistency. Add the sugar, and pass through a fine sieve. This will keep in the fridge for up to six weeks.

For the chaat

Combine all of the ingredients together in a bowl.

To serve

Place aloo tikki patties on the plate, spoon over some chaat, then spoon over some mint sauce. Drizzle tamarind over and garnish with pomegranate seeds, sev and mint leaves.

When the opportunity with Beyond Food came up, I felt I had nothing to lose. This is honestly the first job or learning experience that I've actually been excited about.

I heard about Beyond Food from my probation officer. At 23 years old I found myself having served jail time and with no real career prospects. A bad experience with a kitchen porter position had left me feeling deflated about my job prospects and I was struggling to see a way forward.

In my previous life, I'd been in and out of jail, made some bad decisions and ended up being kicked out of my home as a result. The Beyond Food apprenticeship offered me the opportunity to do things I'd never done before and a chance to act upon a passion for food. I'm really grateful to Simon and the team.

In light of the Covid-19 pandemic, the apprenticeship at Brigade – currently being undertaken remotely - isn't exactly what I had in mind when I signed up, but I'm feeling grateful, positive and inspired about what lies ahead.

Jollof rice with shrimps

800ml chicken stock
2 bay leaves
500g long-grain rice, rinsed
2 tablespoons olive oil
2 ripe plantains, peeled and diced
600g large shrimp, peeled and de-veined
Small handful of coriander leaves,
roughly chopped
Sea salt and freshly ground black pepper
green salad, to serve

Get stuck in

Put the passata, tomato purée, chillies, onions, peppers, garlic, rosemary, thyme, ground coriander and paprika in a blender or food processor and blend until smooth.

Heat the olive oil in a large saucepan over a medium heat. Add the cherry tomatoes and the blended tomato sauce. Bring to the boil, then reduce the heat slightly and simmer for 5 minutes, stirring occasionally.

Add the stock, bay leaves, rice, 1½ teaspoons salt and a large pinch of black pepper. Stir to combine and bring to the boil. Reduce the heat and simmer for 10–12 minutes, stirring frequently to prevent the rice from sticking, until the rice is cooked through. Turn off the heat, cover with the lid and leave to steam for 15 minutes

Meanwhile, heat the sunflower oil in a frying pan over a medium heat. Fry the plantain and shrimp for a few minutes on each side until golden and tender.

Spoon the jollof rice onto warmed plates and add the plantain on the side. Garnish with the chopped coriander and serve with a green salad.

Nigel Adams

Stuff you'll need

Roast strawberries

1kg strawberries, ripe, hulled and halved
1 tablespoon caster sugar
1 tablespoon vanilla extract

Ice cream mixture

395g sweetened condensed milk
500ml double cream, for whipping

Brownie biscuits

165g butter, plus extra for greasing
200g dark chocolate, grated
3 free-range eggs
2 free-range egg yolks
2 teaspoons vanilla extract
165g soft light brown sugar
2 tablespoons plain flour
1 tablespoon cocoa powder
A pinch of salt
154g chocolate digestive biscuits, crushed
Icing sugar, for dusting

I'm a good person who's made some mistakes in life and paid the consequences. Beyond Food gave me a second chance.

After serving time in jail and struggling to readjust to life outside of the prison system, I was introduced to Beyond Food and given the opportunity to pursue a long-held dream of working in a kitchen.

My teenage life was turned upside down when my father was diagnosed with Parkinson's Disease. I had to leave school and act as a carer for my father and younger siblings.

Dad's death had a huge impact and I ended up homeless, taking solace in drink and embarking on a path that would ultimately lead to prison.

Coming out of the prison system was a shock, but having undertaken vocational courses whilst inside, I wanted to build a career and set my sites on hospitality. Finding long term employment with a record wasn't easy. I'm a hard worker but, until Beyond Food, it had always come to nothing.

The apprenticeship has given me so much – not just a job and a support network, but also a future.

Brigade's roasted strawberry ice cream brownie sandwich

Get stuck in

Roast strawberries

Preheat oven to 160°C

Pile strawberries on a tray. Sprinkle over sugar. Toss through, then spread strawberries out on the tray.

Roast for 45 minutes, rotating tray halfway. Remove from oven, toss strawberries, then return to oven for 15 minutes. Keep an eye on it - you don't want juices to become toffee and stick to tray.

Remove from oven, use spatula to scrape into a food processor, being sure to get all the juices and caramelised bits off the tray.

Blitz until smooth as possible (caramelised bits won't blitz smooth), scrape through a sieve into a bowl, then cool completely.

Ice cream mixture

Add condensed milk and vanilla into the strawberries. Beat well for 1½ minutes on high to aerate and combine.

Place cream in another bowl. Use electric beater to beat into stiff peaks - about 3 minutes on high.

Add a dollop of cream into the strawberry mixture. Fold through gently - don't beat in furiously. When mostly mixed through, add another dollop and mix for about 5 times.

Tip strawberry mixture into the cream bowl. Gently fold through until it's a uniform pink colour - about 15 to 20 folds max.

Pour mixture into a container with airtight lid.

Place sheet of baking paper on surface and press out air bubbles (stops icicles forming). Cover with lid, freeze 12+ hours.

Remove the ice cream from freezer, remove paper. Scoop into disc moulds, flatten with a palette knife and refreeze.

Brownie Biscuits

Pre-heat the oven to 180°C .

Grease 2 20cm square baking tins with butter, then line with baking paper with the paper overlapping the sides a little.

Melt the butter in a pan over a medium heat. When the butter has melted, remove the pan from the heat and add the grated chocolate. Leave to stand until the chocolate melts, and then stir together.

Whisk the eggs, egg yolks and vanilla together in a large bowl until the eggs begin to get light and fluffy. Add the sugar in two additions, whisking between each.

Pour it around the side of the egg mix so as not to knock out the air that has been whisked in. Keep whisking until the mixture becomes stiffer. Once the egg mixture is ready, pour the chocolate into it - again around the sides so as not to knock the air out.

Add the flour, cocoa powder, salt and a third of the biscuits and stir until fully combined, then split the mix into two and pour the mixtures into the prepared tins.

Scatter the remaining biscuits over the top, pressing them in slightly. Bake on the middle shelf of the oven for 25–30 minutes. The middle should be very so slightly gooey. Leave to cool in the tin. Cut out using the same cutters as the ice cream discs. When ready to serve, sandwich two brownie cookies around one strawberry ice cream disc. Spoon some chocolate sauce and serve with fresh strawberries.

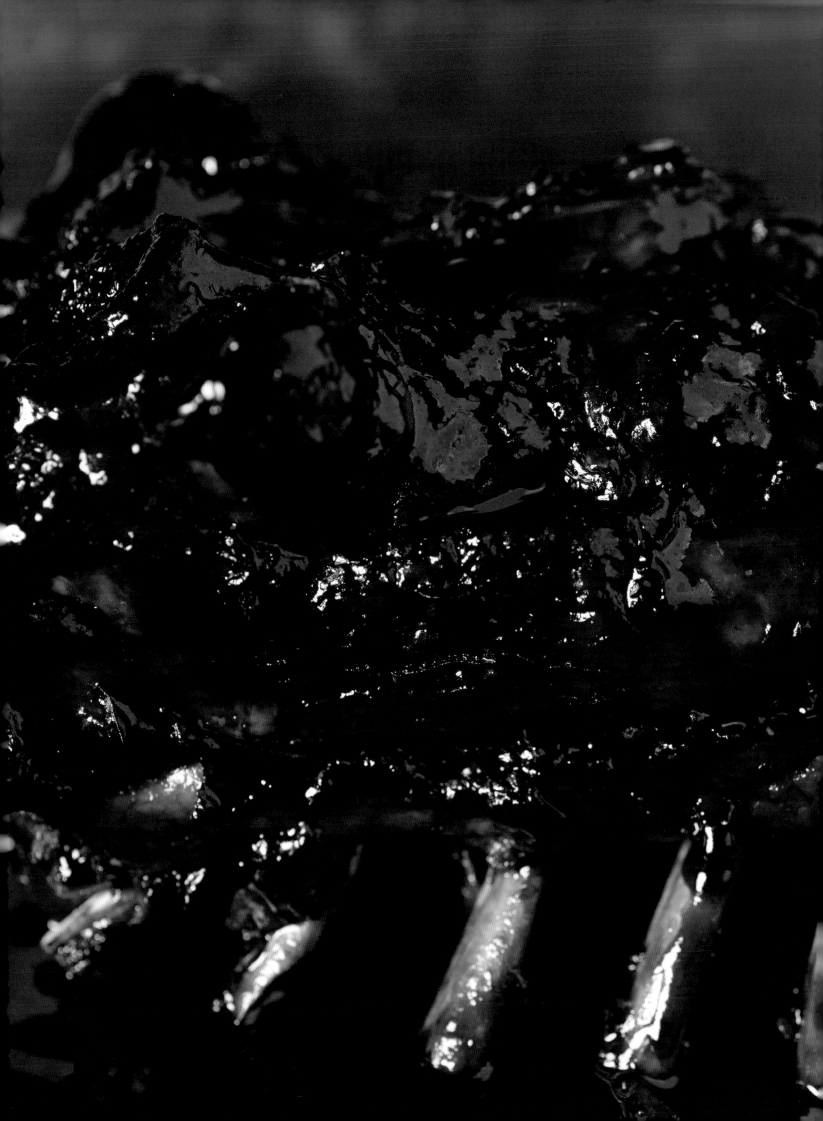

> Manage the heat, let the **meat** cook,
> and you'll get fantastic results.
>
> Guy Fieri

Meat Recipes

Adam Simmonds

Adam cut his teeth at Le Gavroche as an apprentice and then commis chef. He would follow this with positions at a number of London hotspots - The Ritz Restaurant, The Halkin, The Conservatory at The Lanesborough, Les Saveurs and L'Escargot. Leaving London, he then worked at Heathcotes in Manchester, and then for three years at Le Manoir aux Quat'Saisons. Adam's first head chef position would be at The Greenway, then at Ynyshir Hall, where he won a Michelin star in 2006, and at Danesfield House, near Marlow, winning its first Michelin star in 2010. In November 2013, after leaving Danesfield House, Adam started at Pavilion on High Street Kensington, London. He later joined the Capital Hotel in London as executive chef, leaving in the spring of 2020 to become a director of the Little and Large Pub Company.

Stuff you'll need

Foie gras

1 x 500g foie gras lobe milk, as needed
water, as needed, salt, as needed

Eel stock

47g smoked eel, 1cm diced
166g fresh eel, skinned and gutted, 1cm diced
50g olive oil
10g carrots
10g leeks
12g spring onion
1/4 clove of garlic
42g dried chickpeas, soaked
1g white peppercorns
375ml water

Compressed apples

50g granny smith, peeled, cut and diced
0.5g salt
2.5g sugar
1.5g lemon juice

Pickling liquor for turnip

100ml of white wine vinegar
100ml of water
25g sugar
1/2 teaspoon of salt
1/2 a large turnip pickling liquor

Apple purée

3 granny smith apples, cored
6g Ultralex Sugar, as needed

Smoked eel

Olive oil, as needed
18 slices of smoked eel

To serve

Raw turnip, thinly sliced and cut using a 1.5cm cutter. Sorrel leaves, as needed

Get stuck in

Foie gras

Allow the lobe to soften in cold water. Once soft devein without opening the foie gras too much. Place into a bowl of milk, water and salt and leave for 10 minutes. Drain well and cut into 80g pieces. Vac pack and cook at 80°C until the core temperatures reaches 60°C, which takes approximately 7-8 minutes. Once cooked, remove from the bag and cut into four to five pieces.

Foie gras, smoked eel, granny smith apple, turnip

hot before adding the fresh eel and fry until golden brown. In a clean pan, fry the vegetables in the olive oil starting with the carrot, leeks, spring onion and garlic. Allow them to lightly colour. Add the eel and chickpeas to the pan and mix well over the heat. Place the eel and vegetable mix into a clean pan and add the peppercorns. Cover with the water and bring to the boil. Simmer for 3 hours. Remove from the stove, pass and strain through muslin cloth. Place in the fridge to allow to set. Once set, remove the fat and place into a clean pan and reduce by half. Cool quickly over ice.

Compressed apples

Marinade the apples in the salt, sugar and lemon juice for 10 minutes.
Portion into five pieces per bag and compress.

Pickling liquor for turnip

Bring all ingredients to the boil. Chill before using.

Pickled turnip

Using a mandolin, slice the turnip thinly. Using a 3.5cm cutter, cut into discs. Add 10g of pickling liquor to 12 slices of turnip into a vac pack bag. Vac pack on full and leave for at least 12 hours.

Apple purée

Juice the apples. Place in a pan on the stove and bring the juice up to the boil quickly. Pass the juice through a muslin cloth and cool quickly over an iced bain-marie. Once cool, weigh out 100g of the juice and whisk in the Ultralex. Adjust with sugar if required.

Smoked eel

Place a pan on the stove and allow to get hot. Drizzle the olive oil into the pan and place the eel in the pan. Fry quickly on one side. Remove from the pan and drain.

To serve

Place five slices of the pickled turnip on the bottom of the plate followed by three pieces of the compressed apple.
Arrange the foie gras on the plate and add three slices of the smoked eel. Add the remaining two pieces of compressed apple and six pickled turnips. Finish with six thin slices of raw turnip.

Agostino Builas

Agostino created this fresh egg and mountain spinach tagliatelle dish especially for Courmayeur Mont Blanc. Combining delicious Alpine flavours, this is one to perfect now and use for dinner parties in the future.

Stuff you'll need

Ragu

500g Aosta Valley beef
(shoulder cuts) or equivalent beef
50g extra virgin olive oil
50g carrots
50g onions
Salt and pepper to taste
Cooking juices

Cream

200g Alpine pasture,
Fontina Dop or equivalent cheese
200ml single cream

Pasta

400g fresh egg and mountain
spinach tagliatelle
40g ground walnuts
Wild thyme sprigs

Fresh egg and mountain spinach tagliatelle

Get stuck in

Ragu

Peel and chop the onion and the carrot, then mince them with the meat.
Brown the mix in a pan with extra virgin olive oil. Baste with cooking juices
and let it simmer for approximately 2 hours.
At the end of the cooking period, season with salt and pepper to taste, keep
the ragu warm and set it aside.

Cream

Cut the Fontina cheese into pieces and add the single cream. Pour the mix
into a glass or polycarbonate container and put it in the microwave for one
minute or more depending on the power of the oven, being careful not to
bring it to a boil. Filter the cream obtained, keep it warm and set it aside.

Pasta

Put a large pan of salted water on to boil. Once
it is boiling, add the tagliatelle and cook for
approximately three minutes. Drain the pasta,
add it to the pan of ragu and mix well over high
heat.

Plating

Create a bed of sauce on each soup plate with
the Fontina cream, put delicately the tagliatelle
on it, sprinkle with the ground walnuts and
garnish with the wild thyme sprigs.

Alex Harper

Alex has worked in many celebrated establishments, including the Latymer at Pennyhill Park under Marc Wilkinson and Le Manoir aux Quat Saisons, where he rose through the ranks to junior sous chef. Texture restaurant was his first head chef role, working with Aggnar Sverrisson to achieve a Michelin star in 2010. Alex then spent a few years at The Ledbury, working closely with Brett Graham. He gained a newfound love for wild English game and took the head chef role at The Harwood Arms, the only Michelin-starred pub in London. Later, he opened Neo Bistro, with chef and friend Mark Jarvis of Anglo Restaurant. Alex won the YBF's chef award 2017 and is now executive head chef at London's Great Scotland Yard Hotel.

Makes four 125g pies

Stuff you'll need

Hot water pastry
580g T55 flour
3g salt
140g lard or butter
240ml water

Filling
400g pork shoulder (minced)
5g salt
50g black pudding
15g pistachios (coarsely chopped)
50g lardo (1cm dice)
3g thyme (picked leaves only)
4g garlic

Potato
400g pink fir apple potatoes
(peeled and halved)
6g salt
225g unsalted butter melted
100g cream

Pork pie in a hot water crust pastry

Get stuck in

Hot water pastry

Place the lard and water together in a saucepan and bring to the boil.
Add the dry ingredients.
Using a wooden spoon mix thoroughly to make a smooth dough.
Cover the dough with clingfilm and leave in the fridge for 30 mins to rest. Once rested roll out to 1/2cm thickness and cut into disks one 8cm diameter, the other 20cm, for each pie. Weigh the filling into 120g balls, cup the 20cm dough in your hand and place the meatball in the centre. Lightly brush the inside of the pastry with water. Place the small circle of pastry on top and crimp the pastry together to form a crest like a crown.

Filling

Ensure all products are always kept at below 4°C during production.
Mix everything together by hand ensuring that the seasonings are evenly distributed.
To cook the pies brush with egg yolk and milk. Let this set in the fridge for 30 mins. Brush again and set for 30 mins. Place tin foil chimneys into the centre of the pies. Bake at 200°C for 15-20 mins to a core temperature of 75°C or above.
When baking the pies place onto a hot tray and greaseproof paper to avoid a soggy bottom...

Mash potato

Place the potatoes into a pan of water, bring to the boil and turn onto a medium heat to cook for 25-30 minutes until tender.
Check potatoes are cooked, strain through a sieve.
Pass the potatoes through the mouli while gently heating the cream on the stove.
Mash the potato and butter with a whisk on the stove. Slowly add the cream. Adjust the seasonings as necessary.

Alexandros Kapsokavadi

Alexandros, Head Chef at MarBella Nido Hotel, a beautiful five-star adults-only property, nestled into the South-East corner of Corfu in Agios Ioannis Peristeron. The hotel takes its name from the Italian word for 'nest' and this is one of its signature dishes. The Greek dish originated in Corfu: Greek chicken in tomato sauce with cannelloni. This is a meal usually saved for Sundays and shared with family and friends.

Stuff you'll need

Chicken pastitsada

8g chopped garlic
250g onion
300g cooked chicken drumsticks
300g tomato jam
250g onion
200g chicken stock
4g mixed pastitsada spices
8g table salt
1g ground white pepper

Bechamel sauce

80g staka
60g flour
800g heavy cream
200g sliced onions
8g salt
60g melted butter
3g nutmeg
50g grated graviera

Tomato sauce

200g tomatoes
60g sugar
250g virgin oil
16g salt

Chicken pastitsada

Get stuck in

Chicken

Roll the chicken, keeping the skin on the outside, and transfer into vacuum bags with sunflower oil. Cook at 64°C for 12 hours and then shock in an ice bath.

Chicken pastitsada

Put all ingredients into a pan and let it glaze for 10 minutes. Turn off the heat and cut the chicken into medium sized pieces.
Take the pre-made cannelloni tubes and add 15g of pastitsada mix to each portion. Add 4g of bechamel.

Bechamel sauce

Melt the staka in a pan over a low heat and add flour and mix. Stir with a mariz until golden. Add cream gradually and whisk constantly. Then add salt and onions and continue stirring until cooked through for 25 minutes. Empty into a thermomix and mix well for five minutes. Add melted brown butter, nutmeg and cheese and continue mixing for five minutes. Strain in a bowl over ice. Once chilled empty the sauce into u squeezer.

Cannelloni

Boil the cannelloni for 40 minutes (for 4) and shock in an ice bath. Let it cool and transfer to a bowel with virgin oil. Cut at 2.5cm.

Tomato sauce

In a rondeau, saute the onions with oil and garlic until soft. Add tomatoes, salt and sugar - taste for preference and let it set.

Ben Purton

Ben has worked in the hospitality industry for over 25 years, with some of London's most exclusive establishments including The Carlton Tower, The Royal Horseguards Hotel, Selfridges, Hyatt Regency London - The Churchill, Goldman Sachs and The Royal Lancaster London. In 2018 he set up a consultancy business. He works with and mentors students from schools and colleges such as UWL, Westminster Kingsway, and Waltham Forest College. He joined Off To Work in August 2019 as culinary director.

Stuff you'll need

500g of baby plum tomatoes
A drizzle of olive oil
Sea salt and ground black pepper

Serves 3 or 5-6 as a starter

Stuff you'll need

300g of smoked back bacon
3 cloves of garlic, crushed
100g frozen peas
240g Orzo
2pt of vegetable stock
40g grated parmesan
Freshly-milled black pepper

Stuff you'll need

250g fat free cottage cheese
4 medium eggs
100g grated cheddar
2 spring onions finally chopped
150g of thin sliced smoked ham
Optional slow roast cherry tomatoes
A nice amount of seasoning

Slow roast tomatoes

Get stuck in

Cut the tomatoes in half length wise and place cut side up on
a baking tray.

Drizzle with the olive oil so that each tomato has a little on it.

Season with the salt and pepper.

Place in an oven that has been pre-heated to 200°C.

After 10 minutes, reduce the oven temperature to 70°C and leave for 50
minutes.

Remove from the oven and allow to cool.

These will keep in the fridge in an air tight container for 4-5 days.

Lisa's (my wife) orzo

Get stuck in

Cut the bacon into even sized lardons and fry off in a large pan on a high
heat in a little vegetable oil until lightly coloured.

Add the peas and the garlic and mix in well - cook out for 1-2 minutes.

Add the orzo and again mix in well.

Add 3/4 of the vegetable stock, stir in well and bring back to the boil.

Reduce the heat to a rolling boil and stir every 3-4 minutes till the orzo has
softened but still retains a little bite - use the remaining stock if needed until
the orzo is cooked. Season with black pepper to taste.

Turn off the heat and add in 3/4 of the parmesan and stir in well.

Leave to rest for 2-3 minutes, then mix again and spoon into the serving
bowl and top with the remaining parmesan.

Crustless quiche

Get stuck in

Use a 21cm wide x 3cm deep pie dish and oven set at 170°C fan.

Lightly oil the dish and line with the ham, leaving two slices aside and a
small overhang.

Mix the cottage cheese, eggs, spring onion and half of the cheddar. Mix
and season well.

Pour the mix into the ham-lined dish and press in around 12 halves of
tomato.

Shred the remaining ham slices and scatter over the top and then sprinkle
over the remaining cheese.

Fold over the ham overhang and bake in the oven for 34-40 mins or until
the mix has no wobble.

Remove and leave for five mins to firm up slightly.

Brian Turner

Brian trained at Simpson's in the Strand, The Savoy, The Beau Rivage in Lausanne and Claridge's. In 1971 he opened the kitchens of The Capital Hotel with Richard Shepherd, where they won a then rare (for the UK) Michelin star. In 1986 he opened his own restaurant, Turner's in Walton Street, Chelsea. After fifteen years of success he opened restaurants in Birmingham and Slough and in 2003 at The Millennium Hotel in Grosvenor Square, Mayfair. Turner is the president of the Royal Academy of Culinary Arts. In June 2002 Turner was awarded a CBE for his services to tourism and training in the catering industry.

Serves 4

Stuff you'll need

4 partridge
2 tablespoons rapeseed oil
50g diced carrot
50g diced onions
50g diced celery
1 bay leaf
1 sprig thyme
2 cloves garlic
1 glass dry white wine
¼ pt chicken stock
100g butter

Sauce

50g chicken liver
6 pickled onions, cut in half
12 pre-cooked chestnuts
12 good seedless white grapes
1 tablespoon sugar
100g butter
2 tablespoons chicken stock
Splash of Cognac
1 tablespoon chopped chives

Roasted partridge with grapes, chestnuts & pickled onions

Get stuck In

Trim the partridge and season well. Tie legs together.

Heat the oil and the butter in an ovenproof casserole dish, place the bird on each side to colour and take out of the casserole dish.

Add the chopped vegetables, bay leaf, thyme, garlic and fry until golden.

Lay the partridge on top and put in the oven 200°C roast for 8-10 minutes until the juices run clear. Once cooked, remove from the oven and put to one side. Keep it warm.

Sauce

Using the casserole dish with the vegetables, add livers to casserole and sauté.

Add stock and wine and reduce. Sieve all the contents through a fine sieve. Pour the cooking liquor into a clean casserole dish and whisk in 50g of the butter. Season.

Put pan on heat and melt 50g butter. Add pickled onions and cook until golden.

Sprinkle with sugar and caramelize. Add chicken stock and cognac and gently cook.

When cooked, add chestnuts and grapes and warm through.

Pour sauce into the pan with the chestnuts etc.

Pour the sauce into a serving dish, place the partiridge on top. Sprinkle with chives and serve.

Chris King

Chris has spent most of his life travelling extensively with his family, settling in Spain, Portugal, Argentina and England. While at university King continued to develop and expand his love for food at The Pool Court, the only local restaurant to be awarded a Michelin Star at that time. Without any additional training but determined to pursue his passion further, King reached out to Michel Roux Jr. and asked how he could get into cooking. Roux offered King a few days work experience at Le Gavroche, where he later joined full time as a commis. After completing his apprenticeship, King moved to New York City to work alongside Thomas Keller. King remained at Per Se with Keller until July 2010, when he returned to the UK to work with Roux again. Since 2015, King has been executive chef at The Langham.

Serves 4

Stuff you'll need

1 whole, free-range chicken (about 1.6kg)
Cornish or Maldon sea salt
Bay leaf, thyme
Olive oil
100g unsalted butter, diced
500ml fresh chicken stock
½ glass dry white wine
2kg fresh peas in the pod
(or 500g frozen petit pois)
3 young carrots
1 bunch salad onions
(slightly bigger spring onions)
2 heads round lettuce (washed)
350g Charlotte, or other waxy, potatoes
200g smoked bacon lardons

Get stuck in

Preheat your fan oven to 195°C - the chicken must be at room temperature.
Make sure your chicken is nice and dry inside and out. If you like remove the wishbone for easier carving later... Season the chicken generously inside the cavity and place the bay leaf and a good sprig of thyme inside. Truss the chicken with butchers' string. This will help the chicken cook evenly and look neat and tidy.
Place the chicken in a heavy-bottomed casserole and drizzle with a little olive oil. Rub a large pinch of sea salt all over the chicken and put the casserole on the middle shelf of the oven. The chicken will take anywhere from 50 to 75 mins to cook and should be left well alone as it cooks.
Peel the potatoes and carrots and cut them into even, bite size pieces. Trim the tops and

Herb roast chicken with peas and lettuce

roots from the salad onions, then rinse them clean. If they are very big cut them in half lengthways.

Remove the fresh peas from the pod.

Put the potatoes and carrots in saucepans and cover with water and a pinch of salt. Bring them to the boil and simmer only for a couple of minutes until they are just starting to cook. The idea is to give them a head-start so they will cook more quickly later.

After 45 minutes of cooking the chicken it is time to add the vegetables to the casserole. Remove the tray from the oven and put the carrots, potatoes and lardons around the chicken. A good amount of fat will have rendered from the chicken, and this will add a delicious flavour to the finished dish. Continue cooking the chicken until golden brown and cooked through. You can use a meat thermometer, or pinch the drumstick between your fingers. If you can feel the muscles slipping away from the bone then it's cooked. Remove the chicken onto a plate, letting the juices run into the casserole, switch off the oven and leave the chicken inside to rest and stay warm.

Put the casserole on a high heat on the stove. The carrots, potatoes and bacon will have just started to caramelize. With a spatula scrape up any little tasty bits on the bottom of the tray. Add the peas and onions and toss everything to combine. Add the wine to the casserole, scrape up the tasty morsels again then add the stock to the tray and bring up to the boil. Simmer the vegetables for about five minutes, or until tender and the stock has reduced slightly.

Add the diced butter to the stock to emulsify, thicken, and enrich the flavour.

Finely slice the lettuce, keeping the tender hearts for garnish, and add to the stock. Simmer for another two minutes, and check the seasoning. Serve piping hot with a crusty baguette.

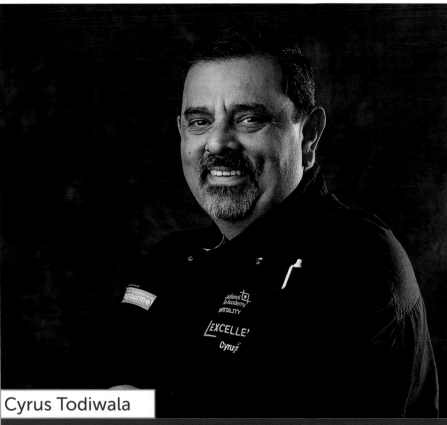

Cyrus Todiwala

Cyrus Todiwala operates four restaurants: Café Spice Namaste, Mr Todiwala's Kitchen at Hilton London Heathrow Terminal 5, Mr Todiwala's Kitchen at Lincoln Plaza London, and a new neighbourhood gem in Buckhurst Hill, Essex, Mr Todiwala's Petiscos. A regular on BBC's 'Saturday Kitchen', Cyrus has written several best-selling cookbooks including' Simple Spice Vegetarian', published in March 2020. A Fellow of the Royal Academy of Culinary Arts, Cyrus works to raise the profile of Asian cuisine in Britain, founding the student competition Zest Quest Asia seven years ago.

Serves 4

Stuff you'll need

8 lamb chops
French-trimmed and flattened
4-5 large old potatoes
(Maris Piper if possible)
2 tablespoons ginger or garlic paste
½ teaspoon turmeric
1 heaped teaspoon cumin (ground)
2 heaped teaspoons coriander (ground)
1 heaped teaspoon red chili powder
2 pieces of cassia bark
3 fresh green chillies
1 tablespoon fresh coriander
1 medium onion finely minced
4-5 tomatoes chopped fine
Salt as desired
1 level teapsoon cumin seeds
(toasted, then finely chopped)

For the coating

100-150g plain flour
3-4 eggs
100-150g fine semolina oil for frying

Cutlet of lamb with potato

Get stuck in

Peel and slice the potatoes roughly 1/8in thick and boil.

When thoroughly boiled, drain the water and return to the same pan onto the hob on a medium heat. Stir continuously scraping from the bottom with a wooden spatula until the potatoes are totally dry.

Now mash or pass through a ricer and set aside in a dish to cool. Refrigerate when at room temperature but do not cover. Remember if you place them in a small bowl the sides will sweat and make your mash wet again.

Blend the powders along with the salt and the ginger and garlic paste and marinate the chops by rubbing the marinade in well. You can do this overnight too for great results, but a couple of hours is sufficient as well.

Heat a tablespoon and a little more oil in a flat pan and when hot add the cassia bark and two of the green chillies slit lengthways into fours. When the bark darkens and the chillies change colour, scrape all excess marinade off the lamb chops (cutlets) and brown them on both sides, taking care not to keep the oil too hot as this will cause the marinade to burn.

Take care not to agitate the pan too much either. By doing so the pan will cool down and the chops will begin to stew rather than sauté.

When the chops are coloured and sealed remove them and add the minced onions to the pan along with the masala that was scraped off the chops. Add some water to deglaze as the masala is very likely to be stuck to the bottom. The water will evaporate and the onions will sauté.

When soft add the chopped tomatoes and cook until both the onions and the tomatoes are thoroughly cooked. Add a bit more water from time to time so as to get gravy with a pouring consistency. Check seasoning and remove the cassia bark and the green chillies and discard. Into the mashed potato now add half the chopped coriander and the other half to the gravy. Finely mince the green chili and mix into the mashed potato and then the cumin seeds which have been toasted and chopped. To get a good crushing effect on the cumin, chop them on the board along with the green chili. That way they will not disperse and you will get a good

texture.

Mix the mashed potato well and season.

Now making equal divisions of the potato, i.e. one ball for each chop, cover the meat area only of each chop and set aside.

For the coating

Roll each chop into some flour, then into beaten egg and then into the semolina. When coated and ready, heat the oil (roughly 1in in depth in a large flat bottom pan) and fry the chops until golden and crisp.

Serve with some salad and the tomato and onion gravy.

Darron Bunn

Darron knows how good all the meat from the Goodwood Estate is - as executive chef he looks after all eight kitchens, with six head chefs and a core brigade of 50 people. He's most typically found at the Goodwood Hotel's main restaurant, Farmer, Butcher, Chef.

Stuff you'll need

2 triceps outer sinew removed
(ask your butcher to do this)
200g Maldon sea salt
50g light brown sugar
20g mustard powder
20g smoked paprika
20g ground black pepper
3 onions, roughly chopped
10 cloves garlic, lightly crushed
1 bottle red wine, rioja or similar
500ml Brownstock
½ bunch thyme

Ash crumb

200g sourdough breadcrumbs, dried overnight
30g beef dripping
1 tablespoon chopped parsley
1 tablespoon finely-grated truffle
3 tablespoons blackened
dehydrated onion powder
½ teaspoon ground black pepper
1 teaspoon thyme leaves
1 teapoon salt

Ash-crusted, slow-cooked goodwood beef, wild mushrooms and red wine

Get stuck in

Mix the salt, sugar, mustard powder, paprika and pepper together to form a rub.

Rub this all over the trimmed triceps and leave to marinate for one hour.

Colour the outside of the beef over hot coals, to get a deep brown colour all over.

Smoke for 6 hours.

Place into vacuum bag, cook at 87°C for 14 hours.

After 14 hours, cut the bag open and pass the liquid through a fine sieve into a pan, reduce this liquid to a glace.

Shred the cooked beef, mix with half of the glace, taste for seasoning.

Roll in clingfilm to form neat cylinders, set in the fridge.

When needed, remove the clingfilm from the beef, cut into portions, brush liberally with the glace, place in the oven on 180°C for 10-12mins, re-brushing with sauce every five minutes.

Once hot and glazed, coat liberally with the crumb and serve with smooth creamy mashed potato, fried wild mushrooms.

A dish of crispy sprouts for the centre of the table will make a nice accompaniment.

Ash crumb

Fry the breadcrumbs until golden brown in the beef dripping.

Drain onto kitchen paper.

Mix with the rest of the ingredients.

David Steel

David's career started when he gained an apprenticeship at 16 years old, working for Shell at their headquarters on the Southbank, London. He joined Bartlett Mitchell in 2016 and was promoted in 2019 to chef director.
In February 2020, he became the director of food at independent caterer, Houston & Hawkes.

Stuff you'll need

20ml olive oil
2 large banana shallots finely diced
¼ bunch of sage, finely chopped
¼ bunch tarragon, finely chopped
125g dried apricots, finely chopped
250g free-range sausage meat
100g smoked free-range chicken breast ,
diced into 1cm pieces
30g wholegrain mustard
75g peeled pistachios
1 free-range egg, beaten
350g puff pastry, all butter is best
Salt and pepper
1 egg yolk, with a pinch of salt
Maldon sea salt
1 teaspoon picked thyme leaves

Pork, chicken, pistachio and apricot sausage rolls

Get stuck in

Heat a splash of olive oil in a frying pan. Add the shallot and sweat down without colour until tender. Remove from the heat. Add the chopped sage, tarragon and apricot. Remove from the pan and place on a tray and leave to cool completely.

Place the sausage meat into a bowl and add the cooled shallot mix. To that, add wholegrain mustard, pistachios and the smoked chicken. Season with salt and pepper and stir well until all ingredients are combined. Put this mixture into a piping bag and place in the fridge, for at least an hour to firm up.

Roll out a rectangle of puff pastry to 70 x 20cm.

Cut a 10cm hole in the piping bag and pipe the mixture down the centre of the pastry, working lengthways. Brush one side of the exposed pastry with egg-wash, then flip one of the long sides of the pastry over to meet the other, enclosing the sausage. Keep the pastry as close to the meat as possible. Press the two edges together with your fingers to seal, then crimp with a fork. Press and massage the sausage roll to form a consistent shape, then rest in the fridge for two hours.

Pre-heat the oven to 190°C. Brush the whole roll with egg yolk and a pinch of salt and leave to dry in the fridge. When the first coat of egg-wash is dry, brush with more egg-wash, then lightly score a pattern on top of the pastry. Sprinkle sea salt and picked thyme then cut roll into desired size. Place on a baking tray lined with parchment paper and bake in the oven in the pre-heated oven for 18 mins or until golden brown. The core temperature should be above 72°C. Best served warm.

Dean Wood

Dean was doing basic food prep from the age of 13. After qualifying as a chef, he spent his early career working around Europe, including as a private chef in France and Switzerland. After moving to Australia in 2012, Dean worked at Mosmans Restaurant, Perth, before travelling to Melbourne and working at Code Black Coffee Roasters and Bright Young Things event catering. Returning to Perth in 2015, Dean secured a job at Mary Street Bakery, taking the head chef position. He later moved to Margaret River, where he worked as head chef at Morries for a year, before moving on to Taylor St Quarters.

Stuff you'll need

500g beef striploin
120g oyster mushrooms
(preferably smaller mushrooms)
Potato starch for dusting mushrooms
Oil for frying
Salt
Cracked black pepper
Ground white pepper
2 spring onion, sliced
1 red chilli, sliced
Small amount toasted white sesame
Micro coriander loosely chopped

Sauce

1 cup soy sauce
½ cup orange juice (fresh)
2 tablespoons rice vinegar
1 tablespoon mirin
2 tablespoons lime juice

Rare beef with salt and pepper mushrooms

Get stuck in

Trim the fat and sinew off the beef and slice the meat length ways into two pieces. Season both pieces with salt and cracked black pepper.

In a hot pan, sear each side of the meat for 2-3 minutes (you want the beef to be a nice dark brown colour) and then wrap in aluminium foil to rest and cool. Once cool the beef is ready to slice and should be rare in the middle with an even brown edge all around it.

Sauce

While the beef is resting, make up the sauce/dressing. Simply mix the soy, orange juice, lime juice, rice vinegar and mirin.

For the mushrooms, season the potato starch with salt and ground white pepper (you want to taste the white pepper). Put the mushrooms into the potato starch and coat, squeeze the mushrooms lightly to ensure the starch sticks.

Heat up about an inch deep of oil in a pot and fry mushrooms for 1-2 minutes, until crisp (they should stay quite white in colour). Strain onto some paper towel.

To serve

Slice 5-6 pieces of beef per serve and spread out around the plate, only slightly overlapping each other. Using tablespoon, coat each piece of beef with the sauce. The sauce will soak into the beef and pool out around the plate, which is what you want.

Place the mushrooms over the top and finish the sliced spring onion, red chilli, white sesame seeds and coriander.

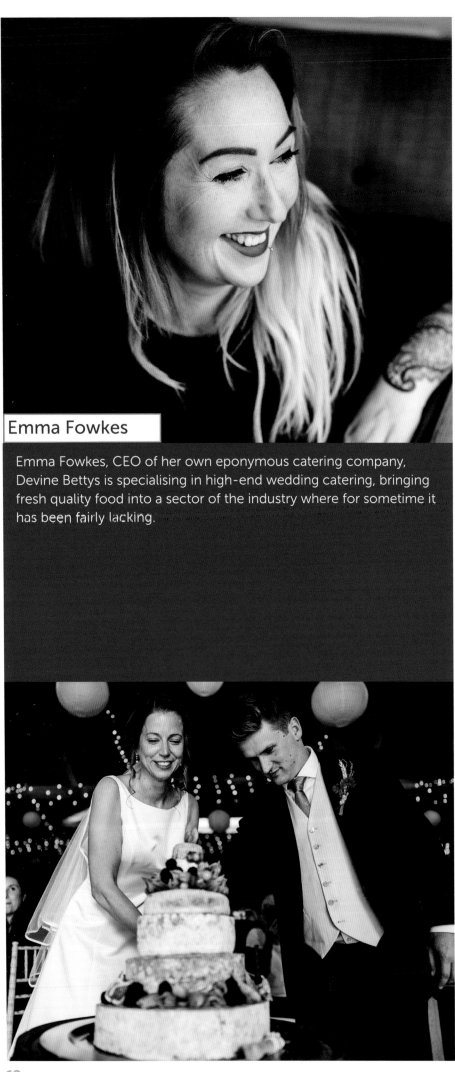

Emma Fowkes

Emma Fowkes, CEO of her own eponymous catering company, Devine Bettys is specialising in high-end wedding catering, bringing fresh quality food into a sector of the industry where for sometime it has been fairly lacking.

Stuff you'll need

1 whole chicken
300g sausagemeat
1 whole lemon zested
Fresh chopped mint leaves
1 large tablespoon of honey
6 finely-diced spring onions
3 teaspoons of dried oregano
1 finely-diced red chilli

Sauce

2 roasted red peppers
Olive oil
2 diced red onions
2 diced sticks of celery
3 sprigs of fresh rosemary
(woody stalk removed)
3 garlic cloves
1 vegetable or chicken stock cube
1 large teaspoon of cumin
1 large teaspoon of dried basil
1 large teaspoon of oregano
2 large teaspoons of paprika
1 tablespoon of ground black pepper
1 teaspoon of salt
250g mascarpone

Polenta

1 cup of polenta
4 cups of vegetable stock
50g butter
Pan juices from the roasting tin
50ml double cream

Rolled lemon and mint chicken with red pepper sauce and wet polenta

Get stuck in

Preheat your oven to 200°C.

De-bone the chicken, remove the drumsticks beneath the thighs and the wings. Lay the bird out skin side down.

In a mixing bowl add all of the stuffing ingredients and combine well, laying the mixture down the center of the bird.

Roll each side in onto itself and tie the chicken. Start at one end - simply slide 30cm of string underneath, pulled around and tie in a double knot. Do this every 2 inches until the rolled bird is secured, turn the chicken over so the knots and seam are unerneath and place in a lightly oiled roasting tin. Season the skin with a generous pinch of salt.

Roast for 20 minutes at 200°C, then turn the oven down to 160°C for 40 minutes. Once cooked, drain the juices into a small jug and rest the bird for 20 minutes before carving.

Sauce

Whilst de-boning the chicken, roast your peppers. Once the chicken goes into the oven, saute all the vegetables for your sauce until soft in olive oil, add in all the herbs and stock cube and mix well. After a few minutes let the mixture cool slightly, then place into a food processor with the peppers and blend until smooth. Pass through a chinois, put back into a pan, and set aside until your chicken comes out of the oven to rest.

Polenta

Cook the polenta and stock - start over a high heat and stir continuously until it starts to thicken, add in the reserved pan juices, turn down the heat and stir every few minutes to prevent sticking. Do this for around 30-40 minutes. When the polenta is pulling away from the side of the pan add the cream and butter, mix well (the chicken should have come out of the oven to rest half way through cooking the polenta).

Rest the chicken, put the sauce back on a low heat and add the mascarpone - this will slowly melt into the sauce and be ready in time to carve your bird.

Serve with a sprinkle of toasted pinenuts and fresh parsley.

Heshan Peiris

Heshan was raised by culinary parents in Melbourne, Australia. His career as a chef started when he was an apprentice at Melbourne Racing Club whilst pursuing a degree in culinary arts at William Angliss Institute. Over the last 16 years, he has lived and worked internationally with Hilton Hotels in Melbourne, Sydney and Seychelles. Prior to joining Banyan Tree Bangkok, Heshan worked in Laguna Lang Co in Vietnam. His favourite cuisines are French, Vietnamese and Thai.

Stuff you'll need

400g tuna loin, fresh
2 chillies diced
2 cucumbers diced
1 garlic clove minced
5g ginger minced
1 lime juiced
10g choped parsley
60ml soy sauce
60g white miso
20ml rice vinegar
90ml olive oil, extra-virgin
1 tablespoon sesame oil
2 tablespoons chopped almonds
2 tablespoons chopped cashews, roasted
2 live sea urchins, or 8 pieces
½ cup thinly-sliced spring onions

Stuff you'll need

4 duck legs, excess skin and fat removed
15ml vegetable oil
4 shallots, finely sliced
4 cloves garlic, finely chopped
2 stems lemongrass, white part only
2 star anise
5cm cinnamon sticks
¼ tablespoon Chinese five spice
An orange, freshly zested
4 oranges, freshly juiced, about 400ml
2 tablespoons Chinese rice wine
2 tablespoons fish sauce

Morning glory

1 bunch water morning glory
(cut into 4-6in pieces, about 4 cups)
4 Thai hot chillies
3 large cloves garlic
½ tablespoon yellow soybean paste
½ tablespoon light soy sauce
½ tablespoon oyster sauce
1 tablespoon vegetable oil

Sea urchin, ahi aok

Get stuck in

In a large bowl, whisk together soy sauce, rice vinegar, sesame oil, ginger, miso, parsley, garlic, chili, green onions, and all the nuts. Add tuna and toss to coat. Refrigerate for at least 15 minutes, up to one hour.

To serve

Top with tuna with sea urchin, and lime juice to taste, serve in sea urchin shells on top of crushed ice.

Slow-cooked crispy duck leg, morning glory and chilli jam

Get stuck in

Place duck in sous vide bag with shallots, garlic, lemongrass, star anise, cinnamon and chinese five-spice, orange zest and juice, wine and fish sauce, seal and refrigerate for 24 hours. Place the bag in the water bath for 12 hours. Sous vide at 76°C. Add water intermittently to keep the duck submerged.

After 12 hours remove from liquid, leave to cool down and then refrigerate.

To cook, remove the confit duck legs from their fat. Put an ovenproof frying pan on the stove. When hot add the duck legs, skin-side down, cook for 4 minutes. Turn the legs and transfer the pan to the oven for 30 mins, until crisp.

Morning glory

Cut the morning glory into 4in-long pieces and place in a bowl. Measure all the sauce ingredients and separate. Chop up the garlic and chillies and reserve.

Heat the oil in a large wok until very hot, add all the morning glory, garlic chilli and sauce ingredients. Stir and fry quickly, turning until the morning glory is wilted.

To serve

Top the morning glory with duck leg, finish with chilli jam and prawn salt.

Serves 8

Stuff you'll need

500g lambs' liver
175g back fat
5g juniper berries
210g oats, blitzed not quite to a powder
500g minced lamb
25ml brandy
50ml port
Breadcrumbs, fresh or dried
½ teaspoon onion powder
½ teaspoon garlic powder
A pinch of brown sugar
A pinch of freshly grated nutmeg
A pinch of sweet mixed groundspice
Caul fat (optional)
Salt and pepper

James Golding

James was first employed by The Savoy Hotel, attending its specialised chef course. On completion, in 1998 he was offered the position of chef de partie at Le Caprice, working under Mark Hix and later Elliot Ketley. James stayed at Le Caprice until 2001 when head chef Tim Hughes offered him a new position at the seafood restaurant J Sheekeys, where he would become sous chef. James left London to become head chef at Soho House New York. In 2006 he returned to his home on Britain's south coast as both group chef director at The Pig Hotels and a Fellow of the Royal Academy of Culinary Arts.

Get stuck in

Preheat the oven to 200°C.
Mince the liver and back fat.
Toast the juniper berries under a medium-hot grill or in a hot dry pan and blitz with 50g of the oats in a blender. Then combine all the ingredients (except the caul fat) in a bowl and stir until the mix comes together and is mouldable. If it's too wet, add some breadcrumbs.
Season and cook a small sample to check the texture and flavour.
When you're happy with the mixture, divide it into 8 equal portions. Lay out a section of the caul fat and wrap it tightly around the faggots one at a time (if you don't have caul fat, just form each portion into a ball-shape with your hands).
Bake them for about 16 minutes until the centre of the faggots registers at least 75°C on a food thermometer.
Serve with mashed neeps, wilted chard and red wine sauce.

Faggots and bashed neeps

James Knappett

James is head chef and founder of Kitchen Table. He attended a Cambridgeshire catering college and worked at a range of top local restaurants, before moving to London and landing formative positions at the likes of Restaurant Gordon Ramsay, The Berkeley and The Ledbury, as well as stints at restaurants further afield, including Rick Stein's The Seafood Restaurant in Padstow, Noma in Copenhagen and Thomas Keller's Per Se in New York. He opened Kitchen Table and Bubbledogs in 2012.

Stuff you'll need

1.5kg chicken wings
3 tablespoons soy sauce
3 pinches white pepper
Tapioca starch (or corn starch)

Sauce

10g minced garlic
20g minced ginger
60ml hoisin sauce
40ml soy sauce
60ml whiskey
60ml honey
1 tablespoon sesame oil
1 star anise

Garnish

Red chillies, thinly-sliced
Mint, picked
Coriander, picked leaves
Spring onions, thinly-sliced

Get stuck in

Marinate the chicken wings with soy sauce and white pepper. Mix until all the wings are coated.
Toss the wings with enough tapioca starch until each wing has a nice light coating.
Let the wings marinate for one hour.

Sauce

Combine all the ingredients in a small sauce pot. Bring it to a boil and them simmer for five minutes. This sauce can be made in advance and can keep in the fridge for up to three days.
Heat frying oil to 190°C and fry the wings in batches until they are crispy and cooked through. After it is fried, toss the wings with the sauce. If the sauce is cooled or cold, reheat it until its warm before dressing the wings.

To serve

Garnish with the herbs and chillies.

James Martin

After catering college James worked in London under the guidance of chefs including Antony Worrall Thompson and Marco Pierre White, travelled around France, and on returning to the UK took up the position of junior pastry chef at Red Star, Chewton Glen. Just a few weeks short of his 22nd birthday, James opened the Hotel and Bistro du Vin in Winchester as head chef. In 2013 he opened James Martin Manchester, and in 2017 The Kitchen Cookery School back at Chewton Glen. James also operates a cafe chain, James Martin Kitchen, at various major transport hubs across the UK.

Stuff you'll need

Portobello mushrooms

4 Portobello mushrooms
(about 8cm in diameter), stems trimmed
and reserved, skin peeled and reserved
110ml olive oil
3 garlic cloves, crushed
4 sprigs fresh thyme, leaves only
Salt and freshly ground black pepper

Crispy eggs

5 free-range eggs
2 tablespoons white wine vinegar
Salt and freshly ground black pepper
110g plain flour
200g fresh breadcrumbs
Vegetable oil, for deep frying

Shallot purée

150g shallots finely chopped
2 garlic cloves, finely chopped
300ml red wine
40ml olive oil
Salt and freshly ground black pepper

Duck confit

110g small red onions, such as red pearl onions,
peeled and halved
30g butter
60ml chicken stock (or water)
salt and freshly ground black pepper
4 teaspoons olive oil
150g mixed wild mushrooms,
trimmed and rinsed
Trimmings and skin from Portobello mushrooms
(see above)
1 ready-made confit duck leg, meat picked from
bone and roughly chopped
2 tablespoons sherry vinegar

Deep-fried egg with mushroom and duck confit

Get stuck in

Portobello mushrooms

Place the mushrooms into a bowl, drizzle over the oil and sprinkle with the garlic and thyme leaves. Season, to taste, with salt and pepper. Mix until the mushrooms are coated in the marinade mixture. Set aside to marinate for at least one hour.

Crispy eggs

Bring a large pot of water to the boil. Add the vinegar and a pinch of salt. Set a bowl of ice water alongside.

Boil 4 of the eggs in the water for exactly 5 minutes, then remove from the pan using and chill in the ice water.

Crack the remaining egg into a bowl. Whisk and add a pinch of salt and pepper.

Sprinkle the flour and breadcrumbs into two separate shallow dishes and season with salt and freshly ground black pepper.

Peel the cooled boiled eggs. Dredge each one first in the flour, then dip it in the whisked egg, then roll it in the breadcrumbs until completely coated. Chill in the fridge.

Shallot purée

Bring the shallots, garlic and wine to a gentle simmer in a small saucepan. Simmer until the shallots are tender and the wine has almost completely evaporated. Transfer the mixture to a food processor, add the olive oil, blend to a smooth purée. Season, to taste, with salt and freshly ground black pepper, then set aside until needed. Keep warm. When the mushrooms have marinated, preheat the grill to medium and grill the mushrooms for 7-8 minutes on each side, or until cooked through.

Cut each grilled mushroom into a perfect circle using a 7.5cm cookie cutter. Then cut a smaller circle inside each mushroom using a 4cm cookie cutter to make a donut shape.

Keep warm. Chop and reserve the trimmings.

Duck confit

Mix together the red onions, butter and chicken broth in a small frying pan. Season, to taste, with salt and freshly ground black pepper. Bring the mixture to a simmer and cook until the shallots are tender, about 3-4 minutes. Heat a

pan and add the mixed wild mushrooms, garlic and thyme and fry for 2-3 minutes, or until softened. Season, to taste, with salt and pepper.

Add the reserved trimmings from the grilled Portobello mushrooms, the confit duck leg meat and the onion mixture and mix well.

Pour in the sherry vinegar and fry for a further 2-3 minutes.

Just before serving, heat the oil in a deep fat fryer to 180°C. Roll the chilled, coated eggs in more breadcrumbs, then deep-fry until golden-brown. Remove from the oil using a slotted spoon and set aside to drain on kitchen paper. Sprinkle with salt.

Plating

To serve, place a spoonful of shallot purée into the centre of each of four serving plates. Spoon a large spoonful of duck confit fricassée on top, then plate one grilled mushroom ring on top. Slice off the wider end of each deep-fried egg to expose the yolk, then set one inside each Portobello mushroom. Sprinkle over a pinch of cracked peppercorns and some of the chives.

Whisk the lemon juice with the olive oil and season, to taste, with salt and pepper. Add the salad leaves and mix to coat the leaves in the dressing. Arrange the salad around the edge of the plate with a few duck cracklings. Serve warm.

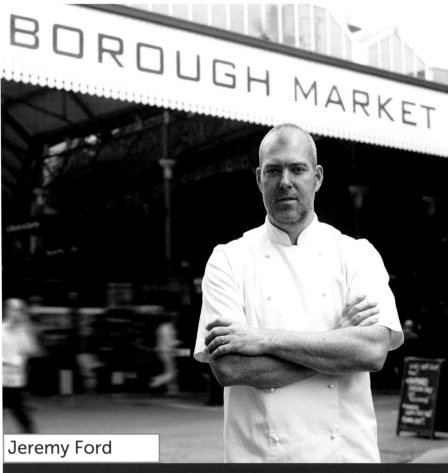

Jeremy Ford

Jeremy is food director of Gather & Gather, which devises new food concepts, menus and chef training sessions. Jeremy started his career with the Academy of Culinary Arts, where he received classical training under some of the industry's top chefs. After a three year stint at the three Michelin-starred Chez Nico, Jeremy began working for Albert Roux in the city under the Roux Fine Dining brand. He achieved the Master of Culinary Arts in 2013 and was given a Fellowship to the Royal Academy of culinary arts in 2015.

Serves 2

Stuff you'll need

300g plain cooked long grain rice

100g cooked chicken diced

75g finely shredded vegetables (cabbage & carrot for example)

2 shallots

2 cloves garlic

1 red chilli

25ml shrimp paste or shrimp sambal

2 eggs

30ml Ketjup manis (Indonesian sweet soy)

25ml veg oil

Garnish

1 lime

35g cucumber

1 spring onion

10g crispy onions

A few sprigs of fresh coriander

Get stuck in

Prepare the paste by blending the chilli, peeled garlic, peeled shallots and shrimp paste till smooth.

Beat the 2 eggs in a bowl and fry in a hot wok or frying pan with the veg oil until cooked, break it into strips in the pan and fry until crispy, remove from pan.

Add the paste to the pan and stir fry for 30 seconds before adding in the shredded veg, cook for 45 seconds until starting to wilt and caramelise, then add the chicken and cooked rice and continue to stir fry until hot.

Add the ketjup manis and stir in until well combined.

Make sure the rice is hot then divide it between two plates.

To serve

Garnish with fresh lime, shredded spring onion, cucumber, crispy shallots and picked coriander leaves.

Nasi goreng

Jeremy Goring

Jeremy is managing director of the Goring Hotel London. He has managed hotels across the globe working for Rosewood, Four Seasons and Belmond. Three years ago he co-founded HotelSchool - a joint venture with London's largest homeless resource centre, The Passage. Like Beyond Food Foundation, HotelSchool inspires refugees, homeless and rough sleepers to get interested in hospitality, teaches entry level skills, and carefully mentors graduates into full time work.

Stuff you'll need

600g Short crust pastry
(or flaky if you must)
50g onions
200g mince beef
(or skirt cut up roughly but small)
200g "turnips"
(Swede in English. Do not use actual turnips)
200g potatoes
Salt, black pepper (plenty of pepper)
50g beef dripping
You can sub in some butter

Cornish pasties

Get stuck in

Roll out the pastry in 4 circles about 20cm across.
Chop the onions, turnips and potatoes in quite small shards.
Mix with mince, salt and pepper.
Heap the above in the middle of the pastry circles.
Close them up. Knit the "handles" of the pastry using thumb and forefingers.
Cut a slit either side of the handle and pour in a spoonful of dripping and a spoonful of water. Apply a light milky eggwash.
Place in a medium oven on greaseproof paper for about 40 minutes.
Ideally, 10 minutes at 180°C. followed by another 20 minutes at 160°C. or until lightly browned.

Notes

Pasty ingredients are always added raw. For this reason do not set the oven too hot. The higher temp at the beginning sets the pastry and prevents it from sagging, the lower temp then cooks the insides without burning the pastry. Hand chopping the potatoes and "turnips" into thin-ish shards further enables this process. Quantities vary according to taste and, traditionally, budget. So use your eyes to judge the correct ratio of meat to vegetables. The term "Cornish" pasty is an appellation controlée in the same way as Château Latour or Champagne. So you will have to cook this in Cornwall, or call it something else.

Jeremy Villanueva

Jeremy Villanueva is executive chef at Romulo Cafe & Restaurant in Kensington, London. Jeremy has worked not only for Holland America cruises but also for London restaurants including Le Gavroche, Brasserie Roux and Le Boudin Blanc. He joined Romulo in 2018.

Stuff you'll need

Adobo sauce

3 cups soy sauce Datu Puti
(Philippine brand of soy sauce)
3 cups vinegar Datu Puti
(Philippine brand of vinegar)
1 cup of oyster sauce
1 cup of dark brown sugar
1 bulb of garlic peeled and crushed
Bay leaves
Handful of whole black peppercorns
150g of silver skin onions or 1 large white onion roughly chopped

Pork belly

250g of pork belly
200g chicken leg (cut into pieces)

Sweet potato mash (garnish)

2 pieces of peeled and cubed sweet potatoes
½ cup of milk
2 tablespoons of butter
Salt to taste

Chicken and pork adobo

Get stuck in

Adobo sauce (marinade) and chicken leg

Add all ingredients together and marinate overnight. Place in a cast-iron casserole or large cooking pot and simmer.

Pork belly and chicken

Place the whole piece of boneless pork belly into the adobo sauce and cook for 2-3 hours until the meat is soft. Meanwhile season the chicken with olive oil, salt and cracked black peppercorn.

Sear the chicken by frying in a hot pan until golden on both sides. Once golden, add to the adobo sauce and cook for a further 20–25 mins with the pork until tender.

Cool down on a tray. Cut into pork into portions.

Deep fry at 170°C the chicken and the pork for about 3 mins. Then finish cooking in the oven for 5 mins at 185°C.

Sweet potato mash

Bring a pot of salted water to a boil. Add potatoes and cook until tender, 20 to 30 minutes.

With an electric mixer on low, blend potatoes, slowly adding the milk. Use more or less to achieve desired texture. Add butter and salt to taste. Blend until smooth.

Plating

Spread the sweet potato mash on the plate. Add the chicken and pork belly on top of the sweet potato mash. Pour some adobo sauce on top. Serve hot.

Joe Sloane

Briton Joe Sloane settled in Thailand over a decade ago after working in the UK, Bermuda and Holland. Having trained as a chef at University College Suffolk, he is a former chef de cuisine at the Landmark, Bangkok, and has also worked in various Michelin-starred restaurants, including many years under Albert Roux.

Stuff you'll need

Beef & stout filling

6kg of braising beef, diced - shank is perfect
300g flour
3l of good beef stock
2kg onions, sliced
10 garlic cloves, large, smashed
2l of a good craft stout
250g of tomato paste
Small bunch thyme, dried
150g of brown sugar
Salt and black pepper

Short crust pie pastry

1kg flour
500g butter
5g salt
250g water

Get stuck in

Beef & stout filling

Slow cook the onions until soft and sweet. Brown beef, then add cooked onions.
Add stout, and reduce.
Add flour and tomato paste, cook out.
Cover with stock, season
with sugar, salt and pepper.
Cook for a minimum of 3 hours.
Check the meat is tender.

Short crust pie pastry

Mix the flour, butter and salt together until fine 'breadcrumbs'. Pour into a large bowl and make a well. Add the water and slowly incorporate without over-working the pastry. Push into a ball, cover and let rest in the fridge for at least 30 minutes.
Roll out the pastry to 2-3mm and line a buttered pie tin. Add the filling and top with a pastry lid, then crimp the edges closed.
Egg wash and pierce a small hole in the top to allow the steam to escape.
Bake in the oven at about 160°C for 25-30 minutes until golden.

Sloane's beef & stout pie

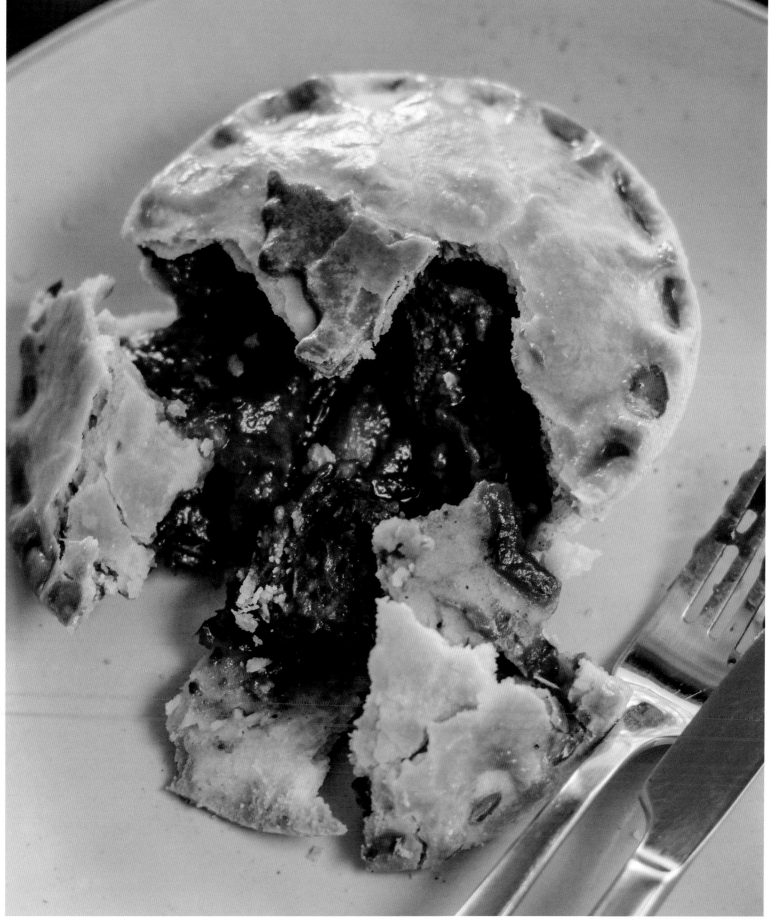

Koj

Koj is a British-Japanese chef based in the Cotswolds with a 'no sushi' casual-dining Japanese restaurant in Cheltenham. After reaching the pinnacle of amateur cooking success in the final of 'MasterChef' 2012, he turned professional after a fast-track training programme in Michelin-starred kitchens across the UK and Europe. He teaches, promotes and demonstates Japanese cookery through his restaurant, cookery schools and food festivals around the UK.

Stuff you'll need

Mabodon sauce

1 tablespoon Jang
(Korean hot pepper fermented bean sauce)
1 tablespoon sugar
100g red miso
2 tablespoons soy sauce
2 tablespoons rice vinegar
70ml sake
400ml dashi stock (or water)

Mabodon

Mabodon

10g garlic, peeled and finely grated

20g fresh ginger, peeled and finely grated

1 bunch of spring onion (white part only), finely chopped

250g pork mince

150g firm tofu, cut into 2cm dice

200g Mabodon sauce

Get stuck in

Mabodon sauce

Whisk the sauce ingredients together until the sugar is dissolved.

Mabodon

Gently fry the garlic and ginger in a little vegetable oil until it softens and smells fragrant, then add the pork mince.

Cook the pork mince through, then turn the heat up a little to drive off any liquid and brown the meat a little.

Add the diced tofu and mabodon sauce and simmer for 5 minutes until the tofu is warm.

You could simmer it for longer and allow it to cool – it's one of those dishes that tastes even better after resting for a day in the fridge.

Serve as a donburi on top of a bed of rice, with some blanched greens.

Leon Seraphin

Leon started his career as an apprentice at the Hoxton Apprentice Academy – a former social enterprise restaurant – in 2004. After gaining experience of working in other restaurants, he wanted to help develop others who had difficult lives and were in need of a second chance and so in 2013 joined the Beyond Food Foundation as a chef trainer at Brigade.

Stuff you'll need

Curry

1kg diced goat meat
2 teaspoons chopped garlic
1 teaspoon chopped ginger
1 teaspoon chopped dried thyme
1 teaspoon ground black pepper
4 heaped teasoons of curry goat seasoning
1 teaspoon all purpose seasoning
1 teaspoon tumeric powder
5 crushed pimento seeds, husks removed
1 teaspoon sliced onion
4 spring onions, sliced finely
8 sprigs fresh thyme
4 sprigs rosemary
1 whole scotch bonnet pepper
2 tablespoons creamed coconut
4 large carrots, peeled and diced
400g potato, peeled and large diced
100ml malt vinegar
1 tablespoon of dark brown sugar
2 limes Juice and zest
Salt and pepper to season

Rice and Peas

200g kidney beans
2 large spring onions, tops sliced in half
8 sprigs thyme
400g long grain/basmati
40g creamed coconut
1 scotch bonnet pepper
1 teaspoon fresh ginger, minced
2 cloves garlic, crushed and pureed
1 teaspoon all purpose seasoning
1 teaspoon ground pimento
1ltr water
Salt and Pepper to season

Goat curry from Dominica

Get stuck in

Curry

Put the goat meat in a large bowl, squeeze lime juice and vinegar over the meat. Rinse carefully and drain.

Transfer the meat into a clean bowl, add all the dry seasoning, the garlic and onions. Allow to marinate overnight, or even better for 48 hours.

Put a casserole pot on the stove and allow to get hot. Add a good glug of olive oil and add the meat into a pan, sealing off until brown. Continue stirring while the meat is browning. Add enough water to cover the meat, then bring to the boil. After 15 mins reduce the heat to a gentle simmer.

Add the scotch bonnet pepper, cream coconut, thyme and rosemary.

Cover the casserole dish and simmer on a low heat for 2 hours, stirring occasionally until the meat is nice and tender.

Strain any impurities that come to the surface to give you a nice clear sauce.

Then add the potatoes and chopped carrots, and adjust seasoning if needed.

Simmer on a medium heat for a further 30 mins until the potatoes and carrots are cooked.

Remove the scotch bonnet pepper and stalks of thyme.

Serve with rice and peas, coleslaw and seasonal steamed veg.

Rice and Peas

Rinse the kidney beans in cold water, then place into a clean bowl and cover with water. Place in a refrigerator and leave to soak overnight.

Keep the kidney beans' soaking water and transfer into a pot.

Rinse the kidney beans again under cold running water and discard any that are burst or discoloured.

Add the kidney beans, scotch bonnet, seasoning, garlic, spring onion tops, ginger and fresh thyme to the pot with the saved kidney beans' soaking water. Bring it to a rolling boil, then allow to boil for 20 mins. Kidney beans have poisonous toxins and need to be boiled furiously for 20 minutes during initial cooking.

Reduce the heat and cover the pot. Allow the

kidney beans to cook for a further 25 mins until they are almost tender – you don't want them to be too soft or mushy. Add the creamed coconut to the pot.

Wash your rice under cold water for 5 mins to get rid of excess starch.

Add the washed rice to the pot and give it a stir to disperse the kidney beans through the rice. Add a little bit more water – you should have at least an inch of water above the rice.

Adjust seasoning, cover the pot, and bring to the boil. Then turn to a gentle heat and allow all the water to absorb for 25 mins until the rice is tender and all liquid is gone.

Discard the spring onions, scotch bonnet and thyme stalks. Add a knob of butter and fluff the rice gently with a fork.

Cover with foil or cling film until ready to serve.

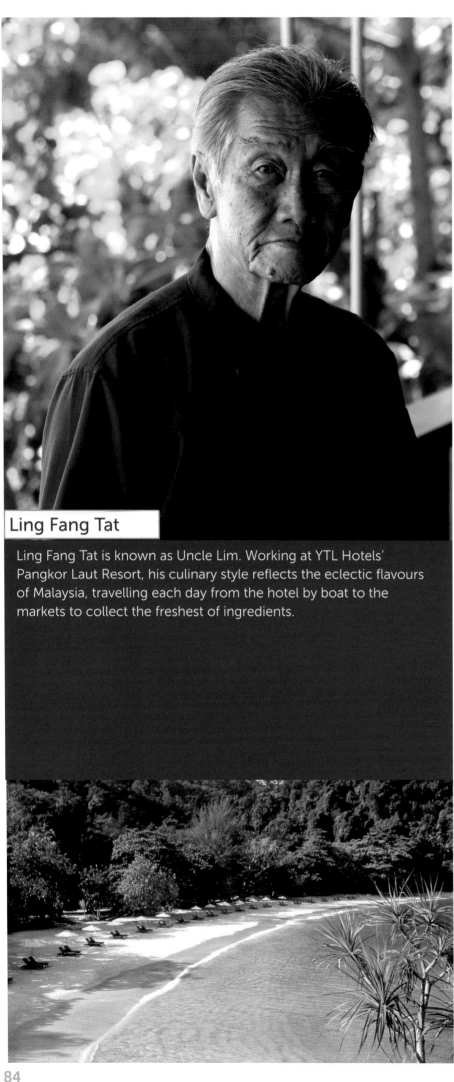

Stuff you'll need

1.2kg boneless chicken

180g corn four

30g sesame seeds

100ml calamansi juice

130g plum juice

120g chilli sauce

600ml cooking oil

Salt and pepper to taste

Ling Fang Tat

Ling Fang Tat is known as Uncle Lim. Working at YTL Hotels' Pangkor Laut Resort, his culinary style reflects the eclectic flavours of Malaysia, travelling each day from the hotel by boat to the markets to collect the freshest of ingredients.

Get stuck in

Slice the chicken legs and coat with cornflower and sesame seeds, then deep fry until they are golden in colour and crispy in texture (approx. 4 minutes).

Heat the oil in the wok, pour in the lime juice, plum juice, calamansi juice and chilli sauce then add the crispy chicken.

Toss together in the pan for about 20 seconds. Season to taste, then serve with hot, steamed jasmine rice.

Calamansi chicken

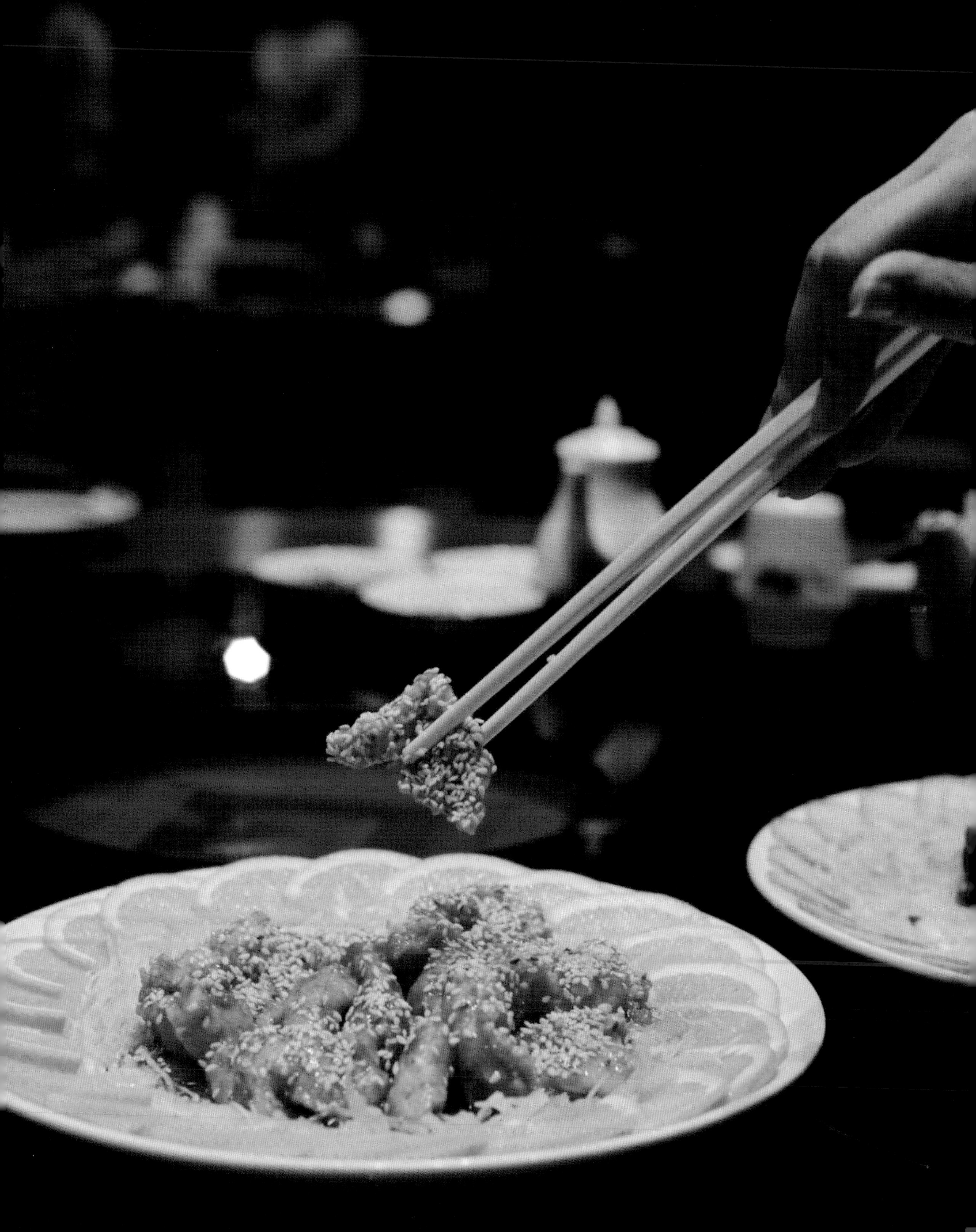

Manuel Mancuso

Manuel Mancuso grew up in Rome - and it was from the traditional Italian home that Manuel realised his destiny was to work with food in a professional kitchen. With his Mediterranean culinary influence, he travelled to London seven years ago. He is now a senior sous chef at Credit Suisse in Pall Mall, with Baxter Storey.

Serves 2

Stuff you'll need

Gnocchi

200ml cold water

200g semolina, extra fine

3g of salt

Wild mushrooms

140g wild mushroom

10g of parsley

1 beard eye chilli

1 garlic clove

Extra virgin olive oil

Salt

Bacon chips

4 slices of streaky bacon

Taleggio fondue

100g of taleggio cheese

100g of lactose-free cream

1g of smoked Cornish salt

Pan-fried semolina gnocchi, wild mushroom, taleggio cheese fondue and toasted black pepper

Get stuck in

Gnocchi

Dust your table or board with flour.

Boil 200ml of water and as soon it starts to boil add the salt, let it boil for 10 seconds and start to add the 200g of semolina flour. With a wooden spoon start to mix immeadiately. It is a 15 second procedure. immeadiately put the mixture on the table previously dusted in flour and while the mixture still hot, start to work your dough for 7 to 8 minutes until you have a smooth texture. Cover in clingfilm. Set aside for 25 to 30 minutes.

Roll out the dough into logs about 2 cm thick and cut them into pieces.

Place the gnocchi at the top of the fork tines and gently press down, rolling it across the fork with your thumb. It will be slightly curled with the indentations on the opposite side.

Arrange the gnocchi on a tray dusted with semolina flour.

Wild mushrooms

Using olive oil in the pan, fry the crushed garlic and chilli until softened. Set aside and using the same pan fry the diced mushroom. Sauté, and add salt and parsley at the end.

Bacon chips

Pre-heat the oven to 200°C . Lay the bacon on parchment paper in a tray and cover with a second piece of parchment. Cover with another tray to keep the bacon pressed between the two trays. Bake for about 12 minutes until flat and crispy.

Taleggio fondue

In a pot simply insert your taleggio cheese and the cream and let everything slowly melt. Season as it needs.

To serve

Blanch the gnocchi in salty boiling water and immerse in iced water. Heat the oil and a knob of butter in a pan and toast the black pepper. Add the drained gnocchi and pan fry.

Spoon the taleggio fondue onto the plate, place the gnocchi and the sautéed wild mushroom. Add the bacon chips. Finish with a drizzle of olive oil and salad cress to garnish.

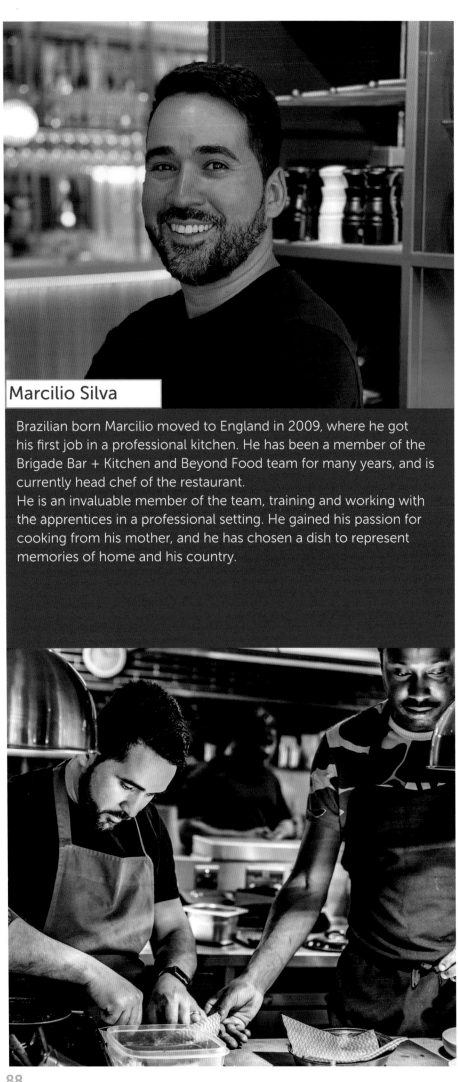

Marcilio Silva

Brazilian born Marcilio moved to England in 2009, where he got his first job in a professional kitchen. He has been a member of the Brigade Bar + Kitchen and Beyond Food team for many years, and is currently head chef of the restaurant.

He is an invaluable member of the team, training and working with the apprentices in a professional setting. He gained his passion for cooking from his mother, and he has chosen a dish to represent memories of home and his country.

Stuff you'll need

Chimichurri

1/2 cup fresh flat-leaf parsley, finely chopped
1/2 cup fresh coriander, finely chopped
2 tablespoons fresh oregano, finely chopped
2 cloves garlic, minced
1 shallot (1/4 red onion), very finely chopped
1/2 tbsp. red chilli, finely chopped
1 tablespoon red wine vinegar
1/2 cup olive oil
Sea salt & fresh black pepper to taste

Picanha Steak

1kg picanha steak, (rump cap)
salt & pepper
2 onions, cut in half
Olive oil
1 bunch of asparagus
1 parsnip

Grilled picanha, burnt onion, charred asparagus & chimichurri

Get stuck in

Chimichurri

Combine all the pre-prepared fresh ingredients with olive oil and vinegar. Season to taste and whisk thoroughly. Do not place in the fridge, it should be served at room temperature.

Picanha steak

Cut your picanha across the grain into 4 strips (between 1.5 and 2 inches thick). Season liberally with sea salt and then cover with cling wrap. Set aside in the fridge for an hour.

Heat a little olive oil in an ovenproof frying pan on high heat. Place the onion halves, cut side down, in the pan and cook until completely blackened. Transfer to the oven for 25 minutes.

Trim bottom of asparagus by holding the tips and ends of the stalk. Bend them gently and the asparagus will snap at the right spot on each stalk. Toss the trimmed asparagus with olive oil, salt and freshly ground pepper. Lay stalks across grill and allow to cook for 2 minutes or so, until asparagus is slightly charred but still firm and bright green.

Shave the parsnip and fry in small pan until a nice golden colour, then dry on paper towel.

To cook your steaks remove them from the fridge and wipe off as much of the salt as possible. Drizzle with olive oil and massage into the meat.

Heat your griddle, grill or braai/barbeque. Season your steak with freshly ground black pepper.

Place the steak fat side down on the hottest part of the griddle or braai/barbeque and cook for 5 minutes. Turn the steaks, searing each side for a couple of minutes with the braai lid down. Once seared all over, move the steak off the direct heat. Cook the steaks at between 130°C and 150°C for 5 to 10 minutes depending on how you like your steak. Personally, I prefer my picanha medium-rare.

Let the steaks rest for 10 minutes before serving with the chimichurri.

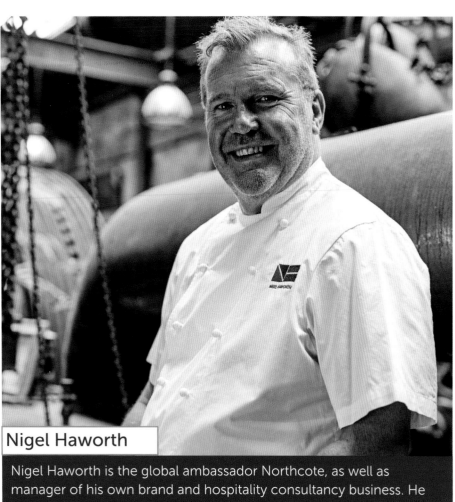

Nigel Haworth

Nigel Haworth is the global ambassador Northcote, as well as manager of his own brand and hospitality consultancy business. He has recently launched a range of supermarket ready meals under the brand, 'Food with Roots'. He was awarded a Michelin star in 1996, maintaining it for over two decades. He is the recipient of the Prince Philip Medal for Outstanding Contribution to the Catering Industry, Egon Ronay Chef of the Year and the Variety Club Legends of Industry Award.

Stuff you'll need

4 tiny cauliflowers or cauliflower florets
4 cauliflower leaves
100ml tempura batter
125g butter
50g black peas
200g black pea houmous (see recipe)
200g smoked onion sauce (see recipe)
4 slices house-cured ham
24 chive batons and some chive flower petals

Tempura cauliflower leaf

100g tempura batter
A few small cauliflower leaves
Extra flour for dusting

Black Pea Houmous

250g black peas, soaked overnight, steam for 1 hour or until soft
Pinch crushed dried chillies
3 cloves roast garlic, peeled and crushed
½ teaspoon salt
20g black treacle
50ml rape seed oil
50ml sunflower oil
Juice 1/2 lemon
50ml tomato juice
70ml vegetable stock, hot

Smoked Onion Sauce

1 med onion in its skin, approx. 200g
250ml whipping cream
250ml milk
100ml vegetable stock
Pinch of salt & white pepper

Ascrofts cauliflower, black pea houmous, house cured rare breed ham, smoked onion sauce

Get stuck in

Prep the cauliflower by removing the outer leaves and trimming the stalk.

Place the cauliflower into a pan of boiling water with the butter and cook for 4-5 minutes until just cooked. The cauliflower should still have a slight bite/crunch to it

Once cooked, plunge the cauliflower into iced water to cool but reserve the cooking liquid for reheating later.

Tempura cauliflower leaf

Lightly dust the cauliflower leaves with flour. Coat each leaf with the batter and place into a fryer a 190°C until lightly golden and crispy. Remove from the fryer and place onto absorbent paper Season with salt and serve.

Black Pea Houmous

Remove 50gms of black peas once cooked, and reserve for the garnish.

Whilst the remaining peas are still hot, place all ingredients into a high-powered liquidiser and blitz until thick, creamy and smooth.

Check the seasoning and place into a container to keep warm for serving.

Smoked Onion Sauce

Roast the onion in its skin for approx 1 hour at 180°C . It should be very soft, remove from the oven and allow to cool.

Once cooled, remove the onion from its skin, saving as much of the liquid from the onion as possible.

Smoke the flesh of the onion for approximately 20 minutes.

In a pan, combine the whipping cream, milk, veg stock, the smoked onion flesh and any onion juices saved.

Bring to the boil and cook for about 2-3 minutes, then place into a liquidiser and blitz until smooth pass through a fine sieve.

Check the seasoning and serve.

Plating

Place the cauliflower into the reserved cooking liquid and boil for about 1 minute until fully reheated. Remove from the liquid and keep warm.

Place a spoonful of warm houmous in the centre of the bowl, place the cauliflower head side down, add the black peas, cured ham and tempura cauliflower leaf, carefully pour the onion sauce over the cauliflower, sprinkle with chive batons and flowers and serve.

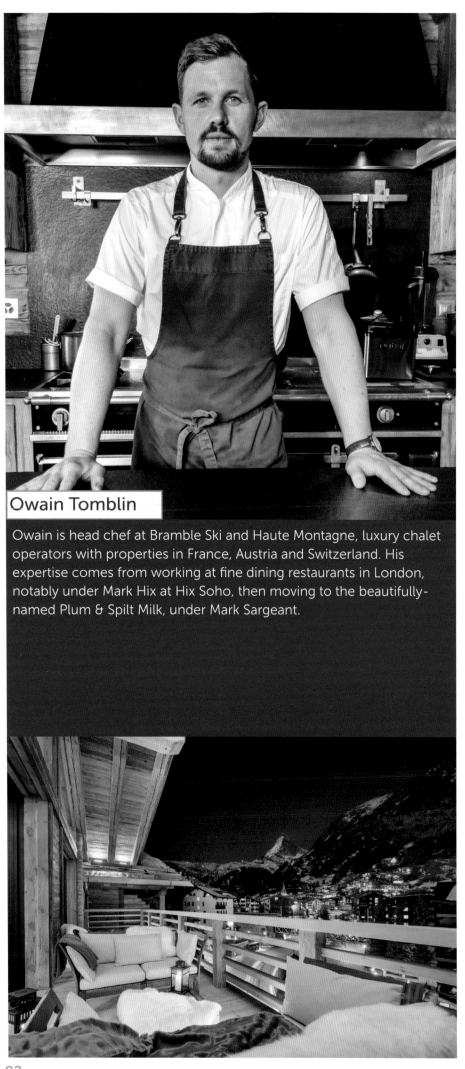

Owain Tomblin

Owain is head chef at Bramble Ski and Haute Montagne, luxury chalet operators with properties in France, Austria and Switzerland. His expertise comes from working at fine dining restaurants in London, notably under Mark Hix at Hix Soho, then moving to the beautifully-named Plum & Spilt Milk, under Mark Sargeant.

Stuff you'll need

4 centre-cut beef fillets (150-200g)

Jerusalem artichoke purée

150g unsalted butter

300g Jerusalem artichoke, washed, peeled and sliced, reserve the peelings for crumb

1 pinch rock salt

500g vegetable stock

50g double cream

2 king oyster mushrooms (these can be substituted for fresh shiitakes)

2 tablespoons oil

Get stuck in

Jerusalem artichoke purée

Add the butter to a large, heavy-bottomed pan over a medium heat and cook until it begins to foam.

Add the sliced Jerusalem artichokes and a pinch of salt, then cover the pan and allow to cook for 10 minutes until soft, stirring occasionally to prevent sticking.

Once soft, add the vegetable stock and bring it up to the boil.

Allow to simmer and reduce by half, then stir in the double cream.

Bring the mixture back up to the boil briefly, then remove from the heat and transfer to a blender. Blend the mixture to form a smooth purée, then season to taste with extra salt and a squeeze of lemon juice if required. Transfer to a piping bag and keep warm until ready to serve.

Truffle jus

Set a large pot over high heat and add the chicken stock.

When the stock has reduced to about 250ml of liquid, reduce the heat to medium and add the sherry along with the truffle peelings.

Let the liquid in the pot reduce until it appears less watery and slightly sticky. The difference will be subtle.

When you are happy with the consistency and texture of your sauce, remove it from the heat.

Beef fillet, jerusalem artichoke

Truffle jus

1ltr dark chicken stock

125ml medium dry sherry

200g black truffle peelings

1 tablespoon butter

1 pinch rock salt

2 black truffles to serve

To finish the sauce, set the pot over low heat, and add the butter.

Stir gently to incorporate the butter into the sauce. Taste the sauce and add salt as necessary. Keep warm until ready to plate.

Beef fillet

Place a large ovenproof frying pan over a high heat and seal the beef fillets on all sides. Transfer to the oven and roast for 8 minutes, then set aside to rest for 10 minutes.

King oyster mushrooms

Trim the base of the mushroom by roughly 2cm. Diagonally score the cut face of the mushroom with a paring knife to a depth of 2mm and then repeat in the opposite direction to create a crosshatch pattern

Place a frying pan over a medium high heat. Add 2 tablespoons of oil and fry the mushrooms, with the cut side down, until golden brown in colour. Flip the mushrooms cook in the oven for 4 minutes or unti tender.

To serve

Pipe a large dot of the artichoke purée onto the plate. Place the oyster mushroom on the purée. Place a piece of beef fillet on each plate, just overlapping the purée, grate or slice some fresh truffle over the plate and serve immediately. For extra effect pour the truffle sauce at the table.

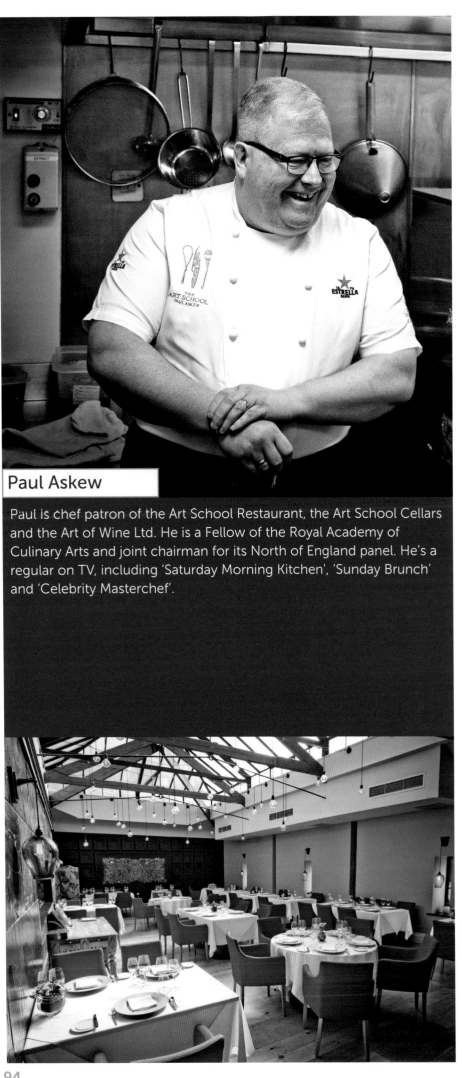

Paul Askew

Paul is chef patron of the Art School Restaurant, the Art School Cellars and the Art of Wine Ltd. He is a Fellow of the Royal Academy of Culinary Arts and joint chairman for its North of England panel. He's a regular on TV, including 'Saturday Morning Kitchen', 'Sunday Brunch' and 'Celebrity Masterchef'.

Serves 4

Stuff you'll need

Rabbit

1 whole rabbit, skinned and gutted
500ml duck fat
2 cloves garlic
2 sprigs of rosemary
4 peppercorns
1 bay leaf
Rabbit/chicken stock
Pre-rolled sheet of butter puff pastry
1 egg yolk

Polenta pastry

400g plain sifted flour
200g polenta
2 sprigs of thyme, stripping the leaves
300g unsalted butter

Pickled vegetable garnish

Carrot, 1/4cm cubed, pre-blanched
Cocktail gherkins (cornichons), halved
Radish, finely-sliced on a mandolin
Baby onions, pre-blanched, quartered
2 tablespoons mirin (Japanese corn syrup)
2 tablespoons rice wine vinegar
Pinch of salt
Pinch of cracked black pepper

Piccalilli

1 cauliflower
3 large onions
8 large shallots
1 cucumber
600ml white wine or cider vinegar
300ml white malt vinegar
1/4 tsp chopped dried red chilli
350g caster sugar
50g English mustard powder
25g ground turmeric
3 tablespoons cornflour
Salt and pepper

Confit of autumn rabbit pie with pickled vegetables & piccalilli vinaigrette

Get stuck in

Rabbit

Separate into the saddle and remove and trim the loins ready to cook. Put the shoulders and legs to one side ready to be cooked.

In a pan, colour each side of the front legs and back legs before placing them into the duck fat with the herbs, and cook them at 150°C until tender, for about 1 hour.

Polenta pastry

Add all of the ingredients into a large bowl, and rub through the cold butter until it has reached a sand-like texture.

Bring it together using ice cold water. Be careful not to overwork your pastry. Wrap in clingfilm and allow it to rest in the fridge for at least an hour before you roll it out.

Remove the pastry from the fridge, and allow it to come back to room temperature before working it.

Roll the pastry out onto a floured surface, to about 3mm thick. This is now ready to be placed into your desired pastry cases.

Bake blind in the oven on 160°C for 10 minutes. Cases can then be left to one side to cool down.

Pickled vegetable garnish

Bring the liquids to the boil add in the vegetables and leave in the picking liquor until needed. Drain onto paper towel before plating as per photograph

Piccalilli

Cut the cauliflower into small florettes. Chop the onions and shallots into 1cm dice and add them to the bowl of prepared cauliflower florettes. Peel and de-seed the cucumber and cut it into 1cm dice. Sprinkle the cucumber with a little salt and leave for a quarter of an hour to draw out some of the moisture. Rinse the cucumber under cold water and leave it to dry. Then add this to the other vegetables.

Put the vinegars into a pan, and add the chilli before bringing it to the boil. Take it off the heat and leave it to stand for thirty minutes. You don't want to pour this over your vegetables as they will start to cook.

Strain and discard the chilli. When the vinegar is cool, mix all of the dry ingredients.

in a bowl and add a little of the vinegar and mix it until it has formed a thin paste. Bring the rest of the vinegar back to the boil and pour it into the sugar/spice paste and stir it well until it is mixed together with no lumps. Return it to the pan and simmer for about three minutes. Pour over the vegetables and mix it well

Store them in a sterilised jar such as a mason jar. Then store them in a cool place. You will be able to keep this for a month or two.

Peter Fiori

Peter is the executive chef of Coutts Bank. He joined the bank in 2002 and has since been made a Fellow of the Royal Academy of Culinary Arts, where he promotes ethically rigorous practices and sustainability within the food industry. Since starting the Coutts Skyline roof top garden in 2011, alongside his colleague Richard Vine, the garden now feeds not only Coutts' clients but is also shared with local charities, as well as providing a home to its very own bees.

Serves 4

Stuff you'll need

2 x 2kg Barbary duck

Duck sauce

30ml olive oil

½ carrot, finely chopped

2 sticks celery, finely chopped

3 cloves garlic, finely chopped

4 sage leaves, roughly chopped

50ml red wine vinegar

175ml red wine

200ml orange juice

500ml chicken stock

1 tablespoon orange marmalade

1 tablespoon brown sugar

Colcannon

500g floury potatoes

½ savoy cabbage, shredded finely

100ml full fat milk

80g unsalted butter

3 spring onions, finely sliced

Salt and pepper

To finish

1 whole orange, peeled, pith removed and segmented

Roast barbary duck, orange and colcannon

Get stuck in

Pre-heat the oven to 200°C. Remove the neck, wishbone and winglets from the duck, then the legs and backbone to create a crown.
Chop the winglets, wishbone and backbone into small pieces and roast in the oven for 15 minutes until golden brown. Strain the bones through a sieve to remove all the fat.

Duck sauce

Add a splash of olive oil to a medium-sized saucepan over a medium heat. Add the carrot, celery and garlic and soften with a lid on. After 3 minutes add the sage, followed by the red vinegar. Reduce by half, add the red wine and reduce by two-thirds, then add the orange juice and reduce by two-thirds. Now add the chicken stock followed by the roasted duck bones. Simmer until you have a nice sauce consistency to coat the back of a spoon. Add the marmalade and brown sugar, check seasoning and pass through a sieve and reserve for later.

Colcannon

Cook unpeeled potatoes in boiling water for 20/25 mins until tender. Drain and return to an empty pan off the heat, cover with a tea towel and leave to steam for 15 mins. Meanwhile cook the shredded cabbage in boiling water until tender but still crisp. Drain and place in iced water then remove from the water and squeeze with your hands to remove as much water as possible. Combine the milk, butter and spring onions in a sauce pan and warm gently. Peel the potatoes and put them through a ricer, add the milk, butter and spring onions and beat into the potatoes, then mix in the cabbage and season with salt and pepper.

To serve

Pre-heat the oven to 160°C. To roast the duck crowns, score the breast fat lightly with a sharp knife and season with salt and pepper, then place skin side down into a pan (no fat required) and fry the crowns until crispy and golden all over. Roast in the oven for 20 minutes, remove and rest for a further 10 minutes. Reheat the duck sauce and add the orange segments. Remove the breasts from the crowns using a sharp knife. Pour the finished sauce around the duck breast and accompany with the reheated colcannon.

Pete Redman

Pete started his career working in 5 star hotels and acclaimed restaurants in Oxfordshire and Buckinghamshire. He then moved to work at the Sultan of Oman's private household and lodge before moving into contract catering. For the last seven years he has been chef director of Bartlett Mitchell.

Serves 4-6

Stuff you'll need

Potato terrine

6 Albert rooster potatoes
100g butter, melted
Olive oil for frying
Garnish
200g Cimi de rapa, or tender stem broccoli
100g jus

Red cabbage puree

½ a red cabbage
4g Agar agar
40g cabernet sauvignon vinegar
75g dark brown sugar
1 fresh black truffle

Lamb

600g lamb cannon
2 cloves garlic
6 sprigs of fresh thyme
60g butter

Cannon of lamb, red cabbage puree, potato terrine and cimi de rapa

Get stuck in

Potato terrine

Start with the potato terrine. Line a terrine mould or oven proof dish with a couple of layers of clingfilm. Peel and thinly slice the potatoes on a mandolin and lay about 8 slices in the bottom of the terrine. Brush with some of the melted butter and season, lay more potato slices on top and again brush with butter and season. Continue this until you have used all the potatoes and then clingfilm the whole terrine in a few layers of clingfilm and cook in the oven at 130°C for about an 1 ½ hours or until a knife can be inserted with little resistance. Let it sit for 10 minutes and then lay a piece of grease proof paper on top and stick a few heavy things on top to press the terrine down and chill for at least 4 hours or overnight. Once chilled and pressed, turn out from the mould and cut into 2in thick slices and set aside.

To serve

Fry the potato terrine add in some olive, turning every couple minutes until they are golden brown, crispy and hot.

Place the cimi de rapa in a pan with a splash of water and a touch of butter and season. Heat until just wilted and glazed. Warm some of the red cabbage puree and spoon on to the plate, cut the terrine in half and plate topped with the cimi de rapa and a few slices of fresh truffle. Carve the lamb and season the cut side, drizzle with some jus and serve.

Red cabbage puree

For the cabbage, cut into wedges that will fit in a juicer and juice until you have about 350g of juice. Put the juice into a saucepan with the sugar and the agar. Whisk to disperse and let it sit for five minutes to hydrate. Bring this to the boil while whisking and simmer for 1 minute. Tip out on to a tray to chill and set. Once set put in a blender with the vinegar and blend until smooth and check for seasoning. Trim the cimi de rapa and set aside.

Lamb

Season the lamb well with sea salt and place fat side down into a pan and cook on a low heat to render out the fat, This will take about 8-10 mins. Once the fat has rendered and has a good colour, use some of the rendered fat to baste the other side and add the garlic, thyme and butter to the pan and continue to baste with the foaming butter until the lamb is medium, about 2 mins and allow to rest.

Peter Tempelhoff

Peter started his 22 year career working at Bosmans at Grande Roche, South Africa, before moving to London to work under Marco Pierre White and Giorgio Locatelli, ending up opening and operating the Automat Brasserie in Soho.

Returning to South Africa in 2006, Tempelhoff took over at Grande Provence Restaurant, two years later moving to Greenhouse as Cape Town's first Grand Chef de Relais & Chateaux. He recently opened his latest project, FYN.

Stuff you'll need

Duck
2 Gressingham duck breasts

Endive
2 endives, split lengthwise
5ml extra virgin olive oil
40ml orange juice
15g butter
Rosemary sprig
Kosher Salt

Hibiscus flowers
40g dried hibiscus flowers
30g sugar
100ml port
20g butter

Celeriac cream
200g diced celeriac, peeled
30g butter
30g cream
100ml double cream, scalded

Hazelnut & hibiscus crumble
100g toasted hazelnuts
2 tablespoons chopped hibiscus leaves
20ml maple syrup
Kosher salt

Truffle sauce
100g duck jus
Chopped truffle

Duck, hibiscus, endive & truffle

Get stuck in

Endive

Fry the endives in the olive oil, allowing for a little colour on the face. Deglaze the pan with the orange juice and continue to cook the endive on medium heat until the juice has reduced. If the endive is still firm to the touch and the juice has reduced to a syrup, add a tablespoon of water and continue to cook for a few more minutes. Monte with the butter and glaze the endive with the orange syrup - serve at once.

Hibiscus flowers

Soak the hibiscus in water for 10 minutes. Remove from the water, strain and squeeze out and place in a small saucepan with port and sugar. Cook slowly until reduced to a syrup. Monte with butter. Add a pinch of salt.

Celeriac cream

Place celeriac, butter and cream into a vac pac bag, seal and simmer for an hour in water. Blend till smooth with the cream.

Hazelnut & hibiscus crumble

Chop hazelnuts and combine with the rest of the ingredients. Use immediately.

Cooking the duck

Pat the duck breast dry and place in a hot pan skin-side down for 2 minutes, turn the breast and sear meat for 30 seconds. Return onto the skin side and place pan in oven for 3-4 minutes depending on the size. Rest the breast for two minutes while plating.

Plating

Slice lengthwise in half and take a little off each side so the duck sits face up. Place the endive next to the duck and top with nut crumble. Place the hibiscus on the opposite side of the duck and garnish with celeriac cream, fresh truffle slices and the truffle sauce.

Prue Leith

Prue Leith is a businesswoman, cookery writer and broadcaster. Her restaurant, Leith's, held a Michelin star and she is a past winner of the Veuve Clicquot Businesswoman of the Year. She chaired The School Food Trust, tasked with improving school meals. She is currently a judge on the 'Great British Bake Off', and advisor to the government's Review of Hospital Food.

Babotie

2 thick slices of white bread
150ml milk
3 tablespoons vegetable oil
2 large onions, finely chopped
2 garlic cloves, crushed
3cm piece of ginger, peeled and finely grated
1 tablespoon mild curry powder
1 teaspoon ground coriander
$\frac{1}{2}$ teaspoon ground cumin
450g lamb mince
1 small dessert apple, grated
75g fruit chutney
2 tbsp Worcestershire sauce
1 tablespoon tomato purée
A handful of sultanas

Custard

2 eggs
275g Greek yoghurt
A handful of flaked almonds
2 Kaffir lime leaves or bay leaves
Salt and pepper to season

Babotie

The Babotie

Put the bread into a small tray or shallow bowl and pour over the milk. Leave to soak. Heat the oven to 180°C.

Heat half the oil in a large, heavy-based saucepan over a medium-high heat. Add the onions and fry until soft and just golden. Add the garlic, ginger, curry powder, coriander and cumin and cook for a further minute or so. Remove from the saucepan and empty into a large bowl. Wipe the saucepan clean and pour in the remaining oil.

Turn the heat up and fry the lamb mince for 5–6 minutes, until golden brown. Press the meat down with the back of a fish slice to encourage it to brown properly. When the meat is browned on all sides, add it to the spiced onions with the apple, chutney, Worcestershire sauce, tomato purée and sultanas. Add a little water if it looks too thick. Fork the wet bread into the mixture, season and gently combine. Pile the mixture into a 2-litre ovenproof dish and use the back of a wooden spoon to flatten it.

Custard

Mix the eggs with the yoghurt. Season with salt and pepper. Pour this over the mixture, then place the almonds and Kaffir leaves on top and bake in the preheated oven for about 40–45 minutes, until the custard has set and browned. Remove from the oven and let it stand for 10 minutes before serving.

Note

When we were little this was often made from leftover roast lamb. Don't fry the meat, just chop or mince finely and mix it with the spiced onions. In South Africa the recipe is generally topped with Kaffir lime leaves; in England they are usually bay leaves.

Simon Boyle with Anton Edelmann

Simon Boyle is an award-winning chef, author and social entrepreneur.

His varied career has seen him on BBC's Dragons' Den, as Culinary Ambassador for Unilever and the chef and founder of the homeless and hospitality charity Beyond Food Foundation, where he uses food as a catalyst for social change. Beyond Food's home and social enterprise restaurant, Brigade Bar + Kitchen is on Tooley Street, London. The restaurant set in Tooley Street's Grade II-listed fire station at the heart of London Bridge relaunched in 2019 with a brand new look. The menu offers a contemporary edge to the capital's smoke and grill movement, focussing on straight from source ingredients.

Stuff you'll need

Lamb

1.5 kg middle neck of lamb
50g plain flour
4 tablespoons olive oil
Mirepoix
(2 onions, 2 carrots, 1 leek, 2 stick celery)
4 ripe plum tomatoes
1 cinnamon stick
10 peppercorns
1 bay leaf
150ml white wine
100g Manuka honey
1 ltr veal stock, reduced

Roasted eggplant

4 Japanese eggplants
Olive oil
Salt and pepper
6 cloves of garlic
2 medium chillies, halved,
seeded and thinly sliced
1/2 lemon zested and juiced
150g feta cheese, crumbled
50g Greek yogurt
Fresh mint

To serve

Wafer thin croutes with butter
Sea salt

Braised neck of lamb, manuka honey, japanese eggplant

Get stuck in

Lamb

Heat a couple of tablespoons of olive oil in a deep heavy based pot, add the whole piece of lamb and brown all over. Dust with seasoned flour and continue to brown for a further few minutes to gain that lovely rich brown colour and flavour.

Remove the lamb from the pot and wipe add some fresh oil and brown off the mirepoix. Keep turning to gain an even colour. Once golden, add the freshly chopped tomatoes, cinnamon, peppercorns and bay leaf.

Pour in the white wine and Manuka honey and stir thoroughly, bring to the boil, reduce to a glaze. Place the neck of lamb back into the middle of the pan with the vegetables around.

Pour in the veal stock, enough to cover the neck of lamb, and bring to the boil. Cover and place in the oven for 3-4 hours, until the lamb is tender enough to fall away from the bone. Take out of the oven and leave to cool. Gently take the neck of lamb out of the cooking liquor and place on a clean oven tray. Strain the liquor and return to the boil and reduce.

Take a couple of ladles of sauce and ladle over the neck of lamb. Return the tray to the oven and, for 10 minutes, keep ladling over the sauce to achieve a beautiful glaze over the surface of the meat. Be careful not to burn the meat. Once the glaze is achieved, take out of the oven and leave to rest for at least 30 minutes.

Roasted eggplant

Preheat the oven to 200°C. Halve the eggplants lengthwise and then score a diamond pattern into the flesh of each half on the cut surface, being careful not to cut all the way through. Sprinkle over the crushed garlic and chillies. Pour about 10 tablespoons of olive oil over the cut surface, season with salt and pepper. Roast for 25-30 minutes, covering with tin foil if needed. When tender place on a tray. Scoop out the flesh and fork to deconstruct the filling. Add the lemon juice and zest, feta cheese and Greek yogurt, mix well and check the seasoning. Refill the eggplant skins.

To serve

Serve the lamb with the eggplant, garnished with some wafer thin croutes and fresh mint leaves. Serve the eggplant at room temperature.

Steve Cooke

Steve Cooke has been a professional chef in the catering industry for 30 years. After from college he moved to London for two years and worked at The Chelsea Room in Knightsbridge and at Anton Mosimann's. After then travelling to Europe and Australia, Steve returned home to work for the Devere Company, with which he was appointed to his first head chef role, at Dunstan Hall hotel, Norwich. After a few years Steve moved back to Sussex and became executive head chef for Brighton College for five years. Steve left to set up Cookes Catering, the chef agency he ran before stepping sideways to take on his current role of operations manager for Handcross Catering Butchers.

Stuff you'll need

Venison

400g Borde Hill Estate venison loin
1 teaspoon ground cinnamon
1 teaspoon sea salt
½ teaspoon peppercorns
4 juniper berries
200g brussel sprouts, trimmed and quartered
2 shallots
150g pancetta lardons
1 tablespoon rapeseed oil

Savoury pannacotta

65ml full fat milk
65ml double cream
75g Sussex Slipcote
(organic sheep's milk soft cheese)
1 sheet gelatine
Seasoning
1 teaspoon white truffle oil

Cinnamon, juniper scented venison loin, sprouts, pancetta with truffle pannacotta

Get stuck in

Savoury pannacotta

Place the gelatine leaf in cold water for 5 minutes. Then add milk, cream, truffle oil and seasoning in a pan and bring to the boil. Remove from heat and whisk in Slipcote cheese and then your gelatine leaf which has been removed from the water. Season to taste and then pour into small dariole moulds or small expresso cups and place into fridge and chill until set.

Venison

Next place the sea salt, juniper berries and cinnamon in a pestle and mortar and grind to a coarse mix, place onto a plate and roll the venison loin until covered.

Heat a pan with the rapeseed oil and stir fry the pancetta lardons until coloured, add 2 sliced shallots and cook for about 1 minute until softened, then add the brussel sprouts and stir fry until just cooked and vibrant in colour.

Whilst the sprout mix is cooking, heat another pan with a little rapeseed oil and pan fry the venison loin, turning all the time for even cooking for a couple of minutes. Remove from the pan and place on chopping board to rest.

Plating

Remove the set pannacotta from the fridge and run the back of the mould under hot water to remove and place onto your plate. Next serve the brussel sprout mix next to the pannacotta and then slice the venison loin which should be nice and bloody. Arrange on plate garnished with a little fresh rosemary....simple but extremely tasty!!

Stephen Stevens

Stephen started work as a plumber after leaving school, then - in an unexpected career change - moved to London to cook in some of the UK's best restaurants. Returning home to Anglesey in 2011, with a young family, Stephen decided to venture out on his own at Sosban & The Old Butcher's.

Stuff you'll need

Kale
Kale, whole leaves washed and dried
1 egg
4 anchovy fillets finely chopped

Branches
2 large free range eggs
200g Tipo '00' flour
100g mushroom powder
4 chicken wings

Brine
250g Malden salt
100g demerara sugar
1 tablespoon whole black pepper corns
2ltr water
5 cloves
50ml buttermilk

Cheddar paste
125g Hafod cheese grated
25g plain flour
25g unsalted butter
300ml milk

Chicken skin
4 rashers smoked bacon
100g chicken skin

Spice mix
150g plain flour
50g cornflour
1 tablespoon chilli powder
1 teaspoon paprika smoked
1 teaspoon paprika sweet
2 teaspoons garlic powder
1 teaspoon oregano
1 teaspoon majoram
1 teaspoon basil

Cesar dressing
1 egg
4 anchovy fillets finely chopped
200g olive oil
1 teaspoon Dijon mustard
Ground black pepper to season
2 tablespoons lemon
1 teaspoon Worcestershire sauce
1 garlic clove, finely grated
Parmesan for topping

Umami log

Get stuck in

Kale

Remove stalks, wash and dry all leaves.
Brush the kale leaves with clarified butter, place
in the dehydrator on high for minimum 8 hours.

Branches

Mix flour, mushroom powder and eggs in
processor into a crumb. Tip out onto the work
top, knead for 10 mins until you achieve a
smooth dough. Clingfilm and leave in the fridge
for at least 30 mins.
Once ready, place through pasta machine on the
spaghetti setting.

Brine

Bring all brine mix to the boil until salt and sugar
are dissolved. Leave to cool. Place the chicken in
cooled brine mix for one hour and then drain.
Store, immersed in buttermilk, in the fridge until
required.

Spice mix

Mix all dry ingredients in the bowl.

Cheddar paste

Melt the butter in a saucepan. Stir in the flour
and cook for 1-2 minutes - ensure the flour
is cooked out. Take the pan off the heat and
gradually stir in the milk to get a smooth sauce.
Add the cheddar, whisk in, season to taste.
Simmer gently for 8-10 minutes and season with
salt and white pepper.
Stir in cheese and allow to melt. Allow to cool.

Chicken skin

Place in the oven on a tray at 200°C. Roast until
crisp.
Remove from the oven and allow to cool. Finely
chop the chicken skin and bacon into a fine
crumb.

Cesar dressing

Combine garlic, mustard, Worstecester sauce,
lemon juice, pepper and whole egg in a bowl
with whisk. Gradually add the oil whilst whisking
until emulsified.

Plating

Remove the chicken wings from the buttermilk,
coat in the spice mix. Shallow fry in a pan at
180°C for approx 4 mins. Place the blanched
spaghetti straws in the oven, carefully remove
and twist with tweezers, and allow to cool.

Spread the cheddar paste on to the crisp straws, dip into the chopped
bacon and chicken skin mix - try to cover as much area as possible for
maximum flavour.
Dress the kale with the prepared dressing. Grate on the parmesan.
Serve all three elements together.

Sujira Pongmorn

Sujira 'Aom' Pongmorn published a cookbook dedicated entirely to phadthai, the iconic sweet-and-savory noodle dish that can be found in countless Thai restaurants around the world. Saawaan - the fine dining restaurant where she is chef de cuisine and co-owner - also received a star in the 2019 edition of Thailand's Michelin Guide. Pongmorn's parents ran a small restaurant in Bangkok and she recalls that when she was six her father taught her how to make a Thai omlette. She instantly fell in love with cooking. At 18, after completing high school, she enrolled at the Mandarin Oriental Bangkok hotel's chef school apprenticeship programme. In 2016, with the backing of local restaurateur Frederic Meyer, she launched Baan Phadthai, putting a gourmet spin on Thailand's iconic wok-fried noodle dish.

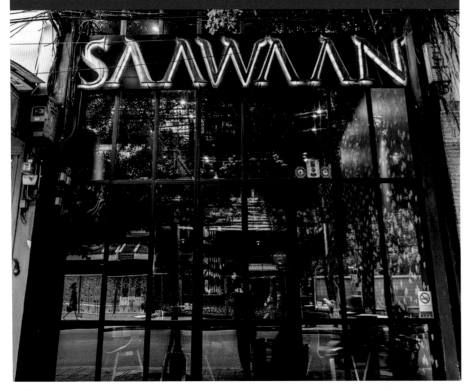

Stuff you'll need

Phadthai gai yang

2 tablespoons vegetable oil for phadthai

1 tablespoon vegetable oil for egg

3 tablespoons vegetable oil

80g dried Chanthaburi noodles

2 teaspoons dried shrimp

1 tablespoon tofu, cut into small chunks

1 tablespoon pickled turnip, chopped

1 tablespoon shallot, chopped

8 tablespoons chicken stock

½ cup phadthai sauce (see below)

1 tablespoon ground roasted peanuts

½ cup bean sprouts

¼ cup garlic chives, cut into 2.5cm pieces

1 egg

1 teaspoon chili powder

1 lime wedge

1 chicken thigh or chicken breast

1 garlic clove, smashed

1 teaspoon black pepper

1 tablespoon Golden Mountain Seasoning Sauce

1 tablespoon palm sugar

Sauce phadthai

¼ cup shallot, thinly sliced

1 tablespoon garlic, finely chopped

1 cup tamarind concentrate

1 cup palm sugar

½ cup fish sauce

1 tablespoon salt

1 cup water

1 teaspoon chilli powder
(or adjust spiciness as desired)

2 tablespoons vegetable oil

Phadthai with grilled chicken

Get stuck in

Phadthai gai yang

In a mixing bowl, mix together palm sugar, seasoning sauce, black pepper and garlic until the palm sugar dissolves.

Add chicken to the bowl, and hand-knead until the marinade is absorbed by the chicken. Set aside to marinate for 20 minutes.

In a heated grilling pan, grill the marinated chicken until cooked. Set aside.

Crack the egg into a small bowl, and beat till smooth. Set aside.

Heat a wok or large non-stick frying pan over medium-high heat. Drizzle two tablespoons of oil into the pan and swirl around. Add shallots and stir-fry until fragrant.

Add tofu and pickled turnip to the pan, and stir-fry for about a minute.

Add noodles and chicken stock and stir-fry until the noodles soften.

Add phadthai sauce and stir-fry until noodles and dry ingredients absorb all the sauce.

Remove noodles and set to one side. Stir-fry the egg in the remaining vegetable oil until cooked.

Add sprouts, garlic chives, dried shrimp and chilli powder and stir-fry until the sprouts and garlic chives are wilted.

Slice the chicken and place over the noodles. Serve with lime wedge, beansprouts, garlic chives, chilli powder and ground roasted peanuts on the side.

Sauce phadthai

Add vegetable oil to a saucepan and place on medium-heat stove.

Add shallot and garlic, and fry until fragrant and the garlic is a bit brown.

Add water, tamarind concentrate, chilli powder, palm sugar, and salt.

Stir constantly until palm sugar dissolves and sauce is mixed well. Let the sauce simmer and thicken.

Remove from the heat and let cool down.

Pour phadthai sauce into a blender and blend until smooth, strain and serve.

Will store refrigerated for up to 1 month

Thomas Frake

Thomas Frake became the MasterChef 2020 Champion, the sixteenth amateur cook to claim the prestigious title, in April 2020. Thomas impressed the judges with his modern elevation of great British traditional dishes and gastro pub classics. Since winning the competition, Thomas has been working with local charities helping to raise awareness, and deliver restaurant-cooked meals directly to NHS key workers.

Makes 6

Stuff you'll need

Eggs

6 quail eggs

Sausagemeat

400g good quality
Cumberland sausages (90% Pork)
1 tablespoon Dijon mustard
1 tablespoon dried parsley
1 tablespoon chopped fresh sage
1 teaspoon ground mixed peppercorns
½ teaspoon ground mace
Sea salt flakes

Coating

75g flour
75g panko breadcrumbs
1 beaten egg
1 teaspoon dried parsley
1 teaspoon chopped fresh sage
Sea salt flakes

Brown sauce

400g chopped tinned tomatoes
2 sliced shallots
100g chopped pitted dates
1 grated granny smith apple
1 tablespoon Worcestershire sauce
1½ tablespoon black treacle
80ml red wine vinegar
30g dark brown sugar
1 teaspoon ground allspice
1 teaspoon garlic granules
1 teaspoon mustard powder
1 teaspoon ground mixed peppercorns
½ teaspoon cayenne pepper
Olive oil
Sea salt flakes

Quail scotch egg with brown sauce

Get stuck in

Eggs

Bring a pan to the boil, and cook the quail eggs for exactly 2 minutes. Remove and submerge in ice water. Leave to cool for 5 minutes, then carefully peel the shells.

Sausagemeat

Slice open the sausages, remove and discard the casings. Mix in a bowl with all the other sausagemeat ingredients and season with a pinch of salt.

Make six balls of sausagemeat, each about the size of a golf ball. Working one at a time, flatten the sausagemeat ball into a disc big enough to wrap around a quails egg. Gently fold the meat up and around the egg, and pinch to seal the top. Roll gently between your palms to shape and ensure the egg is fully enclosed.

Refrigerate for 15 minutes.

Coating

Put the flour in one bowl, the beaten egg in another, and finally mix the breadcrumbs, sage and parsley in a third bowl. Roll the sausagemeat balls first in flour, then the egg, and then the panko breadcrumbs.

Set a fryer to 175°C. When hot, add the scotch eggs and cook for 3 minutes for a soft and golden yolk. Remove the scotch eggs, drain on absorbent kitchen towel, sprinkle with sea salt flakes, and let rest for 10 minutes before serving. They are best eaten warm, but not hot.

Brown sauce

Add a glug of olive oil to a medium hot saucepan and saute the onions until translucent but not brown. Add all of the other ingredients to the pan excluding salt. Stir well, and simmer for 60 minutes until dark and sticky. Season with sea salt flakes to taste.

Place the contents of the pan into a blender, and blend until smooth. Season with sea salt flakes to taste. To make the sauce extra fine and glossy, push the sauce through a fine mesh seive using the back of a dessertspoon. Place in a squeeze bottle and chill before use.

Worapong Panechoo

Worapong Panechoo, better known as chef Kai, has been cooking for 27 years, 25 of which at Banyan Tree Phuket. Today most guests coming to Saffron don't read the menu, and trust him with their meal. Eager to continue developing recipes and spreading Thai flavors, Worapong believes produce and food can be used as medicine and therefore only uses organic fresh produce from local farmers.

Stuff you'll need

250g chicken breast, sliced
2 tablespoons green curry paste
3 cups coconut milk
2 tablespoons fish sauce
1 red chili
2 tablespoons vegetable oil
1 tablespoon palm sugar
2 kaffir lime leaves
100g green eggplant
10 sweet basil leaves
Sliced red chilli for garnish

Get stuck in

Chop eggplant into medium sized pieces, slice the red chilli with a large cross cut, break kaffir lime leaves in half and pick fresh sweet basil leaves.
Warm oil in a pan and sauté green curry paste until fragrant.
Add coconut milk, palm sugar and stir slowly to mix thoroughly until sugar is dissolved.
Add sliced chicken breast and slowly simmer the chicken until cooked.
Add eggplant, chilli, kaffir lime leaves and sweet basil to curry. Keep a few basil leaves for garnish. Warm for two minutes.
Adjust flavour with fish sauce and serve in a warm bowl.
Garnish with sliced red Thai chilli and sweet basil leaves.
Serve with steamed jasmine rice.

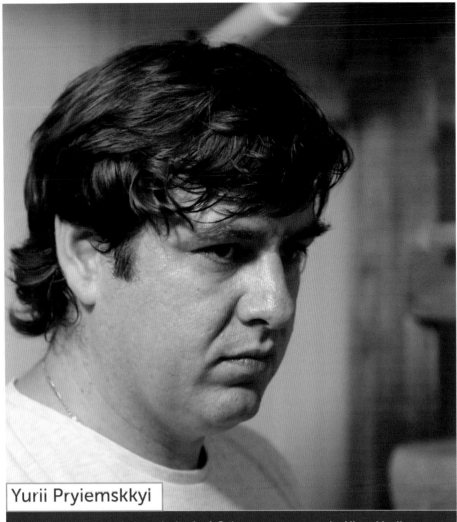

Yurii Pryiemskkyi

Yurii Pryiemskkyi is head chef of Odessa restaurant in Kiev. Yurii dreamed of becoming a football player but soon found that his real passion was to cook, using the amazing ingredients available to him in his beloved Ukraine. Sport's loss was cuisine's gain and his career began when he migrated to Italy and started to learn his craft at the restaurant Benihana, enjoying the challenging environment of chefs cooking in front of the guests. After six months training in London, Yurii headed to Moscow where for the first time, he created his own menu and was able to put his ideas into practice.

Stuff you'll need

Borsch

150g beetroot

40g carrots

30g onions

80g white cabbage

120g potatoes

20g parsley root

100g pelati tomatoes

10ml vinegar

Pinch of salt

Pinch of pepper

10g sugar

Bay leaf x 1

4g garlic

700ml meat broth

5g paprika

30ml Vegetable oil

40g salo/fat

4g dill

Smoked sour cream

100ml sour cream

Plating

Large whole beetroots x 4

Borsch with smoked sour cream

Get stuck in

Borsch

Wash and peel all the vegetables. Dice the potatoes and put into water.

To make a broth, cut the beetroots into thin strips, and pre-fry a little in vegetable oil. In a pan of simmering water add the beetroot, sugar, salt and pelati tomatoes. Simmer until the beetroot is cooked. Chop the onion, carrot and parsley root into strips and fry in vegetable oil until cooked, seasoning with salt and pepper. Cut the cabbage into strips.

Bring the rich broth to the boil, add potatoes and bring back to the boil, add the cabbage and boil for 10 minutes.

Add the cooked beetroot fried onions, carrots and parsley root.

Finally, add the chopped salo/fat with garlic and dill, a bay leaf and season with salt, pepper and sugar.

Leave to infuse for 20 minutes.

Use some vegetables and make puree in a blender and pour back into the soup.

Smoked sour cream

Smoke the sour cream in a smoking device for 10-20 minutes.

Plating

Wash the 4 whole beetroots, cut the tops off and clean out the insides. Pour the soup into the hollowed-out beetroots and top with smoked sour cream. Cover with the tops of the beetroots and serve.

Nothing is more exhilarating than fresh **fish** simply cooked

Rick Stein

Fish Recipes

Adam Gray

Adam Gray is a chef with over 35 years' experience, holding a Michelin star for over a decade, working alongside Gary Rhodes as head chef at City Rhodes and then Rhodes 24. Adam is a Master Craftsman with the Craft Guild of Chefs and a member of the Royal Academy of Culinary Arts. He has worked as executive chef at Skylon in London's Royal Festival Hall and the Bourne and Hollingsworth Group, where he also opened the B & H Kitchen Cookery School before joining the Devonshire Club as executive chef in 2017.

Stuff you'll need

4, 150g sea bass portions
skin on and pin-boned
200ml British rapeseed oil
800g fresh clams in the shell,
washed in cold running water
1 large glass of white cooking wine
500ml fish or chicken stock
Curly parsley, leaves picked and finely chopped
and stalks saved
100ml double cream
50g unsalted butter
1 lemon, juiced
2 sticks of celery, cut into 1 cm dice
2 spring onions
trimmed, peeled, and cut into 1cm pieces
12 Jersey Royal new potatoes,
cooked and cut into 1cm pieces

Roasted sea bass clam and jersey potato chowder

Get stuck in

Cooking the clams

Place a heavy-bottomed saucepan on the stove and heat to a medium heat.

Add the clams and parsley stalks.

Pour over the white wine and fish/chicken stock, place a lid on the saucepan and steam the clams until they are all fully open.

Discard any clams that do not open.

Drain the cooked clams into a colander to separate the cooking liquor from the cooked clams.

Pass cooking juices through a fine sieve and reserve.

Pick the clams from the shells, discard the shells and keep the cooked clams.

Making the clam sauce

Pour the clam cooking liquor into a saucepan and place on the stove.

Reduce the liquor by half and add the cream.

Bring back to the boil and whisk in the cold unsalted butter.

Add half of the lemon juice.

Pass the sauce through a fine sieve and season with salt and pepper.

Roasting the sea bass

Heat a non-stick frying pan to a medium heat.

Add the rapeseed oil to the frying pan.

Sear the sea bass fillets on the flesh side with salt and ground pepper.

Place the sea bass in the frying pan skin side down.

Press the sea bass down gently in the pan with the back of your hand or a fish spatula.

After 2 -3 minutes turn the fish over, so the skin side is facing upwards.

Turn the heat down on the stove to a low heat and continue cooking the fish for a further five minutes. Add the remaining lemon juice.

To serve

Heat up the finished sauce in a saucepan and add the diced Jersey Royal new potatoes, sliced spring onions and diced celery.

Simmer for 2-3 minutes to ensure the diced vegetables are hot.

Now add the cooked clams and finely chopped curly parsley.

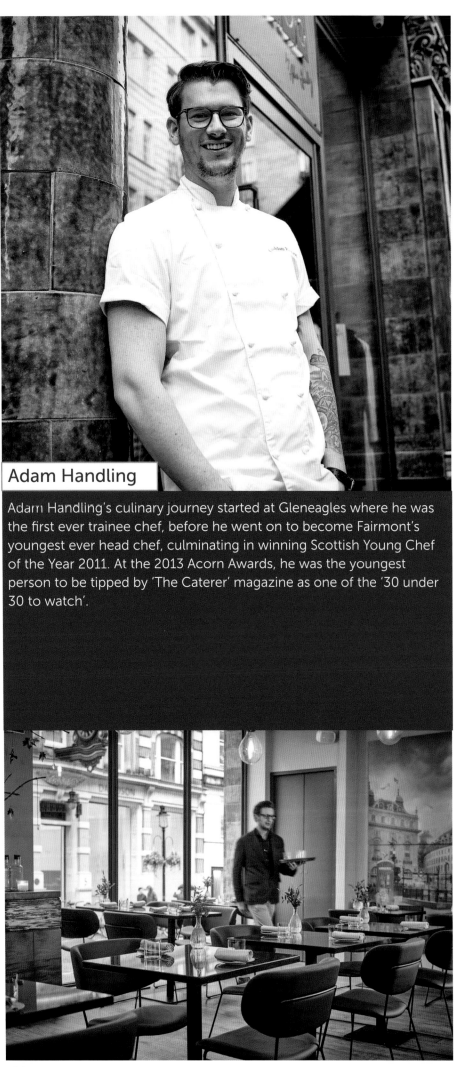

Adam Handling

Adam Handling's culinary journey started at Gleneagles where he was the first ever trainee chef, before he went on to become Fairmont's youngest ever head chef, culminating in winning Scottish Young Chef of the Year 2011. At the 2013 Acorn Awards, he was the youngest person to be tipped by 'The Caterer' magazine as one of the '30 under 30 to watch'.

Stuff you'll need

Broccoli puree

2 broccoli heads
(save stems for the garnish)
30ml vegetable oil
100ml water
6g sea salt
1g white pepper

John Dory

1 lemon juice
50ml extra virgin olive oil
3kg John Dory, filleted and skinned
200g Whey

Whey butter sauce

1 banana shallot, thinly sliced
50ml Chardonnay white wine
50ml double cream
200g whey
250g diced salted butter
150g Ossetra caviar

Garnish

Brazil nuts
Unsalted butter
2 finely-sliced broccoli stems
Extra virgin olive oil
Fresh goat's curd
Scurvy grass
Pennywort
Common sorrel

John dory, whey, caviar and broccoli

Get stuck in

Broccoli purée

Trim the broccoli florets. Pan-roast the broccoli in vegetable oil on a medium heat. Add 100ml of water to the broccoli, for steaming. Put the broccoli in a blender and blend until smooth. Season with salt and pepper. Pass through a fine chinois. Refrigerate until needed.

Whey butter sauce

Add the sliced shallot into a saucepan and pour in the white wine. Reduce until a syrupy consistency is achieved. Add the cream and 50g of whey. Bring to the boil. Whisk in the cold butter until a sauce consistency has formed. Pass through a chinois. Do not chill.

John Dory

Remove the John Dory from the bone, remove the skin and cut into eight equal pieces. Place the John Dory fillet into the whey. Cook for 12 minutes at 55°C, or until tender.

Garnish

Thinly slice the Brazil nuts, using a mandolin. Shallow fry in foaming butter, until golden. Dress the broccoli stems in olive oil.

To serve

Heat the broccoli purée in a small saucepan, on a medium heat. Place 35g of goat's curd onto the plate with a spoon of broccoli purée next to the curd. Top the curd with 55g of dressed broccoli salad. Blowtorch the John Dory. Place the fish on top of the salad. Scatter brazil nuts and sea herbs on top. Warm up the whey butter sauce, ensuring not to make it too hot, as you don't want to cook the caviar. Remove from the heat, add the caviar. Spoon the whey caviar over the fish.

Adam Newell

Adam Newell is one of New Zealand's two Michelin star rated chefs, having been inspired by his Cornish grandmother to carve a culinary career. After stints in London, New York, and Tokyo, Adam moved to New Zealand in the late 1990s and set up award-winning restaurant Zibibbo in Wellington. After some 20 years he sold up and moved north to the wine village of Martinborough. His restaurant Union Square Bistro & Bar is located at the historic Martinborough Hotel.

Stuff you'll need

Celeriac puree

1 peeled celeriac, cut into rough cubes
6 garlic cloves
1 bouquet garni:
sprig of thyme, bay leaf, rosemary
500ml cream
Salt and white pepper

Truffle currants

¼ cup dried currants
25ml port
50ml truffle oil

Seared scallops

3-4 large scallops per person or 6 small, cleaned
Oil for frying
Salt and pepper

Parmesan crumble

50g panko bread crumbs
25ml butter
3 tablespoons grated parmesan
1 garlic clove, crushed
1 tablespoon fresh chopped parsley

Scallops, celeriac puree and truffle currants

Get stuck in

Celeriac puree

Put all the ingredients in a pot. Simmer until the celeriac is soft.

Remove from heat, discard bouquet garni and liquidise the rest in a food processor until smooth.

There will probably be left over purée. It's delicious added to mashed potato, served with roast meat, or thickened with cornflour and used as a pasta sauce.

Truffle currants

Place the currants, port and truffle oil in a small pan and heat until almost at a simmer. Remove from heat and allow currants to steep in the warm liquid for five minutes.

This will keep refrigerated for months and can be used on grilled meat.

Seared scallops

After cleaning the scallops, pat dry gently with kitchen paper. Roll each scallop in oil and season with salt and pepper.
Sear both sides in a hot pan.

Parmesan crumble

Melt the butter and garlic together. Mix panko and parmesan together in a bowl. Add the garlic and butter. Mix well to bind.

Line an oven tray with baking paper and spread the breadcrumbs in a thin layer. Bake at 180°C for 2-3mins, then mix, spread out again and return to the oven for another 2-3 minutes until lightly coloured.

Add parsley when cooked.

To serve

Place the purée on each plate, top each spoonful with a scallop. Drizzle the currants onto the scallops and the port truffle sauce around the outside of each plate. Sprinkle a little parmesan crumb on each scallop. Garnish with a drizzle of lemon infused extra virgin olive oil and fresh micro-herbs.

Adam Thomason

Adam co founded Flavour&Some and develops the menus and concepts for this multidisciplinary company. He was recognized by the Royal Academy in 2017 and awarded an MCA, Master of Culinary Arts. Adam recently competed with the England national team in the culinary Olympics 2020 winning silver across two categories. He is currently working as executive head chef of Wimbledon Tennis Club.

Stuff you'll need

Salmon
1 Royal smoked salmon fillet (King Lax)

Dressing
100g buttermilk
5g dashi granules
1 lemon
Dill oil (see recipe below)

Dill oil
200ml oil pomace
3 dill bunch

Compressed cucumber
1 cucumber
5g activated charcoal
5g rapeseed oil

Fennel salad
1 fennel bulb
30ml rapeseed oil
1 lemon

Dressed watermelon radish
1 watermelon radish

To garnish
Avruga caviar, 1 teaspoon per portion
Salmon caviar keta, 1 teaspoon per portion
1 punnet herb micro fennel cress
20 sprigs bronze fennel cress

Cured & charred king lax smoked salmon fillet, smoked caviar, english butter milk & dill

Get stuck in

Salmon

Salmon - Slice into 1cm thick pieces. Blow torch one piece on one side. Then glaze with rapeseed oil.

Dressing

Season the butter milk with the dashi, lemon zest and juice.
To serve split with the dill oil.

Dill Oil

Blanch dill leaves and dehydrate.
Blend with oil.
Pass through double j-cloth with blue roll in middle. Keep in bottle for service

Compressed cucumber

Scoop small and large cucumber balls. Roll the large balls in charcoal, rapeseed oil and salt and the small balls vac pack with a little dill oil.

Fennel salad

Finely slice on a mandolin, dress with rapeseed oil lemon juice and salt Drain excess juice before service.

Dressed watermelon Radish

On a mandolin thinly slice the watermelon radish and cut out with a round cuter. To serve season with sea salt and rapeseed oil.

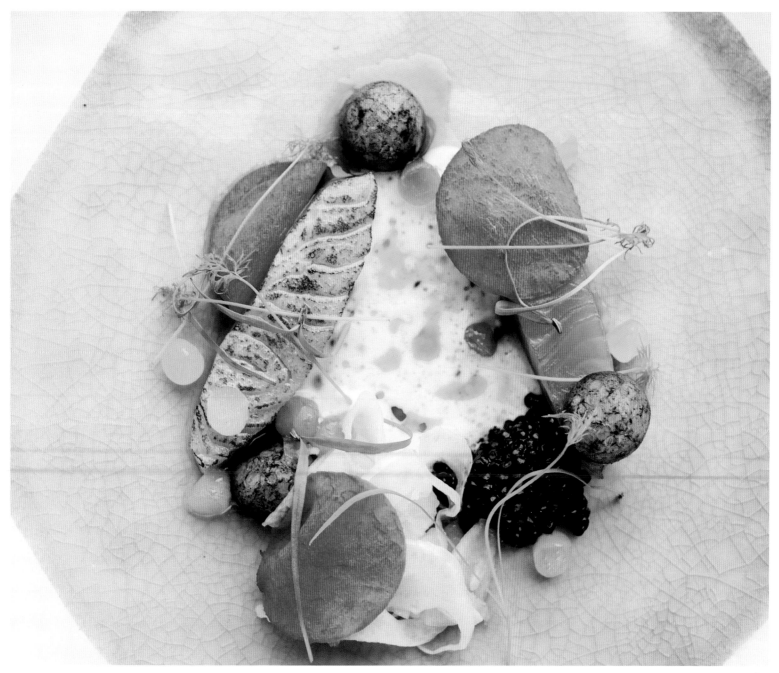

Ahmed Sivath

Ahmed 'Sea Bass' Sivath reckons there is no better way to sample seafood delicacies than aboard an authentic Maldivian boat, or Ba'theli, which also gives its name to his fine dining restaurant. The restaurant and its own kitchens sits within a sailing boat docked in an azure lagoon. There's history in this setting. Boats such as this were the vehicles used to transport cargoes of cinnamon, cardamom, turmeric, cloves, ginger and pepper along the Maldivian Spice Route. Locals bartered coconuts, sun-dried fish and shells, once used as currency for rice, silks and ceramics.

Stuff you'll need

200g red snapper or any meaty white fish
0.5kg fresh lobster
2 medium onions, finely sliced
2 tomatoes
300g grated fresh coconut
½ teaspoon turmeric powder
½ teaspoon cumin powder
½ teaspoon salt
1 teaspoon ginger garlic paste
4 curry leaves
1 teaspoon lemon juice

Maldivian grilled lobster and red snapper fish

Get stuck in

Add the onions, lemon juice, tomatoes, ginger garlic paste, salt, curry leaves, cumin and turmeric powder into a blender and blend until it becomes a paste. Marinate the lobster with the paste, and keep for at least one hour in the fridge.

Take a pan, add a dash of vegetable oil and grill the lobster and fish till it's golden brown and crispy.

Serve the grilled lobster and the fish on a thin bed of curry sauce with white rice and grilled vegetables of your choice. Serve it with cucumber raita, as well as some preserved lemons and green chilli. As garnish, fried onion and fried curry leaves are a great fit.

Alistair Dibbs

Originally from Leicester, Alistair got hooked on cooking after being sent for a three month work experience stage at a Michelin-starred seafront restaurant in Brittany, France, while at chef college. After gaining a taste of some of the finest food and produce France had to offer, he went on to work in several Michelin starred restaurants in the UK, including Fisher's at Baslow Hall and Pied a Terre in London, before opening his own restaurant and events business. He has since worked alongside Simon Boyle at Brigade, and is currently the main kitchen executive chef at Harrods.

Serves 4

Roast cauliflower

1 large cauliflower
10g turmeric
10g cumin
25g vegetable oil

Cous cous

200g cous cous
25g olive oil
Squeeze of lemon juice
Salt and freshly-ground black pepper

Hummus

100g dried chick peas,
soaked overnight in water
15g raw garlic
50g tahini paste (sesame paste)
30g extra virgin olive oil
5g turmeric
Salt and ground black pepper

To serve

30g smoked almonds
A handful of watercress or rocket
Half a pomegranate – remove the seeds by
bashing the skin with a spoon

Roast cauliflower with turmeric hummus and cauliflower cous cous

A couple of tips before you start. Use a really good food processer to blend up the hummus - it should be very smooth. Also soak the chick peas in plenty of water - about 500g of water will be enough. There are three steps to the recipe - the roast cauliflower, the hummus and the cous cous. Just prepare them separately and then combine them at the end.

Roast cauliflower

Cut out the central stem of the cauliflower and cut the rest of it into medium sized pieces (florets). Reserve about 100g of the cauliflower for the cous cous. Toss the remaining cauliflower in the seasoning, spices and oil, place on a baking tray with a few drops of water and roast in the oven at 175°C until just cooked and a light golden brown. Remove from the oven and set aside.

Cous cous

Place the cous cous in a bowl. Bring 300ml water to the boil and pour over the cous cous adding the olive oil, lemon juice and seasoning. Leave for about 30 minutes until the cous cous has absorbed the liquid and has cooled to room temperature. Next place the reserved raw cauliflower in the blender and blend until it is broken down and the texture of breadcrumbs.

Squeeze out any moisture and mix into the cous cous and set aside.

For the Hummus

Place the dried chick peas into a pan and cover with 300 ml fresh cold water. Bring the pan to the boil and simmer gently for about an hour, until the chickpeas are very soft. Next pour the chickpeas along with about 50ml of the cooking water into the blender and add the other ingredients. Blend until smooth. It should be a vivid yellow colour. Season with a little more lemon juice or salt.

To serve

Place the hummus in the centre of the plate, add three tablespoons of the cous cous, place three or four of the cauliflower florets on top of the cous cous. Finish with some of the smoked almonds, a few pomegranate seeds and watercress.

Allen Susser

Allen was named by the James Beard Foundation as the best chef in America in 1994. Born in Brooklyn, New York, his training took him to Paris where he ended up working at the Le Bristol Hotel before returning home. He has now made his mark at the idyllic Jade Mountain resort on the paradise island of St Lucia. There is still a rich French-based Creole culture on the island of St. Lucia, and there is, he reckons, no dish more traditional than Green Fig & Salt Fish (or as it is known in Creole, fig vet e lanmowi), the country's national dish. Every family on the island has its own variation, served on weekends, special occasions and of course during the Jounen Kweyo (Creole Day) festival on 28th October.

Stuff you'll need

3 small cod, (or any white fish) fillets
prepared in sea salt
1 tablespoon coconut oil
1 small onion diced
1 tablespoon diced seasoning peppers
1 clove garlic crushed
2 spring onions sliced
2 small tomatoes, seeded and diced
2-3 drops hot pepper sauce
2 green bananas, boiled until tender and skins
have split, peeled and diced
1½ tablespoons mayonnaise
1 tablespoon torn coriander
3-4 sprigs fresh celery leaf

Green fig (banana) and salt fish

Get stuck in

Liberally season the fish fillets with plenty of sea salt to cover completely and allow to cure a minimum of 1 hour and up to 24 hours. Rinse the salt off under running cold water before cooking and dry the flesh well.

Warm the coconut oil in a heavy pan over medium high heat. Cook the fish on each side for about 2-3 minutes. Remove the fillets and set aside to cool.

In the same pan add the onion, seasoning peppers, garlic, spring onion, cooking slowly for about 3-4 minutes until aromatic. Flake in the cooked fish in thumb-sized pieces and continue to stir in the tomatoes, hot sauce and diced banana.

Remove from heat and fold in the mayonnaise and coriander.

To serve

Spoon the mixture on to a large colourful platter and garnish with sprigs of celery leaves.

Angel Zapata Martin

Barcelona-born Angel Zapata Martin joined Barrafina in April 2017, bringing extensive cooking experience to the Spanish tapas restaurant from all over the world. He was previously Sous Chef at Santi Santamaria's three-Michelin-starred Catalan restaurant, Can Fabes in Barcelona as well as Head Chef and teacher at Barcelona's internationally recognised Hofmann School and its one-Michelin-starred restaurant.

Angel previously worked a private chef in Ibiza, San Tropez, Mégeve and London but he always felt the call of the buzz of a restaurant kitchen. He has recently opened Barrafina Coal Drops Yard, with a new menu reflecting his Catalan upbringing.

Stuff you'll need

Bun
300g plain flour, sieved
200g mash potatoes
140ml milk
10g fresh yeast
9g salt
30g extra virgin olive oil

Stuffing
500g squid
250g butifarra de pagés
1 tablespoon garlic mashed
1 tablespoon parsley, chopped
80g white sour dough bread

Squid and butifarra bun

All i oli Chimichurri

1 clove garlic

2 tablespoons dry oregano

1 teaspoon espelette

½ tablespoon cumin seeds

1 habanero, brunoise

1 piquillo pepper without seeds

½ tablespoon fennel seeds

1 tablespoon coriander, chopped

3 tablespoons parsley, chopped

Salt and pepper

500ml extra virgin olive oil

Lemon juice

1 whole egg

2 yolks

1 clove garlic

Get stuck in

Bun

Dissolve the yeast in warm milk (approximately 30 degrees). Add the mashed potato, salt and evoo to the milk and yeast. Make into a dough knead until smooth and elastic. Split the dough into 40g balls, shape and prove in a warm place for approximately 3 hours. Bake with 85% humidity 175 °C for 8 to 10 minutes.

Stuffing

Clean the squid. Chop the squid wings for the filling, leaving the tubes for stuffing. Soak the bread with milk to soften. Mix everything into a bowl with your hands, add seasoning and place into a piping bag. Its best to keep in the fridge to firm up. Stuff the squid tubes with the filling and place back into the fridge. When the squid is firm cut slices about ½cm then grill or pan-fry each slice with a little olive oil.

All i oli chimichurri

Add the garlic, oregano, espeletter, cumin seeds, habanero chilli, piquillo, fennel seeds and lemon juice to a blender. Put the egg and the yolks into the spices and blend for 3 minutes. Slowly add the oil, whisking constantly in order to get an emulsion (all I oli). Remove from the mixer add the freshly chopped parsley and coriander, check the seasoning.

Anton Edelmann

Anton Edelmann moved from his native Germany in 1976 to work at the Dorchester Hotel. By 1980 he was executive head chef at the Grosvenor Park Hotel, where he launched its Ninety Park Lane restaurant. That would not be his last stop on a tour of London hotels, however. From 1982 to 2003 he was maitre chef des cuisines at the Savoy. Since 2003 Anton has pursued a number of his own businesses as chef and owner or co-owner, including Allium Restaurant, Brompton Bar and Grill and Anton's at Great Hallingbury Manor. He has also operated a consultancy working with the likes of Lords Cricket Ground and the Royal Institution. Anton holds an honorary professorship in hospitality at Thames Valley University, London.

Stuff you'll need

12 razor clams
200ml sparkling wine
1 onion, peeled and finely chopped
1 red chilli, finely chopped
3 cloves of garlic, peeled and crushed
50g unsalted butter
200g white bread crumbs
½ lemon, zested
¼ bunch of flat parsley, picked and shredded
¼ bunch of flat parsley just washed
Vegetable oil for deep frying
2 lemons, halved
Salt and pepper

Get stuck in

Water the clams for about 5 minutes under cold running water and check that they are all tightly closed and not damaged.
Heat the oil to 160°C, add the parsley and fry until crispy.
Remove and drain on a kitchen cloth,
Heat a little of the oil in a small sauce pan, add the onions and the chilli and sweat until soft.
Add the garlic and sweat a further minute, then add the butter. When foaming add the bread crumbs and the shredded parsley, season with salt and pepper.
Cook for about 2 minutes while stirring
Remove and transfer to an airtight container.
In a med size sauce pan heat the wine quickly.
Throw in the clams and cover with a lid.
Cook for 30 seconds until they are open.
Remove from the pan and drain.
Place on a tray and cover with the bread crumb mix.
Pre-heat the grill.
Grill under very high heat quickly till they are slightly brown.
Arrange on plate and top with some of the fried parsley.
Serve with a ½ lemon on the side.

Antony Scholtmeyer

Antony Scholtmeyer honed his craft over more than 30 years in top establishments around the world, including five-star properties in China, Portugal, US and Singapore, among them InterContinental Shenzhen and Ritz-Carlton Millenia Singapore.
Antony came to Bangkok in 2011 as the executive chef at The Sukhothai Hotel. He then moved to the Okura Prestige in 2015 and elevated Elements, the French-Japanese restaurant, to Michelin-star status in the first Bangkok guide. Antony is now at the new Capella Bangkok.

Serves 10

Stuff you'll need

Curing the trout

10 60g ocean trout portions, skin on, pin bones removed
200g rock salt to cover the ocean trout

Pickled vegetables

100g carrots, julienne
100g cucumber, pearls
100g daikon strips

Pickling liquid

20g ginger peeled and diced
200ml rice vinegar
100g white sugar
400ml water

Orange miso sauce

300ml orange juice
1 whole orange for the zest, grated then juiced
100g sweet white miso paste

Cook and serve

400ml olive oil
30g carrot, peeled and diced
30g fennel, diced
30g celery, diced
50g apple, peeled and diced
2g star anise
5g thyme
10g freshly ground white pepper (half for oil, half for ocean trout)
5g fleur de sel
50g trout roe

Tasmanian ocean trout confit, pickled vegetables, orange-miso sauce

Get stuck in

Trout

Cover a flat tray with the rock salt and place the ocean trout portions on top of the salt. Then sprinkle more rock salt over the top of the ocean trout. Cover and refrigerate for one hour. After one hour remove from the fridge and rinse the salt from the salmon under cold running water. Pat dry on absorbent paper and refrigerate until needed. You can do this a day in advance if you like.

Pickled vegetables

Bring the water, ginger, rice vinegar and sugar to the boil and pour 1/2 over the julienne vegetables.
Blanch the daikon strips and then pour the remaining pickling solution over it. Leave out of the fridge until cool. Then chill.

Orange miso sauce

In a stainless steel bowl add all of the above ingredients and cook out over a double boiler until smooth and thick like pastry cream. Pass through a fine strainer and chill. Store in a sauce bottle until needed.

Cook and serve

Bring the ingredients up to the boil and then let cool down to 50°C.
Slowly confit the ocean trout portions in the oil for about 10 minutes.
Peel the skin off the ocean trout. In the centre of each plate place the slices of pickled daikon and top with the ocean trout. Twirl the carrot julienne into a nice shape and place at the top of the plate.
Spread the miso-orange sauce with a spatula and place the cucumber pearls and micro greens on top. Place the trout roe in the corner.
Season the ocean trout with the salt and ground white pepper. Serve.

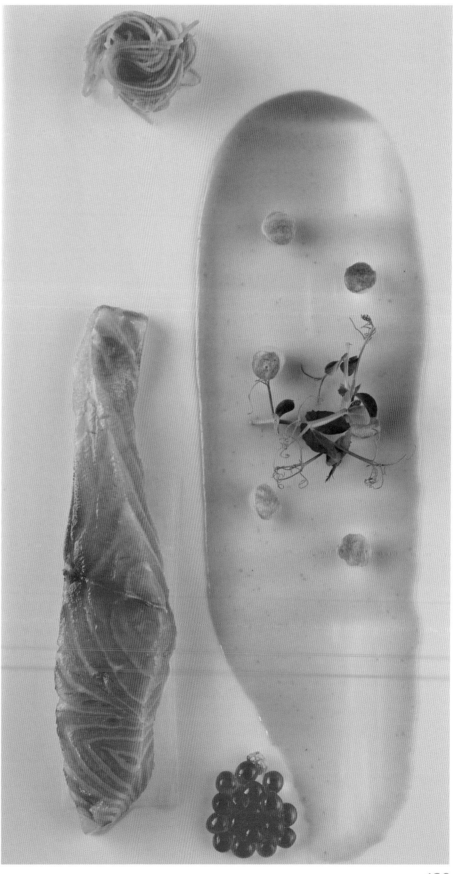

139

Daniel Galmiche with Greg Young

Frenchman Daniel Galmiche's career has since taken him all over the world. In London he worked at Le Gavroche under the tutelage of Michel Roux, then in the two star restaurant Schillinger in Colmar, a spell in three star Marc Meneau in Veselay, and two star Hostellerie du Chateau Servin. When in Scotland Daniel was awarded Master Chef of the Year, gaining his first Michelin star in 1990 whilst working at Knockinaam Lodge. He was also awarded a Michelin Star at Harvey's in Bristol and maintained the Michelin Star at L'Ortolan and Cliveden House in Berkshire. Having been at the helm of The Vineyard at Stockcross for 7 years, Daniel decided to move on to new projects which includes publishing Revolutionary French Cooking. He is currently an ambassador for Norwegian Seafood Council.

Stuff you'll need

Trout

4 140g Norwegian fjord trout pave, skin off
Olive oil
sea salt and freshly ground black pepper
1 large chicory lettuce
40g butter
2 tsp honey

Sauce vierge (makes 150ml)

4 large tablespoon extra virgin olive oil
1 shallot, chopped
1/2 a tomato, deseeded, diced
150g white seedless grapes, skinned and halved
1 tablespoon good balsamic vinegar
Juice of 1/2 a lemon
Micro or fresh tarragon

Get stuck in

Sauce vierge

Pour the olive oil into a small saucepan and briefly warm over a low heat for about 30 seconds, add the shallot and cook for 2 minutes, remove from the heat and gently stir in the tomato and grapes. Add the vinegar and lemon juice and, just before serving, stir through tarragon to taste.

Trout

Heat a pan of water to about 60°C. Meanwhile, wrap the fish in clingfilm and tie up both ends. Poach for 6-7 minutes at a constant heat then remove from the pan. Caramelise the chicory in butter and honey and keep warm. Carefully cut open one side of the clingfilm to release the trout onto kitchen towel. Pat dry then pan fry using a non-stick pan for 2-3 minutes until golden brown, keeping the flesh nice and pink in the middle.

To serve

Position the trout in the middle of the dish, top with caramelised chicory and drizzle over plenty of the grape sauce vierge.

Stuff you'll need

1 whole mackerel
100g asparagus
50g peas
1 sweet potato
1 whole garlic

Avocado purée

1 avocado
2 spoons of olive oil
Season with salt and pepper

Chimichurri

2 shallots
1 red pepper
3 garlic cloves

Daniel Nogueira

Daniel was born in Lisbon and has been a chef for six years.
His career started in Portugal in 2014, working for a catering company
organising events across the capital. After one year, he decided
to move to London. The first door that opened for him was at the
restaurant Lurra in Marble Arch, known for its fine dining Basque
cuisine. Daniel started as a kitchen porter because of his lack of
English, but after two months he was promoted to commis chef. A
year later Daniel joined Percy & Founders in Fitzrovia, where he is now
junior sous chef.

Grilled mackerel with avocado purée, sweet new potatoes, asparagus and chimichurri sauce

Get stuck in

Grill the whole mackerel, steam the asparagus and boil the peas.
Confit the garlic in oil.
Peel and cut the sweet potato into a round shape to look like a new potato and boil until cooked.

For the avocado purée

Blend all the ingredients together in a mixer to make a purée.

For the chimichurri

Brunoise cut the shallots and red pepper. Chop the garlic thinly.
Cook them in a pan with oil and let it cool down.
Chop the fresh coriander and parsley. Add the dry oregano to the mix.
Add salt and pepper and the lemon juice, mix all together well.

To serve

Place the avocado purée on the plate, then add the fish with chimichurri sauce on top. Add asparagus, peas, sweet potato and garlic to present a good-looking dish.

Photos by Noemi Scavo @noemiscavophotographer
www.noemiscavo.co.uk

David Boland

Dave Boland is the founder of the first specialised chefs course for the Academy of Culinary Arts at Bournemouth College, devised to give young, inexperienced hotel chefs a support system, and to help prevent them from dropping out of the industry. The course's alumni have gone on to hold positions at the likes of The Ritz, Claridges and The Savoy. Dave has been a Fellow of the Royal Academy of Culinary Arts for 25 years. He holds the dubious accolade of once having turned down the position of Royal Chef at Buckingham Palace.

Stuff you'll need

2 fillets of salmon
6 cooked peeled king prawns
500g puff pastry, pre rolled
1 egg yolk
2 baby leeks, finely chopped
1 shallot, finely chopped
1/2 glass dry white wine
150ml double cream
25g butter
Chopped tarragon
Pinch of salt

Salmon and king prawns en croute

Get stuck in

Cut the puff pastry to the size of the salmon, then brush it with egg yolk which has a little salt added to it. Mark the puff pastry with the back of a fork for decoration. Place it on a baking tray and cook in a preheated oven at 220°C, until brown and crispy. Remove from oven.

Place the finely chopped shallots and baby leeks in a pan with 25g butter. Cook slowly with no colour, stirring occasionally, until soft. Then add the white wine, stir and reduce by half.

Brush the salmon fillets with a little oil and place on baking tray. Roast in a hot oven for 5 mins. Remove and let it rest.

Add the cream to the leeks and shallots. Bring to the boil and then gently simmer to reduce until thicken. Add the chopped tarragon and king prawns and stir gently. Do not allow to boil.

Cut the puff pastry in half and place on serving plate. Place the leeks, shallots, cream sauce and prawns on the base. Top with the salmon, cover with the lid and serve.

Deepanker Khosla

Deepanker Khosla, DK, as he likes to be called, has had an illustrious career. After studying at the Welcomgroup Graduate School of Hotel Administration in Manipal he joined the Starwood Culinary School and then completed the Starwood Management Training. He later went on to work with Luxury Collection Hotels in Chennai, New Delhi, Jaipur, and Mumbai. In the five-plus years since he's been in Thailand he's been the chef at Charcoal Tandoor Grill in Bangkok. In November of 2017 he launched Haoma, a secluded fine dining restaurant.

Stuff you'll need

2 lobster tails, thawed if frozen
8 new potatoes
4 baby fennel heads, trimmed
8–12 razor clams
30g butter
4 tablespoons water
2 tablespoons coconut oil
4 large scallops, cleaned and roe removed
4 large raw tiger prawns, peeled and de-veined – keep the shells for garnishing
2 red mullet fillets, pin bones removed, each cut into 2 pieces and the skin lightly scored
2 sea bream, pin bones removed, cut into 2 pieces and the skin lightly scored
2 tablespoons lemon juice
30g butter
Sea salt and freshly ground black pepper
Finely-chopped coriander leaves, to garnish
Baby samphire, cleaned, to garnish

Coconut base

2 large tomatoes, a small 'x' cut in the stalk
3 tablespoons sunflower oil
2 garlic cloves, sliced
10 curry leaves
2.5cm piece of cinnamon stick
10 black peppercorns
2 green cardamom pods, bruised
2 cloves
½ star anise
1 bay leaf
15g fresh ginger, cut into julienne sticks
1 onion, thinly sliced
1 green chilli, slit
½ teaspoon ground cumin
2 teaspoons ground fennel
A generous pinch of saffron threads, soaked in 2 tablespoons water for 30 mins
400ml shellfish stock
400ml coconut milk
1 teaspoon tomato purée

Pondicherry poullibaise

Get stuck in

Bring a large saucepan of heavily salted water to the boil and fill a large bowl with iced water. Add the lobster tails to the boiling water and, when the water returns to the boil, blanch for 2 minutes. Use tongs to remove and transfer to the iced water to stop the cooking. When cool enough to handle, peel off the shells. Remove the black intestinal vein and cut each tail into four medallions.

Return the poaching water to the boil. Add the potatoes and boil for 12–15 minutes until they are tender. Use a scoop or large slotted spoon to remove from the water. When they are cool enough to handle, peel them and set aside. Meanwhile, return the water to the boil, add the baby fennel and blanch for 3 minutes, or until tender. Refresh in cold water to stop the cooking and set the color, then set aside.

Bring a separate small pan of water to the boil.

Add the tomatoes and blanch for 2 minutes, or until the skins begin to split. Drain them well and set aside until cool enough to handle. Drain them well and set aside until cool enough to handle, then skin, halve, de-seed and finely dice.

Coconut base

Heat the oil in a pan, add the garlic and sauté over a low heat without colouring. Add the curry leaves, whole spices, bay leaf and ginger, and continue sautéing until the seeds crackle. Add the onion and green chilli, and sauté for 3–5 minutes until the onion is translucent, but not coloured. Stir in the ground cumin, fennel and the saffron threads with the liquid, then add the potatoes and stir until they are coated. Add the stock and bring to the boil. Add the tomatoes, coconut milk and tomato purée, and stir together, then simmer for 15 minutes, or until reduced slightly. Set aside and keep hot until all the seafood is cooked.

Place the razor clams in a steamer and steam for between 30 seconds and one minute until the shells open. Remove the meat from the shells, trim and set aside.

Just before you start cooking the seafood, melt the butter with the water in a separate saucepan, add the baby fennel and potatoes and serve.

Dev Biswal

Dev Biswal is chef-owner of The Ambrette restaurants in Margate and Canterbury, After graduating from catering college in Calcutta, he trained at the Dubai Sheraton, before moving to London in 2003 for spells at Mangoes and Eriki.

After 12 years in London he moved to Margate to run a joint-venture, which he rebranded The Ambrette. In 2019 he was named 'Asian Chef of the Year' at the Asian Restaurant Awards.

Stuff you'll need

1 teaspoon oil
1 teaspoon sea salt
1 teaspoon Fresh green chilli paste
Squeeze of lemon juice
1 teaspoon garlic paste
1 teaspoon chat masala
2 whole crab
1 teaspoon potato starch
Oil to fry

Tomatoe Chutney

750gms tomatoes roughly chopped
5 tablespoons vegetable or mustard oil
2 teaspoons nigella seeds
1 teaspoon fennel seeds
1 teaspoon black mustard seeds
1 teaspoon cumin seeds
2 mild dried chillies
¼ teaspoon kashmiri chilli powder
5 tablespoons light brown sugar
100ml white vinegar
Pinch of salt

Soft shell crab

Get stuck in

Make a marinade using sea salt, green chilli, lemon juice and garlic paste. Marinade the crab in the marinade and leave them to rest in the fridge for half an hour.

Dust the marinated crab thoroughly using potato starch and leave them to rest for five minutes. Dust again.

Heat oil to smoking point. Fry the crab for five minutes or till crispy and golden. Sprinkle chat masala and serve hot.

Tomatoe Chutney

Heat the oil over a medium heat in a large saucepan. Add the whole spices and fry for 30 seconds. Add the chillies and fry for a few seconds too

Add the tomatoes and mix for 1 minute. Now add the chilli powder, sugar and vinegar. Turn the heat down and simmer mixing well. Cook with the lid on for 40 minutes stir often

Now continue cooking without the lid for a further 50 minutes as the chutney thickens and softens. Stir half-way through the cooking and season to taste. Decant in a sterilised jar and seal for a week before serving.

Suggested Accompaniments

Crab Pate, samphire, tomato chutney

Felix Bamert

Felix Bamert, Kagi Maldives' executive chef, developed his passion for Euro-Asian fusion cuisine while working under Andre Jaeger at Fischerzunft, Switzerland. He went on to work in Thailand where he had the privilege of cooking for global leaders including Hillary Clinton, Sergej Lavrov and Javier Solana.

Stuff you'll need

Curry blend

60g fresh coconut ground

2 tablespoons basmati rice

1 small stick cinnamon

3 cardamom seeds

4 dried chillies

1 teaspoon ground turmeric

1 teaspoon fennel seeds

2 teaspoons coriander seeds

2 teaspoons cumin seeds

2 teaspoons black pepper corn

200ml water

Tuna

600g tuna loin cut into 3cm chunks

1 teaspoon turmeric

2 tablespoons olive oil

10 curry leaves

1 medium onion, chopped finely

1 or 2 fresh chili peppers, sliced

2 cloves garlic, sliced finely

1 teaspoon finely-chopped fresh ginger

2 tomatoes, sliced in cubes

2 cups coconut milk

1/4 cup fresh tamarind liquid (80g)

50g fresh coriander chopped

Salt to season

Tuna curry don riha

Get stuck in

Marinade the tuna with 1 teaspoon of turmeric and a little bit of salt for half an hour.

Curry blend

For the curry blend, heat the rice in a pan until lightly golden, add the cinnamon, cardamom, dry chillies, pepper, fennel, cumin and coriander seeds and roast until you start to smell the delicious aromas. Then add the ground coconut and turmeric and cook, stirring continuously until everything is nice and golden. Add the water and place the mixture into a blender to create a curry paste.

Tuna

Heat a frying pan with cooking oil at a medium heat and fry the curry leaves, onion, garlic, chili and ginger until golden.

Add the tuna with the curry paste and braise it until the meat pores are closed, then add the tomatoes and cover the pan. Cook on a low heat for about 8 minutes.

Once the tuna is tender, add the coconut milk, add the tamarind liquid, season with salt to your liking and bring it to boil again.

Sprinkle the curry with fresh coriander.

Serve the curry hot with boiled rice and other vegetable curries for a sumptuous meal.

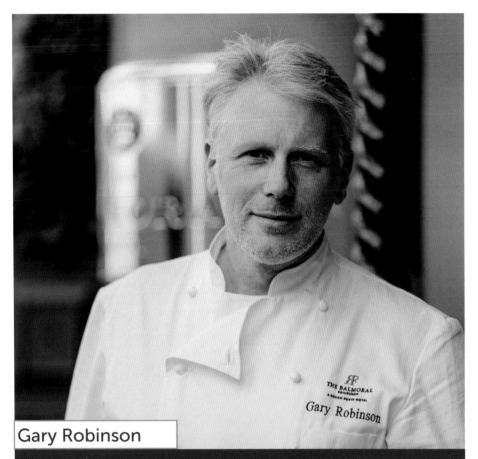

Gary Robinson

Gary arrived at The Balmoral in June 2019 having gained over 25 years of culinary experience, most notably in the honourable position of head chef to H.R.H. the Prince of Wales. Previously Gary held the role of executive chef at the British Embassy in Washington D.C, which saw him cook for numerous presidents, and also spent five years overseeing the entire Condé Nast international restaurants portfolio. Before joining The Balmoral he launched the culinary programme for The Conduit Private Members Club in London, as well as holding executive chef positions at Kowloon Shangri-La and the Aberdeen Marina Club in Hong Kong.

Serves 4

Stuff you'll need

140g fresh Scottish sea urchin
80g crème fraîche
300g dried spaghetti
Plenty of flaked sea salt
25ml extra virgin olive oil
2 cloves garlic, chopped
1 banana shallot, chopped
1 teaspoon gochujang paste
125ml white wine
Freshly ground black pepper
A good pinch of chopped chives and chopped flat leaf parsley

Get stuck in

Keep four of the neatest pieces of sea urchin aside for finishing the dishes and combine the remainder with the crème fraîche and blend to a smooth puree.
Cook the pasta in an abundance of boiling salty water take it not quite to al dente. While the pasta is cooking, heat the olive oil in a pan big enough to eventually hold the pasta comfortably, and add the garlic and shallot. Cook until translucent but without colour. Add the gochujang and wine and cook until almost all the liquid has reduced.
Add the pasta into the gochujang wine reduction and add the sea urchin paste. Keep on the heat and fold in, adding in any pasta water needed to get the consistency just right.
Season with salt and pepper and add the herbs at this stage. Plate the pasta, topping with the reserved pieces of sea urchin, and an extra splash of olive oil.

Hendrik Otto

Hendrik heads up Lorenz Adlon Esszimmer, he and his team offer their guests classic dishes with a modern twist, inspired by the old recipes of his friends and family.

He was awarded two stars in the Guide Michelin 2020. The editors emphasised Hendrik Otto's elaborate combination of classic cuisine combined with modern elements.

Gault Millau awarded the kitchen team with 18 out of 20 points and three chef's hats. He was recognised as Berliner Meisterkoch 2012 and Cook of the Year 2013 by restaurant guide Gusto, which paid tribute to his creativity and individuality. In the 2020 edition Otto and the Lorenz Adlon Esszimmer were recognized with the maximum rating of 12+ pans.

Stuff you'll need

280g salmon
2 sprigs of dill
1g mustard
25g Noan olive oil
10g lemon juice
1gr salt
10g pine honey
0.1g xhantana
20g amaranth
30ml frying fat

To serve

Bavarian flowers,

Rapeseed

1 pinch pepper mixture from Wiberg

Salmon with amaranth and flowers

Get stuck in

Start by filleting and de-boning the salmon.

Afterwards remove the skin and portion the salmon into equal, 70g pieces.

Poach it for 2 minutes at 80°C, steam in a combination steamer.

For the vinaigrette, mix the mustard, oil, lemon juice, salt, pine honey and Xhantana in a thermal mixer to a fine and creamy emulsion.

Afterwards pass the mass through a fine micro sieve and possibly fine tune the taste.

For the puffed amaranth, preheat the fat to approximately 240°C in a saute pan.

Pass the amaranth in a fine sieve and fry it in the fat. Fry until there are no more bubbles. Place the fried amaranth on a dry paper towel to let it drain. Change the paper frequently.

Mix the amaranth one to one with the rapeseed. The cooked salmon gets freed of the fat and drained, then coated with the vinaigrette and sprinkled evenly with the pepper mixture.

To serve

Sprinkle the puffed amaranth and rapeseed on top of the pepper mixture.

Place dried flowers on top. The salmon is served on a white, flat plate.

Jason Atherton

Jason Atherton started out working alongside great chefs including Pierre Koffmann, Marco Pierre White, Nico Ladenis and Ferran Adria at el Bulli, before launching Maze restaurant, first in London and then another five globally. In 2010 Jason launched his own restaurant company, Jason Atherton Ltd. His flagship restaurant Pollen Street Social opened in April 2011 in Mayfair and was awarded a Michelin star within just six months of opening, alongside 4 AA Rosettes. Since then, Jason's 'The Social Company' has grown into a globally renowned restaurant group, with a portfolio of restaurants which include the Michelin-starred Social Eating House and City Social, as well as 5 Social, The Betterment and Berners Tavern.

Stuff you'll need

Roast red mullet

1 large red mullet or
2 smaller fillets, per portion

Stock

200ml pommace oil
1kg large frozen prawns in the shells with heads on, roughly chopped
2 onions
2 carrots
4 plum tomatoes, chopped
6 cloves garlic
1kg langoustine bones, well roasted in the oven
3l chicken or fish stock
Grated zest and juice of 1 orange and 1 lemon

Rice

500g bomba paella rice
3 shallots, diced
3 cloves garlic, diced
1.5ltr prawn stock
3 red gambas prawns per portion, deveined and diced parsley, chopped

Seaweed butter

1kg sea lettuce, washed well, blanched and cooked
500g soft unsalted butter

Seaweed roast potatoes

Baby new potatoes
Olive oil or duck fat
Garlic and thyme, as desired

To serve

300g rice
Chopped prawns, to taste
Butter and olive oil, to taste
Lemon, to taste
Salt and pepper, to taste
Cockles, washed under running water to release sand
Samphire, picked and blanched

Roasted red mullet, prawn rice, seaweed potatoes

Get stuck in

Roast red mullet

Pan roast the mullet to get a little colour. Finish with sea salt and lemon juice.

Stock

In a large pan heat the pommace oil until smoking.
Add the prawns and colour well, add the vegetables roasting until they also colour. Add the langoustine bones and roast for 2 minutes.
Cover with the stock, zest and juice simmer for 1 hour. Allow to cool and infuse then allow the stock to drip through a colander for 10 minutes.

Rice

In a large pan sweat off the bomba paella rice with the diced shallots and cloves of diced garlic. Add the stock to cover the rice.
Cover the pan and place in medium-hot oven about 180°C and leave for 10 minutes. Take out and stir twice then return to the oven for 5 more minutes, still covered - the rice should be just undercooked.
Take out and chill in a tray.

Seaweed butter

Once the seaweed has been washed and blanched, blitz it to a very smooth paste, pass and beat into the soft butter.

Seaweed roast potatoes

Baby new potatoes, confit in olive oil or duck fat infused with garlic and thyme until tender.

To serve

When ready to serve place 1l of the prawn stock into a pan and reduce by half.
Add 300g rice to the stock and mix almost like a risotto, until stock has been absorbed.
Pull from the heat, and add chopped prawns, and then finish with a touch of butter, olive oil, a squeeze of lemon and seasoning.
Roast the potatoes in a pan to give good roasted colour. Add the seaweed butter and fry quite fast.
Add three cockles per portion and allow to open, then add the blanched samphire.
Remove from heat and serve with the rice and red mullet.

Luke Smith

Luke Smith moved into contract catering soon after completing his training and apprenticeship with the Royal Academy of Culinary Arts Specialised Chefs Academy at Bournemouth and Poole College, and with Rowley Leigh at Kensington Place. He worked for the Roux fine dining brand, before going on to hold head chef positions at a number of blue chip companies, and develop concepts and menus for retail and commercial restaurants and events. He is now an executive chef with BaxterStorey.

Serves 10

Stuff you'll need

Crab
400g white crab meat
20g mayonnaise
1 lime zest and juice

Lemon gel
500ml water
125ml lemon juice
125g sugar
9g agar agar

Cucumber oil
100g cucumber skin
200g rapeseed oil

Crispy seaweed
5 sheets nori
Fennel pollen

Seaweed salad refreshed in water
30 slices cucumber, rolled
Sea rosemary sprigs
10 sprigs dill
Rapeseed oil or chardonnay vinegar

Cornish crab, torched cucumber, lemon gel, sea rosemary

Get stuck in

Crab

Pick crab meat at least 3 times with blue gloves removing any shell, mix with mayonnaise, lime and season. Place into small round rings, 40g portions, then remove the ring and rough up the top with a skewer.

Lemon gel

Boil all ingredients for 2-3 minutes, set and bland to a purée

Cucumber oil

Peel cucumbers, blend peelings with rapeseed oil and pass theough a sieve. Cut each cucumber into 3 logs, half each log lengthways and square up. Vac pac tightly in cucumber oil overnight. Remove from oil, cut each piece

in half and blow torch. Season.

Crispy seaweed

Preheat fryer to 160°C, rehydrate nori sheet in water then deep fry until crispy. Sprinkle with salt, sugar and fennel pollen.

Seaweed salad refreshed in water

Assemble and serve, sprinkle the oil or chardonnay at the end.

Maike Menzel

Maike is Germany's youngest chef to hold a star in the Michelin Guide for 2 consecutive years. She became head chef of the Schwarzreiter in August 2018 with her interpretation of "Young Bavarian Cuisine". The central focus is on regionality and innovative lightness. She already knew in her teenage years that she wanted to be a chef, and her love for the profession came from her grandfather and father. Maike has worked in various establishments including the Blauer Bock in Munich, Emiko restaurant and the Pageou Munich restaurant. She has been working at the Schwarzreiter kitchen at Vier Jahreszeiten Kempinski Munich since November 2016, initially as chef de partie and chef tournant, progressing to a sous chef position and ultimately assuming the role of head chef, overseeing a team of nine chefs and five trainees.

Stuff you'll need

Sauerkraut

1 kg pointed cabbage
1 1/2 tablespoon caraway
15 g salt
1 tablespoon sugar
2 pcs bay leaves
1-2 sealable canning jars, cleaned with hot water and dried

Pickled shimeji mushrooms

200g shimeji mushrooms
100g white Balsamico vinegar
180g Champagne vinegar
170ml water
1 bay leaves
5 pcs Piment seeds
2 star anis
1 branch thyme
120g sugar
10g salt

Bacon jelly

300 ml bacon stock/juice
0.8g Gelan (thickener)
2g Agar (thickener)
4g sugar
2g salt

Mustard beurre blanc

250g white onions
125g champignons
100ml white port wine
100ml white wine
50ml fish stock
250g butter
1 tablespoon Dijon mustard
1 teaspoon spicy mustard
sugar, nutmeg, salt

Pike perch

1.5kg of pike perch
60ml olove oil
60g butter
3 gloves of garlic

To serve

1 teaspoon of small crispy potato squares
1 teaspoon crisply roasted diced bacon
Mustard cress
1 tablespoon pickled mustard seeds

Pike perch sauerkraut bamberger hörnla potato mustard tyrolean bacon sauerkraut

Get stuck in

Sauerkraut

Remove the outer cabbage leaves and put them aside for later. Remove the stalk from the cabbage leaves and finely slice, add the salt and sugar and mix together.

Knead the cabbage until water starts to leak out the cabbage. Fill the kilner jars with the cabbage and the juice, make sure to push the cabbage down to the bottom of the jar so it is completely covered in the liquid but still has enough space to allow the gas to develop in the jar. Top with the bay leaves and caraway seeds and cover the top with the reserved cabbage leaves then seal the jar. Let the cabbage ferment at room temperature for about 10 days then store them in a cool place. During the fermenting process, open every jar at least twice a day to let the gas escape.

Preparation of the pike perch

Portion the fish fillet into 110g pieces
Heat up a pan to high temperature add oil and the fish fillets, roast them on the skin side for about 3 to 4 minutes until crispy. Turn the fillets and take the pan off the stove and let the fish sit in the pan, add a little piece of butter and some garlic and hold the pan at a slight angle and spoon the butter over the fish, make sure the fish is covered in the melted butter then take the fish fillet out of the pan onto a drainage plate.

Pickled shimeji mushrooms

Add the shimeji mushrooms to the preprepared kilner jars, then pour the cooled pickling stock into the jars. Leave for five days.

Bacon jelly

Mix up the sugar, salt, agar and galan then blend it with the bacon stock and bring to the boil, while stirring. Pour it onto a tray lined with baking paper and chill. When the jelly firms cut it into 3, 5 centimetre squares put baking paper in between the cut squares and chill until you need them later.

Mustard Beurre Blanc

Fry the onions and mushrooms lightly in oil until glazed, deglaze them with the 2 wines let it boil for 3 minutes to reduce, add the fish stock and simmer for another 10 minutes to reduce to a syrup consistency, whisk in the cold butter. Season with mustard and herbs. Warm gently before serving.

To Serve

Heat up the sauerkraut with a little of the juice. Place the fried fish in the middle of the plate skin side up, add 1 tablespoon of diced bacon add two pickled shimmy mushrooms and cover them with a piece of bacon Jelly then repeat this process add a bit of mashed potato next to and on top of the fish. Place 2 teaspoons of sauerkraut next to the fish on the left and right side, spread the lukewarm butter and pickled mustard seeds around the fish then garnish with the crisp diced potatoes, more shimeji mushrooms and mustard cress.

Marco De Cecco

Marco De Cecco has been a chef for 15 years. He started his journey in his native Italy, then decided to travel to Africa and Asia to look for new flavours. His dreams started to come together in Singapore, where he led Capri to be recognized as one of the top five Italian restaurants. During his stay in Singapore he also won the Diamond and Foodmania awards in 2017. Back in Rome he received the '70 Best Italian Restaurant and Pizzeria In the World' award in 2018. He decided then to move to Prego, Kuala Lumpur, in 2019, where he received further awards.

Stuff you'll need

Pasta

400g tagliatelle

2ltr water

Pasta sauce

4 clams

4 mussels

4 tiger prawns size 21/26

2 scallops

6 squid rings

1ltr tomato sauce

2 lead prawn stock or light fish stock

60g fine salt

12g white pepper powder

50ml extra virgin olive oil

100ml white wine

Basil leaves

To serve

Lemon zest

20g crushed pistachio nuts

20g peeled garlic

20g parsley

Pasta divina

Get stuck in

Pasta

Put the water and 20g of salt in a pot on maximum heat.
Once water is boiling, pour in the pasta and stir.
Wait until pasta is almost cooked.
Drain the water and put the pasta in a sauté pan,
together with the pasta sauce.

Pasta sauce

Put the garlic and the olive oil in a sauté pan, medium heat.
Sauté the garlic until it starts to get golden.
Add the clams and the mussels, drizzle with white wine. Cook until they
have opened.
Remove them from the pan and put them to the side.
Sauté the squid, the scallops and the prawns in the same pan.
Drizzle the seafood with white wine.

Remove the seafood from the pan when it is
almost cooked.
Pour the tomato and the prawn stock in the same
pan.
Adjust the flavour with salt and pepper.
Finely chop the parsley.
Pour the cooked pasta into the sauté pan and
toast it together with the lemon zest, the sea-
food, the parsley and extra virgin olive oil.
Stir in briefly and remove from heat.

To serve

Plate and finish with the pistachio, basil and a
drizzle of extra virgin olive oil.

Mark Mosimann

Mark joined Mosimann's in 2007 after four years in Shanghai where, as the general manager of the highly-regarded Laris restaurant at the Three on the Bund complex, he took the company from pre-opening to winning the 2005 and 2006 Best Restaurant of the Year. Mark is also a graduate of the Lausanne Hotel School and has extensive international hotel and catering experience at establishments such as the Sheraton Park Tower in London, the Villa Principe Leopoldo in Lugano, Switzerland, the Palace Hotel in Beijing and the Campton Place Hotel in San Francisco.

Serves 4

Stuff you'll need

500g salmon fillet

100g picked white crabmeat

5g sliced chives

12 leaves coriander

20g spring onions, finely sliced

12 pieces pickled ginger

Lemon dressing

Juice of 4 lemons

50g caster sugar

A little arrowroot

100ml olive oil

100ml sunflower oil

20ml light soya sauce

Marinated salmon with Cornish crabmeat

Get stuck in

Slice the salmon into thin slices and arrange on a plate in a 5 ½in ring.
Keep the ring on the plate.
Sprinkle the crabmeat evenly over the salmon.
Garnish with the rest of the ingredients and remove the ring.

Lemon dressing

Bring the lemon juice and the sugar to the boil. Combine arrowroot and
soy sauce, thicken lemon juice to sauce consistency. Whisk in oil slowly.
Clean plate and drizzle the dressing over the top of the salmon and crab.

Martin Blunos

Martin made a name for himself with ventures Lettonie and Blinis, which each earned two Michelin stars. With his signature walrus-moustache and Union flag trousers, he became a regular on British cooking TV. Blunos later ditched the stars and moved to Bangkok to open Blunos, his first restaurant abroad.

@eastingrandsa

Stuff you'll need

500g live lobster

2 hot dog buns

20g unsalted butter

1 small clove of garlic

1 orange

60g mayonnaise

1 dessertspoon chopped parsley

Little (pomace) olive oil

Salt and pepper

Lobster roll

Get stuck in

Bring a large pan of slightly-salted water to the boil.

Put in the live lobster and cook briefly for two minutes. Remove and put in a bowl of iced water to stop the cooking process.

Cut lobster in half down the length of its body through the shell, remove all meat and set aside.

Take a coffee spoon-sized piece of the butter and put in a small saucepan over a medium heat to melt, adding a squeeze of orange juice and a splash of olive oil. Put in the lobster meat. Season with salt and pepper. Heat gently and keep warm.

Chop the garlic finely and cream together with the butter and most of the

chopped parsley (keep a little to scatter over).

Spread in each side of the cut faces of the hot dog roll. Fill with the warm lobster meat. Using a micro plane, grate over a little of the orange zest and sprinkle the reserved chopped parsley.

Serve accompanied with orange mayonnaise. Use orange rather than lemon with this dish as the acidity of orange is softer and complements the lobster's delicate sweetness.

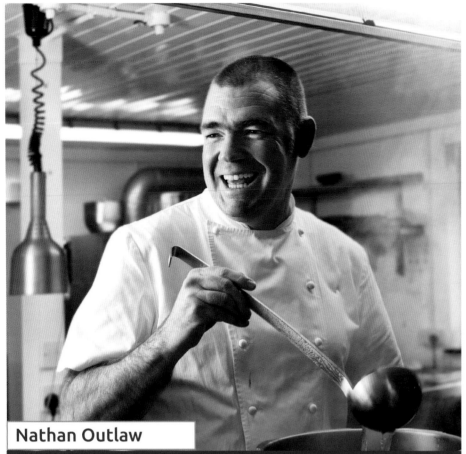

Nathan Outlaw

Originally from Kent, Nathan began his career in London, his interest in seafood cookery saw him move to Cornwall as a young chef to work with Rick Stein in Padstow.

Nathan's style of cooking is one of simplicity, but with complex flavour combinations. He currently has two restaurants in Cornwall. Restaurant Nathan Outlaw holds two Michelin stars and number one spot of the in the Good Food Guide in 2018 and 2019, having scored a perfect 10 for cooking for the past three years. Outlaw's Fish Kitchen offers diners small plates of seafood in an informal setting. It holds one Michelin star. Nathan's regularly appears on TV programmes such as 'Saturday Kitchen' and 'Masterchef Professionals'.

He has written five cookery books, the most recent being 'Restaurant Nathan Outlaw', published by Bloomsbury in 2019.

Nathan Outlaw's fish pie

Serves 8

Stuff you'll need

For the mash

1.5kg floury potatoes, such as Maris Piper

100g butter

200ml milk

For the filling

300g cod fillet, skinned

300g smoked haddock fillet, skinned

300g salmon fillet, skinned

1 litre whole milk

100g butter

100g plain flour

2 tablespoon finely diced shallots

2 tablespoon gherkins, chopped

1 tablespoon small capers in brine, drained and rinsed

2 tablespoon chopped parsley

1 tablespoon chopped tarragon

1 tablespoon chopped chives

1 tablespoon chopped chervil

Sea salt and freshly ground black pepper

For the topping

150g Davidstow Cheddar, grated

8 medium eggs

Get stuck in

For the mash, peel the potatoes and cut into even-sized chunks. Place in a large pan, cover with cold water, add a large pinch of salt and bring to the boil. Lower the heat and simmer for about 20 minutes, until tender.

Drain the potatoes and let them sit in the colander for a few minutes, then return to the pan. Mash until smooth and beat in the butter and milk. Season well with salt and pepper and set aside.

Preheat your oven to 180°C. For the filling, pour the milk into a large pan and bring to a simmer. Meanwhile, cut all the fish into chunks.

Melt the butter in a medium pan over a fairly low heat and stir in the flour. Cook, stirring, for a couple of minutes, being careful not to let it brown. Gradually stir in the hot milk. Bring to the boil, lower the heat and simmer for about 20 minutes. Take off the heat and stir in the shallots, gherkins, capers and herbs. Season the sauce with salt and pepper to taste. Add the fish and toss to combine.

Tip the seafood and sauce into a 30cm square (or similar) baking dish. Spoon or pipe the mashed potato on top and scatter over the cheese. Bake for 20 minutes until the topping is golden.

Meanwhile, bring another pan of water to the boil, then carefully lower in the eggs. Cook for 6 minutes, then drain and place under cold running water until the eggs are cool enough to handle. Peel and cut in half.

When the pie is ready, remove from the oven and poke the halved boiled eggs into the potato topping. Serve straight away.

Nirranjan Tastè

Nirranjan 'Ninja' Tastè is responsible for the culinary operations at Sealy Queensland, one of the leading manufacturers of luxury mattresses. Nirranjan made this career deviation from mainstream hospitality after spending over 23 years managing kitchens of leading hotels of the World and luxury small cruise ships. After completing his studies in food technology, he was selected as a kitchen management trainee for The Taj Mahal Palace, Mumbai. After working at the Taj for four years, he joined P & O Cruises, UK. spending the next 12 years with Swan Hellenic. In 2005 Nirranjan moved to Australia and started at the Sheraton Grand Mirage in Port Douglas, then at Gambaro's, Brisbane's best and busiest seafood restaurant, and finally with the Sofitel Brisbane in Queensland.

Stuff you'll need

Fresh live mud crab

Grade A male crab weighing approx 1.5 – 2 kg

Marinade

Small bunch lemon myrtle and lemon balm leaves (fresh if possible, if not dried)

5 or 6 finger limes

Small piece fresh turmeric root

1 inch piece buderim ginger

4 cloves peeled garlic

Salt and pepper

Sauce

20g chopped spring onions

Curry leaves

50g lightly roasted chopped macadamia

6 bush tomatoes, chopped coarsely

500ml coconut milk

1 medium brown onion, finely chopped

2 peeled mareeba or bowen green mangoes cut into fine juliennes (mango must be comparatively raw but not unripe)

Fresh coriander

Queensland mudcrab with native herbs in a bush tomato and coconut sauce

Get stuck in

Marinade

Peel the ginger, garlic and turmeric.
Wash and chop the lemon balm, lemon myrtle, finger limes, buderim ginger and garlic.
Blend this to a fine paste using a blender or with a mortal and pestle. Add salt and pepper.

Fresh live mud crab

The crab must be put down when alive. Cut out the belly portion. Cut into 4 halves. Detach the claws and keep separate. If you wish you can give then a gentle crack so that cracking them later is easier. Clean them thoroughly and then mix this in the marinade. The marinade should coat the cut crab well. Cover and leave in your fridge for about 45 minutes.

Sauce

Heat a wok until smoking, then add oil, chopped onion, curry leaves. Toss rapidly. Add the chopped macadamia nuts and bush tomatoes and toss well.
Add the marinated crab and mix well so that all the ingredients are combined.
This all must be done on high heat.
Cover the wok with a lid, lower the heat and let it cook for 5 minutes.
Gently lift the lid - the crab should be simmering in its juices. Add the coconut milk, increase the heat and stir until the sauce thickens.
Add the chopped spring onions and check the seasoning.
Mix in the mango juliennes before transferring into your serving dish. Garnish with fresh coriander springs.

Richard Cook

Richard decided, at the age of 19, that the valuable fish resources of the Rivers Severn and Wye, namely wild salmon and eels, were not reaching their full potential. From the beginning in 1989, Richard's Severn & Wye Smokery has avoided the retail sector, preferring instead to supply direct to chefs. Much of its work involves developing bespoke cures and products for specific chefs and venues including The Ritz, The Savoy, Gordon Ramsay, Marco Pierre-White, Wimbledon, Royal Ascot, and many more besides.

Stuff you'll need

3.5inch breakfast muffin cut in half, toasted
80g sliced cured smoked salmon
2 eggs large, poached in acidulated water
30g baby spinach
5g unsalted butter
Milled salt and pepper to taste
50g hollandaise sauce
2g chives, finely chopped

Hollandaise sauce for 4 portions

2 egg yolks
200g warm clarified butter
10ml white wine vinegar reduction
(30ml reduced to 10ml)
Milled salt and cayenne pepper to taste
Lemon juice to taste

Eggs royale

Get stuck in

Cook the spinach in the butter and place on the toasted muffin.

Place the smoked salmon on top of the spinach.

Drain the poached eggs and put on top of the smoked salmon.

Warm the hollandaise and spoon over the eggs.

Sprinkle with the chopped chives.

Hollandaise sauce

Whisk the egg yolks in a metal bowl with the white wine vinegar reduction to a light sabayon. Place the bowl over a pan of gently simmering water and continue to whisk to ribbon stage. Remove from the heat and gently whisk in a trickle of the warm clarified butter.

Correct the acidity with lemon juice and season to taste with cayenne pepper and salt.

Rick Stein

Rick is an English chef, restaurateur, cookery book author and television presenter. He has written over 20 cookery books, an autobiography and made over 30 cookery programmes. He has also cooked for The Queen and Prince Philip, Tony Blair, Margaret Thatcher and French President, Jacques Chirac. Rick is best known for a love of fresh seafood and made his name in the 90s with his earliest books and television series based on his life as chef and owner of The Seafood Restaurant in the fishing port of Padstow, on the north coast of Cornwall.

Stuff you'll need

450g dried linguine or spaghetti
3 vine-ripened tomatoes, skinned, seeded and chopped
300g fresh white crab meat
1 tablespoon chopped parsley
1½ tablespoons lemon juice
50ml extra virgin olive oil
A pinch of dried chili flakes
1 garlic clove, finely chopped
Sea salt and freshly ground black pepper

Crab linguine

Get stuck in

Cook the pasta in a large pan of boiling, well-salted water
(1 teaspoon per 600ml/1 pint) for 7–8 minutes or until al dente.
Meanwhile, put the tomatoes, crab meat, parsley, lemon juice, olive oil,
chili flakes and garlic into another pan and warm through over a gentle
heat.
Drain the pasta, return to the pan with the sauce and briefly toss together.
Season to taste.
Divide between four warmed plates and serve immediately.

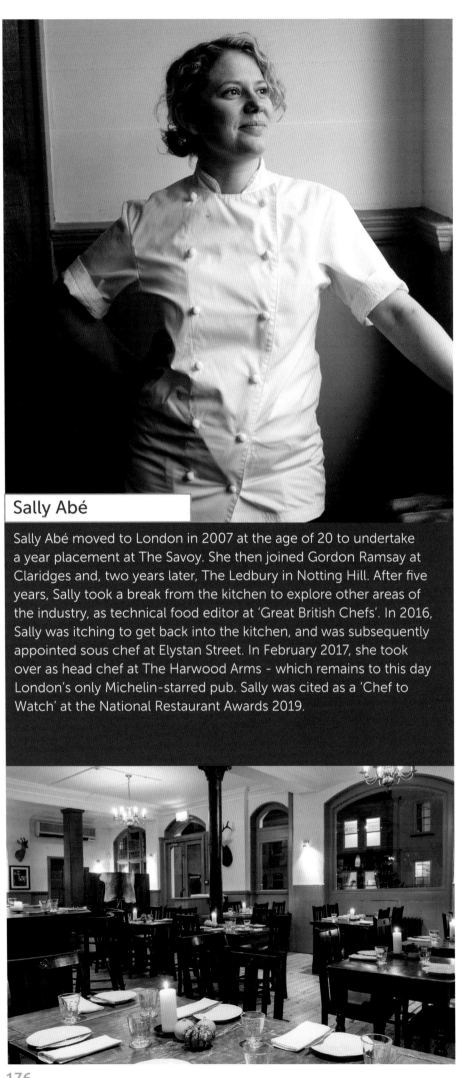

Sally Abé

Sally Abé moved to London in 2007 at the age of 20 to undertake a year placement at The Savoy. She then joined Gordon Ramsay at Claridges and, two years later, The Ledbury in Notting Hill. After five years, Sally took a break from the kitchen to explore other areas of the industry, as technical food editor at 'Great British Chefs'. In 2016, Sally was itching to get back into the kitchen, and was subsequently appointed sous chef at Elystan Street. In February 2017, she took over as head chef at The Harwood Arms - which remains to this day London's only Michelin-starred pub. Sally was cited as a 'Chef to Watch' at the National Restaurant Awards 2019.

Stuff you'll need

2 lemon sole 350-500g skinned

1 bunch baby leeks

1 bunch baby carrots

1 bunch radishes

1 bunch English spinach

2 lemons

2 cloves garlic, peeled

1 tbsp capers

50g parsley, julienne

Vegetable oil

Butter

Salt

Flour, for dusting

Get stuck in

Blanch the vegetables in salted water for 2-3 minutes until cooked, then refresh in iced water. Segment the one of the lemons and cut the other one into quarters.

To cook the lemon sole, place a large frying pan over a high heat and add a tbsp of cooking oil. Season the fish and dust both sides in flour. Place into the pan and fry until golden brown before turning over and frying the other side. Do not move the fish around or turn it over before it is coloured, as this will result in losing heat from the pan and it may stick.

Once the fish is browned both sides add 50g butter, crush the garlic cloves with the heel of your hand and add these to the pan also. Baste the fish with a spoon for a couple of minutes before removing it from the pan. By this point the butter should be golden brown or 'noisette'. Add the capers and lemon segments to the pan and finish with another good squeeze of lemon from one of the quarters. Remove the fish from the pan, spoon over the capers and lemon and sprinkle over the parsley

Pan fried lemon sole with spring vegetables, capers, lemon and parsley

Simon Boyle

Simon has written several life affirming books published by Penguin Random House.

This dish is included in 'How to cook and keep on cooking' and has now become Beyond Food's primary engagement signature dish on the Freshlife programme. It teaches Freshlife's homeless attendees that looking after themselves is so important in their transition to a better way of life. Cooking for themselves and eating good fresh food is really the best start they can give themselves. The rest just follows.

We all know fresh mackerel, pomegranate, spring greens and wild honey are ingredients that can do the world of good, providing positive energy that motivates our mind, body and soul.

Serves 4

Stuff you'll need

2 fresh mackerel, filleted, pin boned
1 tablespoon extra virgin olive oil
Salt and freshly ground black pepper

The dressing

½ pomegranate, cut in half width ways
1 small shallot
1 tablespoon red wine vinegar
¼ teaspoon salt
½ red pepper, diced
1 teaspoon baby capers
Pinch dried chilli flakes
2 tsp Bermondsey honey
1 tsp grain mustard
¼ large bunch fresh mint
4 tablespoon extra virgin olive oil

Cabbage

½ spring green cabbage, washed
25ml olive oil
Salt and freshly ground black pepper

Crackling Cornish mackerel on spring greens, with pomegranate Bermondsey honey dressing

Get stuck in

Wash and pat dry the mackerels. Fillet both sides and carefully cut out the pin bones. Lightly cut the skin five times. This will stop the fillets curling when cooking later. Brush lightly with olive oil, clingfilm and reserve until cooking.

The dressing

Using a rolling pin, gently bash the pomegranate to enable the seeds to fall out. Pick out any white segmental pieces. Add the chopped shallots and red wine vinegar, season with salt and marinate whilst you prepare everything else.

Quarter the red pepper, trim and cut into a fine dice, add to the pomegranate seeds along with the capers, chilli flakes and honey. Pour in the olive oil, mix well. Spoon in the grain mustard. Chop the mint and stir into the dressing, check for seasoning.

Cabbage

Cut in half and shred finely. Heat a pan with a splash of water the olive oil and lemon juice, add the shredded greens and season with salt and freshly ground pepper. Heat quickly and stir for 2-3 minutes, until only just cooked. Check for seasoning.

Cooking the mackerel

Place the mackerel fillets onto a non-stick frying pan, skin side down, season with salt and pepper. Place the pan onto a high heat. As the pan heats the natural oils in the skin will render out and the skin will become very crisp. The flesh will start to become pale around the edges. It is now time to carefully turn the fillets. Cook for 30 seconds and take each fillet out of the pan and onto a reserved plate. Season with Malden sea salt and freshly ground pepper.

Plating

Add the cabbage into the centre of the plate, place the mackerel fillets on top and spoon the dressing around. Serve immediately.

Stephen Marsh

Stephen Marsh grew up in Kent, the garden of England. He has worked in restaurants and hotels throughout the UK, from high end London eateries to a waterside hotels in Cornwall and from, a Michelin-starred hotel to a gastro pub on the Isles of Scilly. He is now the executive chef at the Pickwick.

Stuff you'll need

2 mackerels filleted and pin-boned

The quick cure

100ml white wine vinegar

75ml fruity white wine

50g caster sugar

The salad

1 aubergine

Pink stem radish leaves

4 heritage tomatoes

100g salty fingers

2 Pink Lady apples

Mackerel and salad

Get stuck in

Firstly for the mackerel - two fish will give us four fillets, one fillet each. Make sure that the fillets have no bones left in them.

The quick cure

Let's set up the cure for the mackerel. It's a basic technique called 'ceviche' - using the white wine vinegar to cure/cook the fillet. Add the white wine and sugar to the vinegar and whisk together allowing the sugar to dissolve. If it's too sharp, add a little more sugar if you need to. Place the fillets in the liquid, flesh down. Perhaps use a little plastic container for this.
Now let's prepare the salad. Peel and finely-cut the skin of an aubergine, and deep fry for a little crunchy garnish for our salad. Cut up the tomatoes randomly and the apples into small 'matchstick' pieces. To flame the mackerel, firstly remove the mackerel from the liquid. You will see it has changed colour and texture of the fillets. They are now 'cured'. Light your blow torch and lightly scorch the skin of the fish, making it nice and crunchy. If you don't have a blow torch, place under a very hot grill.

The salad

Now it's time to assemble our salad.
Add all the elements randomly on a small plate and sprinkle a little pesto dressing on the radish and chicory leaves.

Tom Kerridge

Tom Kerridge worked as a chef in restaurants across Britain before deciding to overhaul a pub in Marlow, Buckinghamshire. He opened The Hand & Flowers in 2005 and it went on to become the first pub to be awarded two Michelin stars. In 2014 Tom opened The Coach, his second pub in Marlow, which was awarded a Michelin star in 2017. The same year he opened The Butcher's Tap, a fully operational butchers and pub, also in Marlow. In 2018, Tom opened Kerridge's Bar & Grill at Corinthia London, followed in 2019 by The Bull & Bear in Manchester.

Serves 2

Stuff you'll need

1 tablespoon vegetable oil
1 large onion, finely diced
3 garlic cloves, finely chopped
2.5cm piece fresh ginger, peeled and finely grated
1 long red chili, finely sliced with seeds
A handful of curry leaves
1 heaped teapsoon ground turmeric
1 teaspoon ground coriander
2 medium tomatoes, diced
400ml fresh vegetable stock
50g red lentils
400g monkfish fillets
100g green beans
100ml tinned coconut milk
2 tablespoons roughly chopped coriander leaves
Sea salt and freshly ground black pepper

Get stuck in

Heat the oil in a large non-stick sauté pan over a medium-high heat. When hot, add the onion and cook for five minutes or until softened and starting to brown.
Add the garlic, ginger and chilli and cook for a couple of minutes. Now add the curry leaves, turmeric and ground coriander and cook, stirring for one minute or until fragrant.
Add the tomatoes, stock and lentils to the pan. Stir, bring to the boil over a medium heat and simmer for 12–15 minutes or until the sauce is thickened and the lentils are tender.
Meanwhile, cut the monkfish into 4cm pieces. Trim the green beans and cut them in half. Add the monkfish and coconut milk to the pan and cook over a gentle heat for 2–3 minutes. Add the beans and cook for a further 3–4 minutes.
Remove the pan from the heat, taste to check the seasoning and stir in the coriander.
Serve in warmed bowls.

Monkfish and coconut curry

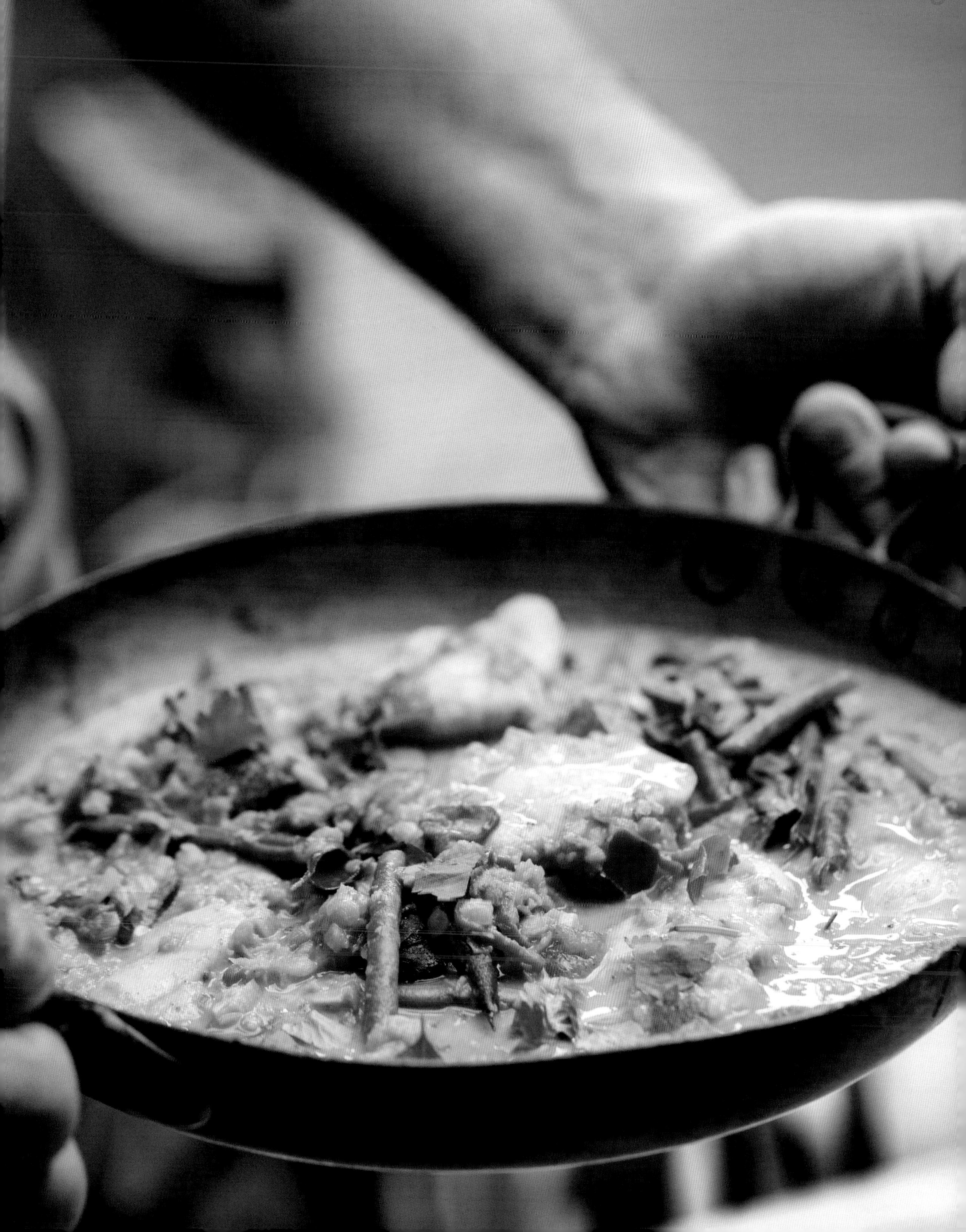

Carefully grown **fruits** and **vegetables**
are an inexhaustible source of emotions and pleasure

Pietro Leemann

Plant Based Recipes

Albert Roux

Albert Roux, OBE, KFO, Legion d'Honneur and Knight of the Order of the Crown of Romania, is one of the world's best-known chefs. In 1967, he and his younger brother Michel Snr opened Le Gavroche, Britain's first three Michelin Star restaurant in London. Albert moved to England in 1953 to spend time as a commis de cuisine within Lady Nancy Aster's country estate at Cliveden. He was later employed as chef to Major Peter Cazelet at the estate at Fairlawne in Kent - and it was the Cazalets who backed Albert to open his own restaurant, Le Gavroche.

Stuff you'll need

45g butter
45g plain flour
500ml milk
5 egg yolks
Salt and freshly ground
white pepper
6 egg whites
600ml double cream
200g Gruyère or Emmental cheese, grated

Get stuck in

Heat the oven to 200°C.
Melt the butter in a thick-based saucepan, whisk in the flour and cook, stirring continuously, for about 1 minute. Whisk in the milk and boil for 3 minutes, whisking all the time to prevent any lumps from forming.
Beat in the yolks and remove from the heat. Season with salt and pepper.
Cover with a piece of buttered greaseproof paper to prevent a skin from forming.
Whisk the egg whites with a pinch of salt until they form firm, not stiff, peaks. Add a third of the egg whites to the yolk mixture and beat with a whisk until evenly mixed, then gently fold in the remaining egg whites.
Spoon the mixture into four well-buttered 8cm diameter tartlet moulds and place in the oven for 3 minutes, until the top begins to turn golden.

To serve

Season the cream with a little salt, warm it gently and pour into a gratin dish.
Turn the soufflés out into the cream, sprinkle the grated cheese over the soufflés, then return to the oven for 5 minutes.
Serve immediately.

Soufflé suissesse

Andrew Aston

Andrew is head of wellness & nutrition at BaxterStorey. He has enjoyed a 28-year career that has taken him across the world. He's been the recipient of a 'Caterer & Hotelkeeper' Acorn Award, and is a member of the Royal Academy of Culinary Arts.

Serves 6

Stuff you'll need

12 British asparagus spears, washed, trimmed and with base snapped away (reserve for nage see recipe below)
100g mung beans
100g white onion peeled and finely diced
1 garlic clove peeled and finely sliced
50g peeled ginger root and finely chopped
½ red chili finely chopped
30g zatar spice
20g fresh turmeric, washed & finely chopped (use gloves)
1 lemon grass stick, washed and crushed
1 cinnamon stick
100g miso paste
4 cardamoms crushed, seeds only
1 lemon for little of the zest
500ml fresh nage
½ bunch of chives, finely chopped
50g set coconut oil
Sea salt
Cracked white pepper

Vegetable stock (nage)

1ltr cold water
Asparagus bases and trimmings
Carrot trimmings
White onion - peeled and sliced
Fennel trimmings, washed
2 garlic cloves, crushed
2 cardamom seeds, crushed
½ lemongrass stick, crushed
4 lemon thyme sprigs
1 bunch washed flat parsley, leaves removed from stalk
1 bunch washed tarragon leaves removed from stalk
1 bunch washed mint, leaves removed from stalks
1 lemon for zest only

English asparagus, mung bean and miso

Get stuck in

Asparagus soup

Soak the mung beans in cold water over night, then refresh in cold water.
Heat the coconut oil in a deep pan, add the onions, garlic, ginger, chilli,
zatar and turmeric. Sauté for a minute or so, add the mung beans,
lemongrass, cinnamon stick and cover with nage.
Allow to simmer for 30 minutes.
Add in the miso paste and cardamom seeds at this stage, stir well and
remove the cinnamon stick. Simmer for a further 20 minutes - the mung
beans should still be al dente. Mix in the chives.
Slice the asparagus stalks to the tip. Heat a non-stick pan with a touch of
olive oil, sauté the asparagus for 30 seconds to take the edge off, season,
then stir through the soup just before serving.

Vegetable stock (nage)

In a deep pot, place the vegetable trimmings
and herb roots into the cold water, bring to the
boil remove from the heat and cool slightly.
Submerge the herbs into the cooled stock. Cover
and allow to infuse for 6-8 hours. Strain before
using.

Andrew Dargue

If someone had told Andrew Darge at the age of 16 he would become a vegetarian he would have laughed. As a keen restaurant visitor even at a young age, the uninspiring options of a mushroom risotto or a halloumi kebab weren't exactly inspiring.

It did however make him think that there must be a better way to create vegetarian food – and he set up his own restaurant to prove it. In 2004 he opened Vanilla Black, determined that there would be no meat substitutes or dishes relying on pasta – just fresh, innovative creations which changed the face of vegetarian cooking.

Serves 2

Get stuck in

Sweet potato
300g sweet potato
Coconut milk
Salt

Lentils
100g puy lentils (or green lentils)
Oil for deep frying

Curry oil
4 heaped teaspoons curry powder
(your choice of heat level)
1 teaspoon tomato purée
100g sunflower oil

Sweet potato 'dhal' and crispy lentils, charred broccoli and curry oil

Stuff you'll need

Prick the skin of the sweet potato, add to the microwave and cook on full power. Turn occasionally. Alternatively bake in the oven until cooked.
Whilst still warm but not hot, peel and blend until smooth.
Add enough coconut milk to give a purée consistency.
Season with salt.

Lentils

Soak lentils in cold water overnight.
Add 1l sunflower or vegetable oil to a large pan and heat to around 180°C.
You need a large pan - if the lentils are wet they will spit.
Drain the lentils and dry very well on a cloth.
Deep-fry in hot oil for around a minute or until crispy.
Remove from the oil with a slotted spoon then add to a cloth to drain.
Season with salt whilst still hot.

Curry oil

Simply mix everything together with a whisk including the broccoli.

Sweet potato

Peel and dice.
Heat a frying pan and add a little oil.
When hot add the sweet potato and cook until brown and charred.
Carefully add a little cold water then cover with a lid and steam. Season with salt.

To serve

Place the sweet potato on a plate. Arrange broccoli on top. Drizzle with curry oil then sprinkle on the lentils.
Add some coriander or parsley as a garnish.

Serves 4

Get stuck in

600g lotus stems
Vegetable oil, for deep frying
70gr raw unsalted peanuts, skinned
1 teaspoon chilli powder
1 tablespoon amchoor (Dry mango powder)
1 tablespoon roasted ground cumin
5 cm inch piece ginger, peeled and cut into
julienne
1 teaspoon salt, or to taste
Juice of 1 lemon
Few sprigs coriander, chopped

Anirudh Arora

Anirudh Arora started his career with Oberoi Hotels as its youngest Indian chef. During this time he opened a number of restaurants for the company. Travelling to London in 2003, Ani worked with chef Atul Kochhar, a fellow Oberoi alumnus, to open Michelin-starred Mayfair restaurant Benares. Two years later he moved on to Moti Mahal, where he spent over a decade as head chef. Ani then went on to open three London restaurants of his own; his most ambitious project, Hankies Haymarket, opened in Spring 2020.

Kararee bhyein

Stuff you'll need

Peel the lotus stems, then thinly slice, preferably with a mandolin. Rinse under cold running water, then drain well and pat dry with kitchen paper. Heat enough oil for deep frying in a wok or deep sauce pan to 180°C, or until a cube of bread browns in 30 seconds. Add the lotus stem slices and deep fry until crisp. Remove and drain on kitchen paper.

Heat a heavy based frying pan and dry roast the peanuts, shaking the pan frequently, until golden brown. Leave to cool, then crush in a food processor or put in a double layer of plastic bags and bash with a rolling pin.

Put the chilli powder, amchoor, roasted ground cumin, roasted peanuts, fried lotus stems, ginger and salt in a large bowl. Squeeze over the lemon juice and mix together lightly, taking care not to crush the lotus stems. Sprinkle with the chopped coriander.

Ashish Tiwari

Ashish is from Kempinski Hotel Muscat's award-winning North Indian restaurant, Bukhara, designed to reflect the heritage and culture of India with a contemporary twist. Best served with mint or tamarind chutney, Bukara's Dahi ke kabab is a melt-in-the-mouth vegetarian kabab recipe. It's easy and quick to prepare too.

Stuff you'll need

150g yoghurt
50g cottage cheese
60g processed cheese
5g salt
3g black salt
5g chopped green chilli
5g chopped ginger

Dahi ke kabab

40g onions, chopped
10g brown onion, chopped
10g fresh coriander roots
3g cumin seeds, roasted
15g roasted gram flour
15g refined flour
Bread crumbs for coating

Get stuck in

Take the yoghurt and hang over night in a cheese cloth.
To make dahi ke kabab, take the paneer and processed cheese and grate them finely. Add chopped brown onion, onion, ginger, green chilli de-seeded, coriander roots and mix them together.
Add roasted cumin seeds with salt and black salt, mix hung curd and add enough roasted gram flour until the mixyure binds.
Make even balls of the mixture and dip them in a flour mixture and add them to bread crumbs. Deep fry them until they turn golden brown.

Ben Tish

Ben is the culinary director of The Stafford London and Norma - the Charlotte Street restaurant inspired by the food and culture of Sicily. He is also the author of 'The Times cookbook of the year 2019, 'Moorish'. In September 2019, Ben and The Stafford London launched a new restaurant, Norma, which draws upon Moorish influences on the cuisine of Sicily. Prior to his role at The Stafford, Ben was chef director of Salt Yard Group, having launched the Soho sites of Dehesa, Ember Yard and Opera Tavern.

Serves 6

Stuff you'll need

8 aubergines, sliced lengthways, about 2cm thick
4 burrata or mozzarella balls, 120g each, drained
5 x 400g cans chopped tinned tomatoes
250g parmesan reggiano, grated
1 bunch fresh basil, leaves removed
250g dried breadcrumbs
Extra virgin olive oil
Sea salt and black pepper

Aubergine parmigiana

Get stuck in

Place the tinned tomatoes in a saucepan over a medium heat and slowly reduce by half. This will take about an hour. Reserve.

Heat a large, heavy-based frying pan over a medium heat, pour in some olive oil and when hot gently fry the aubergines slices, in batches, until they are all tender and golden brown. You will need to add extra oil as you go as the aubergines soak it up quite quickly. When the slices are fried, season well and drain on kitchen paper.

Heat the oven to 180°C. Rub the sides and base of an ovenproof dish with olive oil and add a layer of aubergine slices, then a sprinkle of breadcrumbs and a few basil leaves, followed by a ladle of tomato sauce, a burrata ripped into pieces and a handful of parmesan.

Ensure everything is evenly spread and continue to layer this way until you finish with a layer of aubergine.

Transfer to the oven and cook for 40 minutes, or until the parmigiana is bubbling away and the top of the aubergines have begun to crisp. Remove from the oven to rest for 20 minutes and then sprinkle with the remaining breadcrumbs and cheese, finish under a hot grill for five minutes before serving with a green salad.

Binixa Ludlow

Binixa's mother taught her traditional Gujarati cooking from the age of seven. Bini has since set up the Sweet Cumin cookery school, Bini Fine Foods and a frozen ready meals line. Her longstanding collaboration with Thatcher's Cider, pairing curries with ciders, has been rolled out across the UK, Australia and the US. Bini is also a member of the National Women in Enterprise Taskforce for the Federation of Small Businesses.

Serves 3-4
Heat rating mild/medium

Stuff you'll need

200g cooked canned chickpeas, drained
400-500g potatoes (Roosters or any waxy potato)
3- 4 tablespoons rapeseed oil
30g fresh ginger
3 cloves fresh garlic
1 or 2 fresh finger chillies (to your preference)
10ml lemon juice (or to taste)

Dry spices

¼ - ½ teaspoon turmeric
1 heaped teaspoon coriander
1 heaped teaspoon cumin powder
A pinch of chilli powder
2 teaspoons whole cumin seeds

For garnishing

Lemon juice
2-3 medium fresh tomatoes, chopped
1 small red onion, finely chopped
¼ teaspoon salt (or to taste)
1 tablespoon chaat masala
Chopped fresh chillies (optional)

Channna chaat

Get stuck in

Boil the potatoes in their skins, until they are cooked, allow to cool and cut them into 1cm cubes.

Drain the chickpeas and set aside.

Peel and chop the ginger and garlic. Remove the stalk on the chillies and chopped finely.

Blitz in a food processor until a paste is formed. Set aside.

Oil a frying pan, add cumin seeds, allow to sizzle in the oil. They will brown and release a lovely aroma. Reserve some for garnish.

Next add the ginger, garlic and chilli paste, allow to brown, add the potatoes, chickpeas and stir.

Add the dry spices. Stir well to ensure that the chickpeas and potatoes have been coated evenly.

To serve

Serve into a large bowl, garnish with fresh coriander, chopped tomatoes, red onion, tamarind chutney and yoghurt chutney topped with roasted cumin seeds.

Sprinkle chaat masala on top and, if you are brave, chopped fresh chillies.

Serve warm or cold.

Darren Deadman

Established in 1847, Searcys is one of Britain's longest-running hospitality companies, serving in some of the UK's most spectacular settings. Darren joined Searcys' in 2017 and has been instrumental in creating Searcys sustainability pledges.

Born in Kent to a family of chefs and farmers, from a young age Darren forged his love of British seasonal produce. After college, Darren spent a year in Europe, where he fine-tuned his skills and knowledge of classical cooking. Returning to the UK, he set to work in some of the capital's finest hotels and restaurants under an array of top chefs and mentors. Throughout his career he has worked on some of the biggest high-profile events such as the Farnborough Air Show, the BAFTAs and the London Olympics.

Stuff you'll need

2 tablespoons rapeseed oil
2 leeks, dark green parts removed, chopped
Sea salt and ground black pepper
400ml vegetable stock
1 large potato, peeled and chopped
3 bunches watercress, first reserve some leaves for garnish and then remove thick ends and chop the rest

Leek watercress and pea soup

Get stuck in

In a medium saucepan heat 1 tbsp oil. Add leeks and season to taste. Cook, stirring occasionally until tender. Add stock, all but one handful of potatoes, and 1 litre of water. Bring to boil, reduce to simmer and cook partially covered until the potato is tender.

Meanwhile, cook the reserved potato in some boiling salted water until tender.

Add watercress to the soup and cook until bright green and tender. Process, either with a stick blender or in a food processor until smooth. Check and adjust seasoning.

To serve

Stir the separately cooked potato through the soup. Pour into bowls and top with the reserved watercress. Finish with some rapeseed oil.

Francesco Marrucelli

Tuscany Now & More Chef - Francesco Marrucelli from the Estate of Petroio shares his recipe for Gnudi. Gnudi is a traditional Tuscan dish of gnocchi-like dumplings made with ricotta cheese instead of potato. The result is often a lighter, pillowy dish, unlike the often denser, chewier gnocchi - true Italian comfort food.

Serves 4

Stuff you'll need

500g fresh spinach
350g ricotta
100g parmesan, grated
2 eggs
2 tablespoons flour, plus extra for dredging
Salt and pepper
Ground nutmeg, optional

Gnudi

Get stuck in

While you wash the spinach, place a pot of water on the stove. Bring to the boil, add a handful of cooking salt, and the spinach. Once cooked, drain and squeeze the spinach, making sure to remove any excess liquid. Place the spinach aside, or if you prefer more flavour, saute in a frying pan with olive oil and garlic.

Finely chop the spinach, stir in a medium bowl with the ricotta, parmesan, two eggs, flour, salt, pepper and ground nutmeg (optional). Using a spoon, scoop out portions of the mix (about the size of a walnut) and, using damp hands, roll smooth and round balls. Drench in flour, tapping off any excess, and place on a floured surface. Set aside in a cool place covered with clingfilm until ready to cook, or refrigerate for up to 24 hours.

When ready to cook, bring a pot of salted water to a boil, and slide the gnudi in. Remove the gnudi using a slotted spoon when they float to the surface (after around 3-4 minutes). Toss with a butter and sage sauce, or fresh tomato sauce.

Frédéric Claudel

Frédéric joined the kitchens of the Elysée du Vernet in 1997, where he discovered his love of seafood. In 2006, he took the reins of the Senderes restaurant alongside Chef Banctel, to win two Michelin stars. Frédéric now puts all his experiences at the service of the most beautiful terrace of Paris at the Grand café **Fauchon**, where he works in close collaboration with chefs Sébastien Monceaux and François Daubinet.

Stuff you'll need

80g pasta riso
60g butter
40g white onions
30g white wine
12g fine salt
5g ground white pepper
1ltr vegetable broth
1 bunch spring onions
30g mascarpone
250ml vegetable milk (or soy or almond)
6g black melanosporum truffle,
chopped and shavings
6g old comte
(preferably aged for 14 months)
2g fleur de sel (flower of salt)
3g Chervil
2g Fauchon olive oil (or any good olive oil)

Get stuck in

Cooking the riso

Chop the white onions and sweat them in butter.
Add the riso and coat in the fat, as you would for a risotto.
Season with fine salt and pepper.
Add the hot vegetable broth and gradually cook the risotto (for approximately 11 mins).
Drain the pasta riso, reserving the cooking broth.
Once cooked, spread the riso in a plate and fork it lightly.
Chop the white and the green of the spring onion finely.

Truffle

To prepare the truffle, peel and keep the trimmings.
Finely chop the trimmings.
Mandolin the truffle and carve five shavings.

Vegetable broth

Simmer the vegetable broth until it is reduced by half. Add the milk of your choice and 30g of butter, bringing it to a simmer and cook for approximately 3 minutes.
Season and then mix together with the cooked pasta riso. Remove from the heat.

Truffle pasta riso

Finishing the riso

Cut the Comte cheese into fine slices.

Add the chopped spring onion, chopped truffle, mascarpone and adjust the seasoning.

Place the riso in a deep plate and scatter the truffle and old Comte shavings in the centre.

Decorate with chervil, parsley or watercress.

Gavin Roche

Gavin has spent the last two years as executive sous chef at Gleneagles Hotel and Golf Resort in Scotland and is now the first 'culinary coach' for the London business for BaxterStorey. His career highlight was gaining three AA Rosettes as a young head chef, more recently being part of the culinary team to win Global Golf Resort of the Year.

Stuff you'll need

2kg salad tomatoes
Washed and cut into 8ths
200g black lentils
50g caster sugar
20g sea salt
20g dried oregano
50ml balsamic vinegar
50ml cold pressed rapeseed oil

Twilight tomatoes

Get stuck in

Marinate the tomatoes in all other ingredients
for 20 mins.

Mix then drain all the liquid.

Place on parchment in a warm oven on low heat
for up to 1 hour. Turn off the oven and leave the
dish over night in the oven to finish.

A tip: try starting the tomatoes in a hot oven for
6 mins - don't forget about them.

Keep the juice from the tomatoes as a dressing.

Grace Regan

Grace is the founder of the UK's first vegan curry house, SpiceBox in Walthamstow, London. After being named one of the UK's best young entrepreneurs in 2015, she won a place on a top Silicon Valley accelerator and moved to California, where she became vegan. Grace moved back to London and started SpiceBox from her home kitchen. She quickly fell into the world of street food, trading with Kerb at markets and festivals across the UK and was named a Young British Foodie Street Food finalist. Grace opened the first SpiceBox curry house in Walthamstow in January 2019.

Stuff you'll need

1 medium sweet potato

3 tablespoons vegetable oil

1 tablespoon cumin seeds

1 tablespoon mustard seeds

3 cardamom pods, crushed

2 bay leaves

1 white onion, peeled and sliced into half moons

1 tablespoon salt

1 tablespoon sugar

1 green chilli, slit lengthways

4 cloves garlic, peeled and grated

A thumb of ginger, grated

½ tablespoon turmeric

1 tin butter beans, drained and rinsed

400g tin of coconut milk

2 large handfuls of spinach

¼ lemon, juiced

Butter bean, sweet potato and spinach coconut curry

Get stuck in

Dice the potato, drizzle it with oil and some salt and roast it in an oven set at 180°C for 25 mins.

While the potato is cooking, heat the oil in a large frying pan and add the cumin and mustard seeds, cardamom and bay leaves. Fry until the seeds begin to pop. Add onion, salt and sugar and fry on a gentle heat until it's soft and caramelised.

Once the onion starts to soften, add the chilli, ginger and garlic and cook out with the onion for 10 minutes.

By now your sweet potato should be cooked. When it's cool enough to handle, roughly dice it into one inch chunks. Add these to the frying pan along with the turmeric and beans. Give everything a good stir and then add the coconut milk. Turn down the heat and simmer for five minutes, then stir through the spinach and lemon juice. Take the pan off the heat and season.

Stuff you'll need

1 head of puntarelle or chicory
500g fresh broad beans

Anchovy dressing

75ml extra virgin olive oil
2 cloves of garlic peeled and halved
7 anchovy fillets in oil
Dried chilli (optional)
Juice and zest of a lemon
A pinch of salt
Ground black pepper to taste

To serve

Lemon thyme and thyme flower
(optional)

Graziano Pagliarulo

Graziano, hailing from southern Italy, has had a varied chef career since moving to London at 18. He has worked both at fine-dining establishments, such as Aquavit London, and innovative cocktail venues, including Untitled in Dalston. He joined the team at Beyond Food Foundation's restaurant Brigade Bar + Kitchen last year, before taking the opportunity to intern at three Michelin star restaurant Maaemo, in Oslo. Since returning to London he has been the head chef for wine bar Top Cuvee.

Puntarelle and broad bean salad with anchovy dressing

Get stuck in

First thing to do is to prep the puntarelle salad. Take off the external leaves, cut off and keep the tenderest leaves from the inside and cut off each point of the salad.

Wash the salad, then slice each point longways around 4-5mm thick. Keep the salad in ice water for half an hour at least.

Start cleaning the broad beans, then remove them from their pods and rinse.

Anchovy dressing

Warm 75ml of good quality extra virgin olive oil in a small pot, then add the garlic, dried chilli to taste and the anchovy fillets.

Once the oil is hot, turn off the heat and let it cool a little bit. Remove the cloves of garlic and then add the juice of a lemon. Whisk the oil and lemon juice until emulsified and thickened.

To serve

Drain from the water and dry the greens.

In a large mixing bowl put the puntarelle, broad beans, anchovy dressing, zest of a lemon, black pepper and a pinch of salt (be careful with salt because the anchovies are already salted).

Mix well and plate the salad in a plate.

Finish it with a couple of flowers and lemon thyme leaves to give that extra herbal kick.

Ian Human

Ian is executive chef at The Coach House and The Church Hall, two new hospitality concepts by Restaurant Associates. With over 20 years' experience in various kitchens, Ian has been with Restaurant Associates since 2001 working as head chef for a number of different venues. Ian was also directly responsible for the food served to high profile guests at the London Olympics 2012 including Princess Anne, David Cameron, Boris Johnson, and Lord Sebastian Coe and the International Olympic Committee.

Stuff you'll need

3 aubergines
60g smoked chimichurri
100g fregola
Half a bunch spring onions, thinly sliced
60g Greek yoghurt
2 lemons
20ml lemon oil
Bunch of watercress, washed
10g flat parsley, thinly sliced
30g red chillies, deseeded and sliced
60g olive oil
Salt and pepper

Get stuck in

Cook the fregola as per packet instructions.
Peel, seed and slice the chillies thinly.
Wash and thinly slice the spring onions.
Mix the zest and juice of two lemons with the Greek yoghurt, lemon oil and a pinch of salt.
Cut the aubergines into a large dice and dress generously with olive oil, salt and pepper. Roast for 20 minutes at 230°C.
Dress the fregola with the chimichurri.
Now build the salad, layering the aubergine with the yoghurt, watercress, fregola, chillies and spring onions.

Aubergine, smoked chimi churri,
spring onions, watercress, toasted fregola

Stuff you'll need

4oz royal trumpet mushroom, thinly sliced

¼ cup fennel, brunoise

25g parmesan, shaved

1 cup baby arugula

2 tablespoons hazelnuts, chopped

¼ teaspoon fleur de sel

4 teaspoons hazelnut oil

1/4 teaspoon black pepper

1/4 teaspoon caraway seeds, toasted and lightly cracked in a mortar & pestle

¼ teaspoon nutmeg

¼ tsp lemon zest

4 tablespoons lemon vinaigrette

Fennel brunoise

4.3 ounces fennel, brunoise

1 bulb fennel, chopped into medium-size pieces

Olive oil

¾ cup white wine

23oz vegetable broth

⅔ cup lemon juice

1.5 teaspoon salt

John Fraser

John's restaurant group, JF Restaurants, is behind New York City's only vegetarian Michelin starred restaurant, Nix; Times Square's first and only fine dining restaurant, 701West at the Times Square EDITION hotel; as well as Ardor at the West Hollywood EDITION; and his signature neighbourhood brasserie, The Loyal in West Village.

Mushroom carpaccio

Get stuck in

Fennel brunoise

In a medium saucepan over medium heat, sweat the fennel with a bit of olive oil for around 10 minutes, until the pieces start to become tender. Season lightly with salt.

Once tender, add the wine and continue cooking off the alcohol.

Add the vegetable broth and bring to a boil. Reduce heat to medium-low and simmer for eight minutes. Turn off the heat and add the lemon juice and salt. Strain the fennel and reserve the liquid. Cook the fennel brunoise in the liquid until tender.

To serve

Layer slices of royal trumpet mushrooms on a plate to give them the appearance of a shingled roof. Brush with the lemon vinaigrette.

Top with fennel brunoise, parmesan cheese, baby arugula, hazelnuts, and garnish with fleur de sel, hazelnut oil, black pepper, caraway seeds and nutmeg.

John Williams OBE

John Williams OBE is executive chef of The Ritz London. His career includes 17 years in the kitchens of Claridge's. John has received numerous honours during his time at The Ritz, including a Michelin star in 2016, an MBE and a Chevalier de l'Ordre du Merite Agricol (the first British chef to receive such an honour).

Serves 6

Stuff you'll need

6 gulls eggs

Pecorino foam

50ml olive oil

20g butter

60g shallots, roughly chopped

½ celery stick, finely sliced

2 garlic cloves, crushed

50g button mushrooms, trimmed and finely sliced

6 black peppercorns

50ml dry white wine

4 tablespoons fish stock

400ml milk

4 tablespoons double cream

450g pecorino cheese, grated

Asparagus

18 green and 24 wild asparagus spears (or just use green)

2 pinches of salt

2 pinches of caster sugar

40g butter

Morels

18 morels, cleaned and stalks trimmed

20g butter

100ml water

100ml chicken stock

Purée & glazing

120g broad beans, skinned

40g butter

50g peas

100ml chicken or veal stock

To finish (optional)

10 bean flowers

Wild garlic flowers

50g mixed wild herbs, such as wild chervil or wood sorrel

Soft-boiled gull eggs, asparagus and pecorino foam

Get stuck in

Pecorino foam

Heat the oil in a large sauté or frying pan. Add the butter, then the shallots and sweat them over a medium-low heat until softened but not browned. Stir in the celery, garlic and mushrooms. Add the peppercorns and season with salt, then pour in the wine and leave to bubble away until reduced by half. Stir in the nage and, again, reduce by half. Add the milk and cream and bring to the boil.

Remove from the heat and leave to cool for 5 minutes (or to 70°C) before returning the pan to the heat and adding the pecorino. Remove from the heat, leave to infuse for 30 minutes then pass through a fine-mesh sieve, stir well and set aside. Immediately before serving, use a stick blender to aerate the sauce to make it foamy.

Asparagus

Break the asparagus spears at their weakest point to ensure tenderness. Peel off the outer skin of the asparagus stems and slice about 4cm (1½in) from the base to ensure every piece is succulent. Reserve the trimmed pieces for the purée. Place the green asparagus spears in a pan of water so that they are submerged by three-quarters. Add half the salt, sugar and butter and cook over a high heat for 3–4 minutes, or until tender. Set aside. Repeat the process with the wild asparagus, but cook these for only 1 minute.

Morels

In a pan, braise the morels in the butter and measured water over a medium-low heat for 2–3 minutes. Pour in the stock. Cook for 5 minutes, turning the morels gently in the stock until they are perfectly glazed and have absorbed the stock's flavours. Set aside.

Purée & glazing

Add the beans to a large pan of boiling salted water. Cook for 3 minutes until tender. Drain and set aside. Cook the asparagus trimmings in the same way. Using a stick blender, blend the asparagus trimmings with one-quarter of the

beans to form a purée. Mix in half the butter and season to your taste. In a frying pan over a high heat, melt the remaining butter, add the reserved beans and the peas, then pour in the stock. Turn the beans and peas so that they are well coated and glazed. Set aside.

Finally, the gulls' eggs

Bring a large pan of water to the boil. Reduce to a simmer and carefully lower in the eggs. Cook for 4½ minutes. Shell the eggs in a bowl of icy water, then they're ready to serve.

To finish

Spoon the purée into the centre of each plate. Top with the eggs, add the asparagus and morels, scatter with the glazed beans and peas, flowers and herbs, then spoon over the pecorino foam. Serve hot.

Paul Gayler

Paul Gayler was until the end of December 2013 executive chef at London's Lanesborough hotel on Hyde Park Corner. Paul opened the hotel in 1991. His early career included working at the Le Crillon in Paris, Royal Garden hotel and Dorchester in London. He left the Dorchester in 1982 as executive chef and deputy to Anton Mosimann. In 1982 Paul was appointed chef director at London's Inigo Jones restaurant. In 1989, he was asked to open the Halkin Hotel in Belgravia. On the side Paul was responsible for the development and introduction of Tesco's Finest range. In 2012 he was awarded an MBE for services to the hospitality industry and charities.

Serves 4

Stuff you'll need

Tandoori carrots

12 large carrots with stalks, carefully peeled whole
300ml thick vegan yoghurt
1 teaspoon ground turmeric
3cm piece root ginger
4 garlic cloves, crushed
30ml lemon juice
20g fresh coriander
20g fresh mint
A little salt

Carrot pickle

300g carrots, peeled, cut into thick julienne strips
50g fresh ginger, cut into julienne strips
50ml rice wine vinegar
50g sugar
1 teaspoon ground cumin
8 cloves
1 tablespoon fresh lemon juice

Puy lentil & date dal

300g puy lentils
1 tablespoon veg oil
2 small onions, finely chopped
1 teaspoon ginger paste
1 teaspoon garlic paste
1 teaspoon Kashmiri red chilli powder
1 tablespoon tomato puree
1 teaspoon garam masala
½ teaspoon dried fenugreek leaves
½ teaspoon sugar
3 tablespoons vegan yoghurt
50g vegan butter
50g stoneless medjool dates, cut into small cubes
50g chopped coriander

To serve

Micro coriander leaves
Radish, thinly-sliced

Tandoori-scorched carrots, lentil and date dal, carrot pickle

Get stuck in

Tandoori carrots

Place all the ingredients in a blender (except the carrots), blitz to a smooth paste. Transfer to a large bowl, add the carrots and gently mix them well with the yoghurt marinade. Cover and refrigerate overnight.

Carrot pickle

Heat the sugar and vinegar together in a pan, add the ginger, cumin and cloves and cook gently for 5 minutes.

Add the carrots and remove from the heat to cool. When cold, refrigerate overnight. Remove cloves and drain well, place in a bowl, season and add lemon juice.

Lentil & date dal

Heat the oil in a pan, add the chopped onions and cook over low heat until golden brown. Add the garlic and ginger paste and the red chilli and cook for 5 minutes.

Add the tomato purée, and cook together for 2-3 minutes. Then add the lentils and half the butter, cook over very low heat for 15-20 minutes or until lentils are just cooked and thick in texture.

Stir in the yoghurt, fenugreek, remaining butter and sugar.

Add the herbs and dates, season to taste. Keep it hot.

To serve

Heat the oven to 200°C, line a baking tray with kitchen paper.

Remove the carrots from their marinating juices and lay out flat on the baking tray. Place in the oven to roast for 30-40 minutes until cooked and lightly charred or scorched all over.

Place a bed of the date dal in a serving bowl. Top each dal with three roasted tandoori carrots and some carrot pickle.

Finally, scatter over some thinly sliced radish, garnish with the micro coriander and serve with steamed basmati rice.

Stuff you'll need

500 ml double cream
80g Gruyere
80g blue cheese
80g cheddar
50g Parmesan
50g mascarpone
10g Dijon mustard
1kg macaroni

Get stuck in

Grate all the cheeses and mix them together
along with the mustard.
Bring the cream up to a boil
and pour over the cheese,
then return the mix to the stove
and whisk or blend with a hand blender.
Mix in 2kg of cooked macaroni.
Place in serving dishes and
cover with grated cheddar.
Bake until golden brown.

Phil Carmichael

Phil Carmichael - executive head chef at Berners Tavern - first met
Jason Atherton in 2002 and worked alongside him on the launch
of Gordon Ramsay's Maze. Quickly becoming Jason's right hand
man, Phil headed up the kitchen at Maze in South Africa and then
in Prague, where he won his first Michelin star. Phil then returned
to London to assist Jason with the launch of Pollen Street Social in
2011.

Mac 'n' Cheese

Pietro Leemann

Pietro earned Europe's first Michelin star for a vegetarian restaurant, Joia in Milan. Some 29 years on, it remains the only vegetarian restaurant to own a star in Italy - and still sets a benchmark for vegetarian fine dining. In 2010 he received the Città di Fabriano award. He has also founded - with his friend and co-author Gabriele Eschenazi - the first international festival of vegetarian culture and cuisine, The Vegetarian Chance, now successfully in its fifth edition. In recent years, inspired by Asia, Pietro has been busy developing his personal philosophy of 'natural cuisine' (Alta Cucina Naturale) based around organic produce without meat.

Stuff you'll need

Terrine
650g pumpkin cream
300g toasted cashews
8g agar agar mixed with 400g of boiling water
80g celery
80g carrots
50g leeks
250g porcini mushrooms
40g seed oil
40g extra virgin olive oil

Polenta
500g water
125g corn white flour
1.5g cumin
4g salt

Mayonnaise
200g almond milk
330g deodorised seed oil
25g lemon juice
7g salt
A drop of beetroot water

To serve
Wild herbs
Flowers
Sprouts
Lovage salt

Bavarois with porcini mushrooms, pumpkin and white polenta with cumin

Get stuck in

Terrine

Cut the celery, carrots, leeks and mushrooms into a brunoise and cook them separately in a pan with the seed oil and seasoning. Put them in a bowl to cool.

In a Thermomix, blend the cashews and add the pumpkin cream and bring it to 80°C. Add the agar agar and the vegetables, stirring gently. Season with salt and extra virgin olive oil and put it in buttered mould.

Polenta

Bring water to the boil in a large saucepan. While stirring the water constantly with a wooden spoon, tip in the polenta, cumin and salt in a steady stream. Lower the heat so the polenta isn't spluttering too much, then cook, stirring occasionally, for 10 mins. Meanwhile, line a 40 x 30cm tray with baking parchment. Spoon the polenta onto the tray. Spread to a rough rectangle, making sure the polenta is packed tightly and there are no gaps. Cover with another sheet of baking parchment and a flat baking tray, then top with some cans or jars to press and flatten the polenta while you chill it in the fridge for at least 2 hours, or up 24hours.

Heat a griddle pan, cut the set polenta into neat rounds. Brush both sides of each wedge with a little of the remaining oil and griddle for 5 mins on each side until charred and hot through. Place on paper towel before serving.

Mayonnaise

Whip up the mayonnaise ingredients and colour half the mixture with beetroot water.

To Serve

Set the polenta in the middle of the plate, place the terrine on top. Dress with fresh herbs, petals, sprouts and some points of mayonnaise along the plate circumference, alternating the colours.

Rocky Barnette

Rocky, formerly of The Inn at Little Washington, and his wife, Virginia Lebermann, took a leap of faith when founding The Capri in 2016. It was then one of only a dozen other establishments serving food in Marfa - not counting the gas station. Rocky says he fantasized that one day he would serve seared avocado in place of foie gras at the Michelin-starred vegan restaurant he'd own. In reality, he wound up grilling the avocados and making guacamole for a very discerning crowd here on the border...

Recipe re-printed from
Cooking in Marfa: Welcome, We've Been Expecting You, published by Phaidon

Stuff you'll need

Tostones

Neutral oil, such as soybean or avocado,
for frying
6 green plantains
Sal de Chapulín

Guacamole

120ml fresh lime juice
60ml avocado oil
1 teaspoon citric acid (optional)
6 firm-ripe Hass avocados, halved and pitted
Kosher (flaked) salt
Freshly ground black pepper
½ medium red onion, cut into 3mm dice
2 large jalapeños, seeded and cut
into 3mm dice
20g cilantro (fresh coriander), finely choppe)
½ teaspoon ground cumin
2 tablespoons extra virgin olive oil

Grilled avocado guacamole

Get stuck in

Tostones

Pour at least 10cm oil into a deep-fryer or other heavy pot. Heat the oil to 149°C over medium heat.

Cut off both ends of the plantains. Using a knife, score each one lengthwise and release them from the peel. Slice the plantains crosswise into 5cm lengths.

Working in batches, fry the plantains until they are a light golden brown. Remove them from the oil. While the next batch is frying, flatten the pieces from the previous batch between 2 pieces of parchment paper using a small frying pan (we use a tortilla press).

Heat the oil to 177°C.

Return the flattened plantains to the oil and fry until they are golden brown and crispy around the edges but the centre is still a little soft.

Transfer to paper towels to cool and season with Sal de Chapulín.

Guacamole

Preheat a grill barbecue or a cast-iron grill pan to very high heat.

In a small bowl, combine the lime juice, avocado oil, and citric acid (if using). Season the avocados with salt and pepper. Brush them liberally with the lime juice mixture.

Place the avocado halves flesh side down on the grill until they are slightly charred, about 4 minutes. Flip them and grill on the skin side for 1–2 minutes to heat the avocados through but not char the skin. Remove from the grill and brush the flesh side with more lime juice mixture. Set aside to cool to room temperature.

Squeeze the avocado flesh into a large molcajete or bowl. It should slip right out of the skins from the grilling. Add the onion, jalapeños, cilantro (fresh coriander), cumin, olive oil, and any remaining lime juice mixture from the grilling process.

Process with the mano if in the molcajete or with a spoon in the bowl to get a semi-smooth paste with some small chunks about the size of a pea. Season with salt and pepper.

Serve immediately, with the freshly fried tostones for dipping. Guacamole can be stored in a pastry bag or airtight container for up to one day.

Ruth Hansom

Ruth trained at Westminster Kingsway College and secured a position at The Ritz, where she completed her Royal Academy of Culinary Arts apprenticeship and progressed from commis to chef de partie. In 2017 she was named Young National Chef of the Year. In 2018, Ruth joined Luton Hoo hotel as head chef at its restaurant Wernher, before joining Pomona's in Notting Hill as head chef the following year. She left Pomona's in the spring on 2020 with plans to set up a smaller venture. Ruth also helps deliver the Royal Academy of Culinary Arts' 'Adopt a School' programme to primary school children.

Stuff you'll need

3 green asparagus spears

3 white asparagus spears

Pickled mushroom

200g mushrooms

100ml white wine vinegar

100ml water

100g sugar

5g of salt,

4 cardamom pods

Berkswell shavings

Plating

Pea shoots

Mint leaves

Dressing

50g chopped toasted pine nuts

1 lemon zest and juice

20ml truffle oil

5g chopped mint

5g Maldon salt

5g sugar

100ml rapeseed oil

Get stuck in

Asparagus

Peel the white asparagus.
Remove filo glades from green asparagus.
Blanch the white and green asparagus in salted lemon water and refresh in ice water.

Pickled Mushroom

Cut mushrooms into quarters.
Bring to the boil the white wine vinegar, water, sugar, salt, and cardamom pods.
Pour the pickled liquid over the mushrooms.

Dressing

Mix all ingredients together.

To Serve

Pick small mint leaves and pea shoots.
Shave berkswell with a peeler.

Simon Boyle

Simon received the Craft Guild of Chefs' People's Choice award in 2013, and then the Lord Mayor's Dragon Award in 2015. In 2016 Simon was included in the Evening Standard's Progress 1000 most influential people in London.

In 2017, Simon became a Fellow of the Royal Academy of Culinary Arts, while Beyond Food and Brigade won the 'Education, Training & Jobs' Award from Social Enterprise UK.

In 2018 Simon received a notable Catey Award. The Catey's are renowned as the Oscars of the hospitality world. Simon was recognised for his outstanding contribution to the industry, and for going the extra mile in the world of social impact.

Serves 4

Stuff you'll need

Mushrooms and beans

4 teaspoon olive oil

4 King oyster mushrooms

200g girolle mushrooms

8 baby courgettes with flowers

2 banana shallots

2 teaspoon fennel seeds

½ clove garlic

200g butter beans & haricot blanc soaked and blanched

125ml white wine

60ml Oloroso sherry

2 tablespoons capers

½ lemon, zest

1 handful parsley

2 teaspoons flaky sea salt

Freshly ground pepper

50g crushed hazelnuts

1 tablespoon cold pressed extra virgin olive oil

Chargrilled pepper Ajvar

2 red peppers

2 cloves garlic

1 eggplant

100ml cold pressed extra virgin olive oil

2 teaspoons white wine vinegar

½ teaspoon flaky sea salt

Freshly ground pepper

Sourdough toast

½ sourdough loaf

½ clove garlic

15ml cold pressed extra virgin olive oil

Mushrooms and butter beans on toast

Get stuck in

Red Pepper Ajvar

Load and light the chargrill (a gas flame or hot oven will do the job.) When all the coals are lit and covered with grey ash set cooking grate in place cover grill and allow it to pre heat for five minutes. Oil the grate for grilling. Place the peppers on the hot side of the grill and cook until blackened all over, 10 to 15 minutes. Transfer the peppers to a large bowl, cover with plastic wrap and leave until cool enough to handle, about 20 minutes. Remove charred skin seeds, cores from the peppers.

While the peppers are cooling, prick the skin of eggplant with a fork all over the eggplant, place on the now cooler grill, cover and cook until skin darkens and wrinkles an eggplant is uniformly soft when pressed with tongs, about 30 minutes, turning halfway through for even cooking. Remove the eggplant from the grill. After 10 minutes, or once cool enough to handle, trim ends and split lengthways. Using a spoon, scoop out the flesh of the eggplant and discard the skin.

Place the roasted peppers, eggplant pulp, and garlic in a food processor fitted with a steel blade, pulse until roughly chopped. Add oil, vinegar and salt, and pulse until incorporated and peppers are finely chopped. Transfer sauce into a medium saucepan, bring to a simmer over medium high heat, reduce heat to medium low and simmer for 30 minutes, stirring occasionally. Remove from the heat and season with salt and pepper to taste. Let cool to room temperature then use immediately or reserve.

Mushrooms and beans

Cean the girolles, to do this scrape the stems to reveal the layer underneath and wipe the cap of any dirt, cut into half. Cut the king oysters in half. Trim the courgettes.

Finely chop the shallots and crush ½ clove of garlic. Heat a frying pan until very hot and add the olive oil for frying and immediately add the mushrooms and courgettes Toss quickly and add the shallots and fennel seeds. Keep moving quickly. Throw in the beans and continue to move the pan. Deglaze with the white wine, and bring to the boil and reduce. Aad sherry and heat up then add the capers, lemon zest, parsley and extra virgin olive oil. Check the seasoning.

Sourdough toast

Thickly slice the sourdough and drizzle with extra virgin olive oil and grill, on both sides. on a griddle or chargrill. Rub with garlic and season with Maldon sea salt and pepper. Cut each slice into two. Turn the heat up on the mushrooms, drizzle in the extra virgin olive oil and shake into the reduced sauce,. Taste for seasoning. Place one slice of toast on each plate and arrange the mushrooms, courgettes and spoon the beans and dressing over. Place one slice upright, so it remains crisp.Sprinkle over the hazelnuts and spoon the red pepper ajvar on the side.

Stefano Sanna

Stefano moved from Sardinia to Edinburgh to open his own private chef and catering company Shardana Catering. As a child he watched his Nonna prepare family feasts before he turned his hand to cooking himself. He worked at various local Sardinian restaurants before investing his savings into cookery school. He trained at Italian cookery school, Alma, where Stefano gained an in-depth knowledge of food and techniques. Upon graduating he worked in Michelin star restaurants across Italy before deciding to make the move to Scotland. He chose Scotland as he viewed it as an exciting inclusive nation, with passion and culture. Whilst he specialises in Sardinian and Italian dishes, he enjoys exploring different cuisines – especially modern Scottish cuisine.

Stuff you'll need

Pasta dough

150g flour

100g semolina flour

14ml water

Salt to flavour

1 teaspoon olive oil

Filling

50g potatoes

3 tablespoon of garlic infused oil

70g of Pecorino cheese

8-10 Mint leaves

Salt to flavour

Tomato sauce

300g passata

100g of diced fresh cherry tomatoes

2 tablespoons of olive oil

1 clove garlic

Salt and pepper to taste

Sardinian culurgiones

Get stuck in

Pasta dough

Combine the flour, semolina and salt. Add the oil and water a little at a time, kneading until an elastic, smooth ball is obtained. You know you have added enough water when you can bring the flour together in a ball. Wrap it in plastic wrap and let it rest for 30 minutes.

Filling

Cook potatoes until tender.
Drain the potatoes, peel their skin and place peeled potatoes in a bowl. Then crush with a fork while potatoes are still hot.
Add the garlic infused oil to the mashed potatoes. You can make your own garlic infused oil by adding fresh garlic cloves to oil.
Add the grated Pecorino cheese, mint and a generous pinch of salt and mix to combine. Wrap with cling film and refrigerate for at least 1 hour.

Tomato sauce

Place oil and garlic in a medium saucepan over medium heat. Add the passata, and cherry tomatoes then cover and cook the sauce for 30 minutes, stirring often. Taste and season.

Remove the filling from the refrigerator. Unpack the dough and spread it on a well-floured work surface and roll to a thickness of about 1mm.
Cut 8cm circles of dough – you could use a cookie cutter to get the shapes.
Place a ball of filling in the centre of each dough circle, then pinch and fold the base to seal it on one side. Continue pinching and bending the ends to seal the top.
Place the finished culurgiones on a floured tray
Bring a large pan of salted water to a boil.
Working in groups, cook the culurgiones in batches for 4 minutes or for 2 minutes once they have returned to the surface
Drain and spoon around 60ml of pasta water to your tomato sauce.

To Serve

Lay them on heated plates and drizzle with tomato sauce. Serve immediately and garnish with freshly grated parmesan.

I hope there's pudding

J.K. Rowling

Adam Byatt

Adam achieved both local and critical success with his first owned restaurant, Thyme, before opening Trinity in Clapham Old Town, London, in 2006. He subsequently opened Bistro Union in 2011, and then Upstairs at Trinity, recipient of a Bib Gourmand Award, a Michelin Star and three AA rosettes. Adam has recently been appointed chef director of food and beverage at Brown's Hotel in Mayfair.

Stuff you'll need

200g puff pastry
110g softened salted butter
130g caster sugar
1 star anise
1 vanilla pod, split
4 Pink Lady apples

Spiced apple tart tatin

Get stuck in

Roll the puff pastry out on a lightly-floured surface to the thickness of a pound coin. Rest this in the fridge for 40 minutes.

Slice the butter and place on the bottom of a heavy-based pan and add the sugar, the whole star anise and vanilla pod.

Peel and halve the apples, scoop out the seeds with a Parisienne scoop and carefully turn the edges of the apple with a knife to make it neat and round. Place curved side down in the sugar and butter.

Cut a disc of puff pastry out to the same diameter as the outside of the pan. Dock it all over with a fork and place the pastry over the apples. Tuck the pastry in gently around the apples and allow this to rest in the fridge.

After 20 minutes of resting, place the pan on the stove and gently allow to caramelise. The butter and sugar should combine to create a light butterscotch that will appear around the pastry. Do not leave the tart tatin unattended on the stove - turn continuously to achieve even cooking.

When you are happy with the colour of the caramel allow the tart to cool for 10 minutes, before placing in the oven at 170°C for around 25 minutes, checking after 10 minutes. Bake until the pastry is cooked, the apples are soft and the caramel has reached the correct shade.

Alexander Negro Tsatsaronis

Alexander Negro Tsatsaronis discovered his fascination with pastry at the age of 12, as he worked his summer vacation at a small pastry shop in Lagonissi, Greece. At the age of 18 he went to Dubai to graduate from the ICCA Culinary institute of Dubai, subsequently working at five star hotels both locally and in Turkey. He is now head pastry chef at COYA, London, where he has worked at for the past three years.

Stuff you'll need

Chocolate short crust pastry

420g all purpose plain flour
80g cocoa powder
200g icing sugar
200g butter room temperature
3 small eggs (125g liquid eggs)

Dark chocolate filling

350g dark chocolate
(at least 66% cocoa mass)
220g double cream
1 whole egg
2g salt
15g honey

Dark chocolate tart

Get stuck in

Chocolate short crust pastry

Mix all the dry ingredients together. Once mixed add the butter and mix by hand until you get a crumbly consistency.

Add the eggs and mix to a smooth paste, rest in the fridge for at least 6 hours. Once rested roll to 0.5 cm thickness and mold into your tart case, blind bake it at 160°C for 20-25 min. Cool to use later.

Dark chocolate filling

Make sure all ingredients are at room temperature, especially the egg. Warm the double cream in a sauce pan. Place the chocolate in a separate bowl, pour the warmed cream over the chocolate and allow to melt. Incorporate by gently mixing, then add the egg and mix together until it comes together and it's shiny and smooth. Add the honey and salt and combine. Pour the mixture into your tart case, preheat the oven to 170°C and cook for 5 minutes turn off the oven and leave the tart in the oven for another 15 minutes, then remove and allow to cool down for at least 2 hours to set. Portion and serve with a dollop of crème fresh or fresh berries.

Andrew Scott

Andrew has spent his entire cooking career in Michelin starred kitchens, training initially at Mallory Court, Lords of the Manor and L'Enclume. Moving to the Curlew restaurant in Kent where he achieved a Michelin star in the 2014 guide. Progressing to Sudbury House in Oxfordshire to become Executive Head Chef and achieving 3 rosettes in the hotel's fine dining eatery Restaurant 56. While in charge at Sudbury, Andrew represented the central region on BBC2's Great British Menu in 2016, since this he's moved into the world of food development and customer experience at Miele, a global appliance brand as Head Development Chef for Great Britain.

Stuff you'll need

The jelly
200g cherry puree
100g water
50g sugar
3g agar agar
3 gelatine sheets

Cheesecake
100g white chocolate
100g cream cheese
1 vanilla pod
1 gelatine sheet
160g double cream

Flapjack
50g honey
50g butter
50g sugar
100g porridge oats

Pistachio curd
6 eggs
3 yolks
125g butter
150g sugar
2 teaspoons pistachio paste

Sorbet syrup
210.5g sugar
34.5g sorbet stabilizer
1955g water
909g glucose

Cherry sorbet
809g cherry puree
428g water
428g sorbet syrup

Poached cherries
250g pitted cherries cut neatly in half
250ml port
250ml red wine
300g caster sugar

Cherry gel
250g cherry puree
200g stock syrup
50g water
5g agar agar

To garnish
50g pistachios, pulsed

Cherry cheesecake cannelloni, flapjack, pistachio curd

Get stuck in

The jelly

Soak the gelatine in cold water. Boil the puree, water and sugar. When boiling, whisk in the agar. Ensure to reboil the mixture. Squeeze off the gelatine leaves and add to the mix. Pour into a glass bowl. Allow to cool slightly for 3 minutes. Spray a tray with grease spray, place asotate on top and ladle the mix onto the asotate, then spread to form an even layer. Place in the fridge for at least 20 minutes.

Cheesecake

Soak the gelatine in cold water. Melt the white chocolate in a glass bowl over simmering water. Warm the cream cheese and vanilla pod in a small saucepan. When simmering, add the gelatine to the mix. Then add the cream cheese mix into the chocolate. Lightly whip the cream to form soft peaks. When the chocolate mix has cooled slightly, fold the cream into the mix. Pipe the mix into tubes and set into the fridge.

Pistachio curd

Place the eggs, yolks and sugar into a thermomix jug. Cook at 100°C for 5 minutes. Add the butter and nut paste, then mix all together. Pour the mix into a piping bag and store in the fridge until needed.

Flapjack

In a small saucepan, mix the honey, butter and sugar together. Bring to the boil. Remove from the heat and add the oats. Mix it all together. Bake in the oven at 160°C for 10-12 minutes. Leave to cool

Sorbet Syrup

Mix the stabilizer with 10% of the sugar. Bring the remaining ingredients to 50°C and add the stabilizer mix and whisk until it reaches 80°C pass through a sieve and chill.

Cherry sorbet

Mix all the ingredients together in a thermomix. Pour into a pacojet canister and freeze until solid. Churn as required.

Poached cherries

Bring the port, wine and sugar to a light simmer. Place the cherries in the pan and remove from the heat. Cover in cling film and leave to cool down at room temperature.

Cherry gel

Boil the puree, water and stock syrup. Add the Agar Agar and re-boil. Refrigerate until set, then blitz back to a smooth gel. Transfer to a squeezey bottle.

To serve

Cut 2 squares of flapjack. Remove one of the cheesecakes from the tube. Place horizontally on the jelly sheet and score a knife on the jelly sheet, either end of the cheesecake. Wrap the jelly around the cheesecake and cut into 3. Pipe a circle of the curd onto the plate and spread across the plate with a palate knife. Place flapjack and cheesecake on the curd. Arrange some of the cherries and fluid gel around the cheesecake.

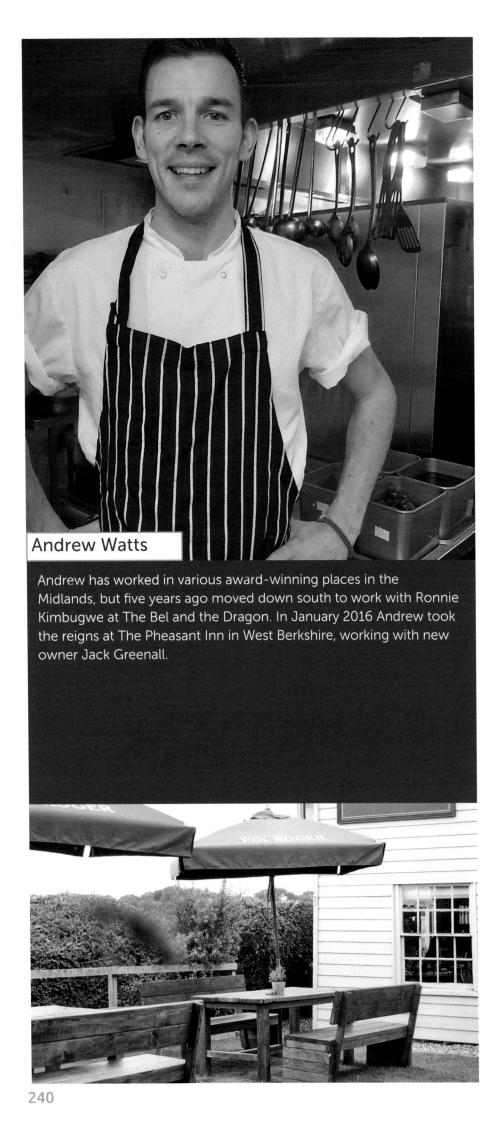

Andrew Watts

Andrew has worked in various award-winning places in the Midlands, but five years ago moved down south to work with Ronnie Kimbugwe at The Bel and the Dragon. In January 2016 Andrew took the reigns at The Pheasant Inn in West Berkshire, working with new owner Jack Greenall.

Stuff you'll need

Pastry

175g unsalted butter

75g icing sugar

2 egg yolks

250g plain flour

Tart filling

500g dark chocolate

3 eggs

200ml milk

350ml double cream

Icing sugar to decorate

Chocolate tart

Get stuck in

Pastry

Cream together the butter and icing sugar in an electric whisk until soft and white. Add the egg yolks, beat in thoroughly then scrape down the sides of the bowl and beat again.

Measure out 25ml of cold water.

Add a little of the water and all the flour and mix together, stopping every now and again to scrape down the sides of the bowl.

Add the rest of the water and mix for a couple of minutes.

Remove from the bowl and shape and chill for one hour.

Roll out the pastry and chill for 20 minutes.

Blind bake at 160°C for 15 minutes then check.

When ready remove the beans and bake for another 5 minutes until golden.

Egg wash and bake for one more minute.

Leave to cool in the tin and trim any excess edges.

Tart filling

Melt the chocolate over a bain marie.

When melted remove from the heat. Whisk the eggs in a large bowl.

Put the milk and cream in a pan and bring gently to the boil.

Pour over the eggs and whisk quickly. Pass through a sieve onto the chocolate and mix well.

Pour the chocolate filling into the cooled case.

Pre heat the oven to 160°C place the tart in the oven, close the door and turn the oven off, leaving the tart for at least 45 minutes, ideally up to one hour.

Dust with icing sugar, portion the tart and serve.

Tart is best kept at room temperature and served on the day.

Glaze with a blow torch if desired for an extra shine and serve.

Serve with raspberry coulis, raspberries, ice-cream and praline.

Anissa Boulesteix

Anissa is a young talent making her mark at the Hotel Crillon Le Brave in Provence, an area of France which is home to the most incredible array of produce.

Date pancakes

Serves 10

Stuff you'll need

250g flour
50g sugar
A vanilla pod
12g baking powder
3 eggs
150ml milk
60ml sunflower oil
Chocolate spread
One banana for topping
Some praline powder
Handful of dates for topping

Get stuck in

Mix the flour, baking powder and sugar.
Add the oil, milk, eggs and vanilla pod.
Mix the ingredients and then let them
stand for an hour.
Pour the mix into a heated pan, add some
chocolate spread and seal with more mix. Heat
your pancakes until they turn brown.
Play with your toppings.

Bruno Augusto

Bruno Augusto is executive chef at the Tivoli Carvoeiro hotel on Portugal's Algarve coast. Bruno started his 15 year career working in Michelin-starred restaurants the likes of Eleven and Ocean, in Portugal, and at the Grand Hotel Du Lac, Switzerland. He also worked in two of the most luxurious hotels in Portugal, Penha Longa Ritz Carlton Resort, in Sintra, and the Ritz Four Seasons in Lisbon.

Stuff you'll need

Pastry
(or use ready-made puff pastry for ease)
250g flour
100g water
Margarine

Filling
500g milk
75g flour
17g Maizena cornflour
500g sugar
250g water
1 cinnamon stick
Rind of ½ lemon
100g egg yolks
50g eggs

Pastel de nata

Get stuck in

Pastry

Mix the flour with a small amount of milk. Boil the remainder of the milk and mix in well.

Filling

Make a paste with water, sugar, cinnamon and lemon and boil for two minutes.

Mix the paste with the flours and milk. Leave to cool then add in the egg yolk and eggs.

Pre-heat the oven to 320/340°C.

Cut the puff pastry sheet into two pieces and place them on top of each other.

Tightly roll the sheets into a log, starting from the short side.

Next, cut the pastry into 12 evenly-sized pieces. Place one piece in each of the 12 wells of the muffin tin. Dipping your thumb in cold water first, press your thumb down into the center of the dough piece and press outwards to form a cup with the pastry. The pastry cup should have its top edge just above the top of the well of the muffin tin.

Fill each pastry cup ¾ of the way to the top with the filling.

Put the tray in the oven and bake until the custard starts to caramelize and the pastry turns golden brown (roughly 10-12 minutes).

Chris Edwards

Chris has been running his own event business, JUS Fine Food, for over 20 years, catering for corporate and private clients. Chris began his career at London's deluxe Claridges Hotel. Wanting to broaden his experience internationally, he moved to South Africa, accepting a post as sous chef at The Carlton Hotel & Carlton Court in Johannesburg, a 5-star Westin International Hotel. Returning to London 4 years later, he went on to work for Prue Leith for over 10 years, most notably as executive chef for the Directors of Sea Containers and The Orient Express Group.

His wife, Jeni, is a foodservice consultant, past chair and board member of the Association of Catering Excellence and sits on the fundraising committee for Springboard UK.

Stuff you'll need

Cake

200g plain flour

2 heaped teaspoons baking powder

½ teaspoon salt

100g dried cranberries, roughly chopped

75g pistachio nuts, shelled

220g caster sugar

250g thick Greek yoghurt

3 large eggs

2 blood oranges,
to make 2 teasponns zest and 80ml juice

5ml vanilla extract or paste

125ml vegetable oil

Syrup

2 blood oranges - peel zest into fine
strips and juice to make 80ml

110g caster sugar

2 tablespoons water

Equipment

22cm springform cake tin

or 21cm x 11cm x 6cm loaf tin

Get stuck in

Cake

Pre-heat the oven to 180°C. Lightly grease the pan and line the base and sides with baking paper.

Sift the flour, baking powder and salt into a bowl.

In another bowl, whisk the eggs and 220g of caster sugar until the mix becomes pale and creamy. Add 50g of the dried cranberries, 25g of the chopped pistachios, grated orange zest, 80ml of juice, vanilla and yoghurt. Whisk on a slightly lower speed for a further minute or two, slowly adding in the dry ingredients until combined and smooth.

Using a rubber spatula, fold the vegetable oil into the batter until it is evenly incorporated.

Pour into the prepared pan and bake for about 50 minutes or until a skewer inserted into the centre comes out clean.

Allow the cake to cool in the tin for 10 minutes.

Syrup

Place the strips of zest into a shallow saucepan of boiling water for one minute to soften, then drain and set aside.

Combine 110g of caster sugar, 80ml orange juice and 2 tablespoons of water into the same pan and stir over a low to medium heat until the sugar dissolves. Add the zest strips and allow to simmer for 2 minutes. Makes about 125ml.

To finish

Pierce the top of the cake with a skewer 10-12 times, pour half the syrup over the cake and allow to soak in for a few minutes.

Remove the cake from the pan and place it gently onto a baking rack over a sheet tray before drizzling over the rest of the syrup.

Sprinkle with the remaining chopped pistachio nuts and cranberries and allow to cool before serving.

Serve with an extra spoonful of Greek yoghurt. This cake can also be made with any citrus if blood oranges are not in season.

Claire Clark

Claire Clark has, over her career, worked at The Ritz, Claridges, Intercontinental and Westbury hotels, Sir Terence Conran's Bluebird and French Laundry in California, and encompassed the likes of setting up the pastry kitchen at the House of Commons. She completed her apprenticeship with two Swiss German/Austrian patissiers, the legendary late Prof. John Huber, and Ernst Bachmann. In recognition of the commitment to her craft Claire was awarded an MBE in 2011.

Stuff you'll need

Sponge

3 tablespoons green tea powder

3 tablespoons hot water

90g plain flour

25g cornflour

8 egg yolks

160g caster sugar plus extra for dusting

6 egg whites

50ml vegetable oil

Filling

300ml whipping cream

25g icing sugar

1 teaspoon vanilla extract

To decorate

50g white chocolate

Sprinkles optional

Get stuck in

Sponge

Heat oven to 200°C. Grease a 35cm x 28cm Swiss roll tin and line with baking parchment. Dissolve the green tea powder in the hot water and leave to cool. Sift the flour and cornflour together and set aside.

Using an electric beater, whisk the egg yolks and 100g of caster sugar until thick and pale. Add the green tea mixture and whisk to combine. In a separate bowl whisk the egg whites and the remaining 60g sugar to stiff peaks. Using a large metal spoon, fold the egg whites into the egg yolk mixture a third at a time. Sprinkle a third of the sifted flour over the surface and fold it in. Repeat until all the flour has been added, taking care not to over mix and lose volume.

Green tea roulade

Finally fold in the oil. Pour the batter into the prepared tin and level the surface with a palette knife.

Bake for 10-15 minutes, until the cake springs back when gently pressed. Do not over cook or the cake will become difficult to roll.

Remove from the oven and transfer the sponge, still on the paper, to a work surface. Place another piece of baking parchment on top of the sponge and roll it up lightly. Leave to cool.

Filling

Whisk the cream with the icing sugar and vanilla until it just holds shape.

Assembly

To assemble, unroll the sponge in a piece of baking parchment - it should be slightly bigger than the sponge, and lightly dusted with caster sugar. Carefully peel of the backing paper. Spread the cream evenly over the cake.

With a long side nearest you, turn over 1-2cm of the cake and start the formation of the roll, keeping it tight. Once you are half way with the rolling it will become easier.

To decorate

Melt the white chocolate in a microwave or in a small bowl set over a pan of gently simmering water, making sure the water doesn't touch the base of the bowl. Put it in a disposable piping bag, snip a small amount off the top and zigzag the chocolate back and forth over the cake. Refrigerate for 30 minutes, then trim off the ends of the roulade to neaten. It's best eaten on the day of making.

Claire Hutchings

Claire got her first job in a Michelin-starred kitchen at 16. At 22 she was the youngest ever MasterChef finalist and finally won the title in 2018 in a rematch with a past finalist. This recipe is the winning dish. Claire is currently working as head chef on a super-yacht in Spain and also works with The Cookaway in the UK, where she has created Spanish recipes that customers can order online and have delivered to home.

Stuff you'll need

Crystalized black olives
25g black olive slices
60g sugar, 30g water

Yogurt
100g Greek yogurt
10g icing sugar

Sheep's yogurt parfait
3.5g gelatin leaf,
150ml double cream
120g sheep's yoghur,
35g caster sugar

Sorrel sorbet
20g Glucos
500g organic pressed apple juice
150g sorrel with stalk
50g pro sorbet cold
20g caster sugar
3.5g xanthan gum
Green food colouring

Yoghurt meringue
90g egg white, 180g sugar
56g water, yoghurt powder

Hierbas Dulce (anise liqueur)
10ml lemon juice
100ml hierbas dulce (anise liqueur)

Compressed apple
½ Granny Smith apple, large dice
1g Citric acid

Herb gel
20g nasturuim,
20g coriander
20g basil
10g sorrel
10g lime, 100g stock syrup
Green food coloring

Extras for decoration
Small nasturtium leaves
Baby red vein sorrel leaves
Yellow sorrel flowers

Sorrel sorbet with wild herbs, crystalized black olives, yoghurt, apple and aierbas

Get stuck in

Crystalized black olives

Bring the sugar and water to 121°C, then remove from the heat and add in the olives stirring constantly until they crystalize. Spread on a tray to cool, break any large chunks.

Yoghurt

Sieve the icing sugar and mix together. Save half in a squeeze bottle and half in a small jar.

Sheep's yoghurt parfait

Warm 60g of cream with the sugar then dissolve in the soaked gelatin. Leave to cool slightly. Whip the cream left over and fold together, then set in silicone moulds. Place in the freezer to set. They should be removed from the freezer once set and left to defrost before serving.

Sorrel sorbet

Blend all the ingredients together then pass through a fine sieve. Add the colour to a small amount of the mix and use this as a colour guide. Churn the sorbet. For best results leave the sorbet over night before churning.

Yoghurt meringue

Make an Italian meringue - put the sugar and water in a pan and bring to 121°C, whip egg whites and add in the sugar syrup. Churn until cold then add in the yoghurt powder. Pipe onto greaseproof paper and cook at 90°C for 1 hour, then leave to cool.

Hierbas dulce (anise liqueur)

Mix the two ingredients and this will be used to infuse the apple .

Compressed apple

Peel and dice the apple equal sizes. Keep the dice covered in citric acid water to prevent oxidation. Put the apple into a sous vide bag with some of the anise liquor to cover and start to remove the air. Don't seal the bag until the third air removal (this helps to penetrate the apple).

Apple batons

Using the left over half of apple, cut into batons leave in the citric acid water, so as not to discolour.

Herb gel

Blend all together, strain through a fine sieve. Calculate 2g of xanthan gum for every 100ml of liquid - blend together with a hand blender. Store in a small bowl.

Clive Howe

Clive started his career at the Dorchester Hotel under Anton Mosimann. From there he took his first head chef position in the North West of England, before becoming executive chef at the Savoy Group's Lygon Arms and then for the investment bank Goldman Sachs. Later appointed its global food service manager role, Clive had the opportunity to set up dining in its Hong Kong, Singapore, Chicago, and other European offices. His current position is at the Garrick Club, where he has been for the last 15 years.

Stuff you'll need

Jelly

400g Yorkshire rhubarb, washed and trimmed
350g caster sugar
400ml water
1 vanilla pod, split
250ml English white wine
5 gelatine leaves

Pistachio and almond clotted cream

200g clotted cream
1 splash of vanilla essence
(to taste preferably with seeds)
100g frosted pistachios and
almonds (crushed)

Frosted pistachios and almonds

50g blanched pistachios
50g flaked almonds
50g caster sugar
1 egg white

English wine and rhubarb jelly with pistachio and almond clotted cream

Get stuck in

Jelly

In a saucepan place the water, caster sugar and the split vanilla pod and bring to the boil. Reduce heat and simmer for 10 minutes to infuse the vanilla.

Cut the washed and trimmed rhubarb into 1.5cm lengths and place into an earthenware or stainless steel baking dish.

Pour the sugar syrup over the rhubarb, cover with aluminium foil and place in a pre-heated oven at 130°C for approximately 20 minutes or until the rhubarb is tender.

Remove from the oven and allow too cool in the syrup.

Strain 500ml of the rhubarb cooking syrup into a pan and re-heat.

Soak the gelatine in water so that it is just covered until soft, remove the syrup from the heat and stir in the gelatine and the white wine. Strain and allow too cool.

Divide the cooked rhubarb between four serving glasses and pour on the jelly. Place in a refrigerator and chill for at least 8 hours or preferably overnight.

Frosted pistachios and almonds

In a mixing bowl combine all the ingredients together until the nuts are coated.

Lay a piece of baking parchment on a tray and spread the nuts out thinly.

Place in a preheated oven at 160°C for 7-10 minutes, until the nuts start to colour.

Remove from the oven and allow to cool.

Take half the nuts and crush them slightly for the ice cream and retain the other half for garnishing the jelly.

Pistachio and almond clotted cream

Mix together the clotted cream and add the crushed pistachios and almonds.

Flavour with a little of vanilla essence.

To serve

Remove the jellies from the refrigerator and place a scoop of clotted cream on top, sprinkle with the remaining frosted pistachios and almonds and garnish with some small sprigs of lemon balm.

Cyrille Michel Boggio

Cyrille initially worked Valencia, developing a network of 'birra and blues' breweries, and 'spaghetti and blues' restaurants. After 10 years he returned to France to work in Nice, qualified as a pastry chef and worked with some of the best confectioners in the world, including Angelo Musa, Frank Michelle and Anabel Lucantonio. He is now the brand-chef of a pizzeria network chain and has his own family restaurant, Spadaro, in Kiev.

Stuff you'll need

Coconut Island

125g Milk

105g Sugar powder

133g Coconut shavings

83gr Torment

125g Eggs

125g Trimolin Butter 82% -102g

10g Frozen lime puree

Creamo passion fruit-banana

87g Eggs

52g Passion fruit puree

78g Sugar powder

26g Frozen banana puree -26g

17g Frozen lime puree

10g Gelatin

130g Butter cream 82%

Shantilles masarpone-coconut

493g Cream: 35%

70g Mascarpone

25g Liquor Malibu

211g Coconut cream

Passion fruit and guayawa balls

300g Passion fruit puree

200g Guayava puree

4g Xanthan

Coconut with shells

500g Chocolate white 35%

1000g Chocolate black-kuverture 64%

300g Coconut shavings

Coconut island

Get stuck in

Coconut Island

Sift the flour and all the powdered ingredients. Add eggs and milk. Melt the butter to 45 °C, add the trimolin, the lime puree. Stir everything without whipping. Cook at 160°C.

Creamo passion fruit-banana

Heat the eggs, icing sugar and all the puree to 85°C. Add the gelatin diluted with water. Introduce the oil 40°C and stir.

Shantilles masarpone-coconut

Mix all the ingredients together and refrigerate at 4°C. Beat before use.

Passion fruit and guayawa balls

Stir the puree with the xantan. Pour into the elastic shape of the hemisphere with a diameter of 3 cm

Coconut with shells

Temper the black chocolate and form 24 semi-spheres with a diameter of 7cm. When the black chocolate is completely crystallized, temper the white chocolate and pour over the black on a semi-sphere. This will create the 24 semi-spheres of the white inner part and black outer part of the coconut. Before the white chocolate crystallizes, fill the coconut shavings inside. The shavings of coconut will be attached to the nut. Bond two different semi-spheres together. Scratch the coconut shell with a metal brush to get the effect of coconut shell.

Dessert montage

Put a coconut on a round plate. Put the coconut chocolate nut on top of the cake. In the nut to make a hole in the effect of a broken shell. Insert pre-frozen balls of passion fruit and guayawa into the hole of the nut. On the plate place a few broken pieces of the shells of chocolate coconut. Place the whipped chantilly on a fresh mango pieces,pre-dip in cold glaze for shine.

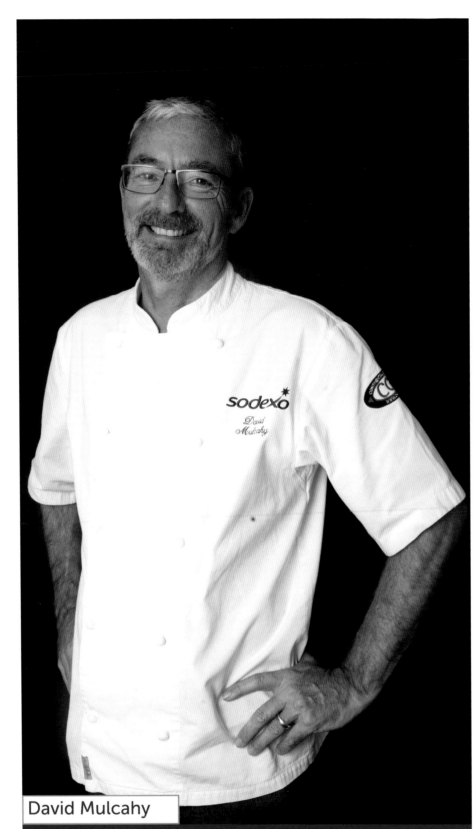

David Mulcahy

David Mulcahy FCFA CG Culinary Ambassador, Food Development & Innovation, Sodexo UK & Ireland Vice President & Past National Chairman, The Craft Guild of Chefs

Highly respected, with a wealth of experience, David has recently taken on the role of culinary ambassador for Sodexo UK & Ireland. In addition to representing Sodexo externally his remit, includes enhancing the reputation and recognition of Sodexo within the wider market place and the hospitality industry. With his team he strives to drive and support initiatives involving food strategy, sustainability, chef development and engagement across the business. David is active in promoting catering industry standards and was past national chairman, and current vice President of the Craft Guild of Chefs.

Makes 12

Stuff you'll need

300g self raising flour
60g spelt or wholemeal flour
50g porridge oats
1 teaspoon baking powder
½ teaspoon bicarbonate of soda
Pinch of salt
1 teaspoon ground cinnamon
140g soft brown sugar
60g whole hazelnuts, toasted, skinned and roughly crushed
100g semi dried, apricots, sultanas, dates, prunes and figs
1 large ripe banana
50g blueberries
2 eggs beaten
220ml milk
80ml yoghurt
100g butter, melted
80g granola

Topping

1 tablespoon porridge oats
1 teaspoon soft brown sugar

Breakfast muffins

Get stuck in

Preheat oven to 180°C and line a muffin tray with paper muffin cases.
In a large bowl, sift the flours, baking powder, bicarb, salt and cinnamon.
Then stir in the sugar. Mix in the nuts, dried fruits and blueberries.
In a separate bowl, mash the banana and whisk together with the milk,
yoghurt, eggs and melted butter.
Pour the liquid into the dry ingredients and mix together, very lightly until
just incorporated. Do not overmix.
Divide the batter between the muffin cases and sprinkle the top with the
granola mixture.
Bake for 20-25 minutes or until a skewer inserted into the muffin comes out
clean.
Leave to cool slightly before serving.

Topping

Mix the porridge oats and soft brown sugar

David Simms

David is the culinary director of the RA Group. He started his career working closely with the Roux family as a protégé from 1992 to 2000. From there, a stint as Alison Price head chef saw David responsible for teams serving politicians the likes of Tony Blair and George Bush, music icon Elton John and the royal family. A career with Restaurant Associates soon beckoned and he held the position of group hospitality executive chef from 200 to 2011. The next eight years of David's career were split between working as managing director for Simon Rogan and then holding the same role for Richard Corrigan. In June 2018 David returned to the RA Group.

Stuff you'll need

Brioche
30ml milk
15g yeast
10g salt
300g flour
4 eggs
20g sugar
250g butter
Eggwash

Custard
500ml whole milk
50g caster sugar
6 egg yolks
1 vanilla pod, split length ways
45g plain flour

Rhubarb jam
180g rhubarb
180g granulated sugar
7g stem ginger
5g unsalted butter
Juice of ½ lemon

Get stuck in

Brioche

Warm the milk to blood temperature, whisk in the yeast then add the salt.
Add the flour and eggs and knead with a dough hook until smooth (approx 10 mins in a machine).
Beat the sugar and butter together until smooth. Add this a little at a time to the dough, making sure it is completely incorporated before adding more.
Continue to mix for 5 minutes until smooth and elastic.
Cover with clingfilm and leave at 24°C for two hours, until the dough has doubled in volume.
Knock back a couple of times.
Cover and refrigerate for up to 24 hours,
Roll out into a 2cm thick rectangle. Place back in the fridge for 30 minutes to firm up.

Brioche rhubarb and custard doughnut

Remove from the fridge and cut into 4cm x 4cm squares. Cover with a damp cloth.

Prove in a warm draught free place until doubled in bulk.

Deep fry at 150°C until golden brown, turning over half way.

Drain on kitchen paper and allow to cool.

Roll in caster sugar once cooled.

Pierce a small whole in the middle of one side, and pipe in equal quantities of the rhubarb jam and custard.

Custard

Place the milk and vanilla in a thick-bottomed pan and set on a low heat to warm.

Whisk the egg yolk, sugar and flour together until smooth.

Pour the warm milk onto the egg mix and whisk until smooth.

Place back onto a medium heat and continually whisk until it boils.

Cook out for 2 minutes.

Transfer to a small bowl, place clingfilm on top (touching the custard) and place in the fridge to chill.

Transfer to a piping bag when cold and set aside until needed.

Rhubarb jam

Wash the rhubarb and cut into 2.5cm pieces. Cover with sugar and leave overnight. The following day, place in a saucepan and add the lemon juice and ginger.

Slowly bring to the boil and stir occasionally until sugar has dissolved.

Boil at approximately 115°C until the jam sets.

Remove any scum then stir in the butter.

Emily Roux with Diego Ferrari

Emily is the youngest to join the Roux family chef dynasty. Daughter of Michel and granddaughter to Albert, Emily has been training across France before settling back in London in 2016, working with Restaurant Associates and her father Michel at Le Gavroche. Her training began in 2010 where she worked in the kitchens of the Michelin-starred La Table du Lancaster in Paris. She then moved to Monaco to work in the kitchens of two of Alain Ducasse's restaurants, La Trattoria and then to Le Louis XV at the Hotel de Paris. She was then demi-chef de partie at Le 395, then junior sous-chef at Akrame. In October 2018, Emily opened her first restaurant with husband Diego Ferrari, Caractère, in Notting Hill.

Stuff you'll need

Chocolate mix
200g dark chocolate
200g butter
4 egg yolks
4 egg whites
15g caster sugar
150g brown sugar
50g flour
75g salted caramel

Salted caramel
100g sugar
120g double cream
30g salted butter

Chocolate pastry casing
450g flour
60g almond powder
180g icing sugar
300g room temperature butter
2g salt
30g cacao powder
2 eggs

Molten chocolate tart

Get stuck in

Salted caramel

Melt the sugar in frying pan until golden colour. Pre-heat the cream before pouring directly over the caramel, whisking continuously. Add the salted butter and leave to cool.

Chocolate mix

Melt the chocolate and butter over a bain-marie.

Whisk up the egg whites and stiffen with the caster sugar. Once the chocolate/butter mixture is completely melted and at room temperature, add the yolks, flour and finally salted caramel to the mix. Delicately add the egg whites to the previous mix.

Chocolate pastry casing

Place butter, salt and icing sugar together in a stand mixer.
Once homogenised add the eggs to the mixture.
Finally mix in the flour and cacao powder knead the dough until smooth.
Set aside for a couple of hours in the fridge.
Thinly roll out the chocolate pastry into 10cm diameter mould/ring.
Blind bake for 5 minutes at 180°C. Once cooled, add the chocolate cake mixture into the tart. Bake once again for 8 minutes at 180°C.
Serve with a dusting of icing sugar and cacao powder with a generous scoop of your favourite ice cream.

Emma Dodi

Emma Dodi always seeks to push boundaries by creating, elegant bespoke cakes and exquisite hand-painted macarons.
Since founding the business in late 2016, Emma has designed unique and luxurious cakes that are personal to each client. Every person has a story and with this in mind Emma translates the vision into a bespoke reality, bringing character and romance to each design.
Another hallmark of Emma Dodi Cakes, are the instantly recognisable hand-painted macarons. Using only the finest ingredients Emma is equally focused on taste and texture.

Stuff you'll need

Tant pour tant

90g egg whites (age for 3-4 days)
250g ground almonds
250g icing sugar
Gel or powdered food colouring

Italian meringue

90g egg whites (age for 3-4 days)
250g caster sugar
60-65 ml water

Aging egg whites

Separate the egg whites 3-4 days before making the macarons and put them in the fridge to age. Bring them back to room temperature before using.

Vanilla ganache filling

130g whipping cream
2 vanilla pods
200g white chocolate

Italian macarons with vanilla ganache filling

Preparation

Have all your equipment ready before you start making your macarons.

Line 2 large baking trays with baking parchment or silicone mats. If using baking parchment, you can secure the paper by using mini magnets or small dollops of the mixture in the corners. You may wish to use a template for the macarons, which you can place under the parchment. There are many free templates online, personally, I like to use 2cm templates. Just remember to remove the templates carefully from underneath before baking.

Prepare a large icing bag with a 1cm round nozzle.

Continued

Get stuck in

Tant pour tant

In a food processor pulse the ground almonds and icing sugar to make a fine powder do not overdo it or you will release the oil from the almonds.

Sift the blended almonds and icing sugar through a fine sieve into a large bowl, this mixture is known as the tant pour tant. Add the first portion of egg whites to the mixture but do not mix. If you want to colour your shells, then add either gel or powdered food colouring now, again do not mix. Set this mixture to one side. Note: Macaron colours lighten when baked, so add a little more food colouring than you think you may need.

Italian meringue

Wipe down your mixer bowl and whisk with a little vinegar to remove any grease. Place the egg whites into the mixer bowl, fix the whisk to the machine but do not switch it on yet.

Combine the the sugar and water in a small saucepan and heat on medium/high without stirring. When the syrup boils and reaches a temperature of 114-115°C, start the whisking the egg whites, slowly to start then building up speed, so they become frothy and start to form soft peaks. When the syrup reaches 118-119°C take it off the heat, put the whisk speed on low and carefully start pouring the syrup down the side of the mixer bowl. Once it is all poured in, put the whisker on high until you get a thick and glossy meringue and the bowl is no longer hot to touch.

Macaronage

Take a tablespoon of the meringue and mix into the tant pour tant. Mix it together well so you achieve a paste consistency. Add 1/2 the remaining meringue folding it in very carefully and gently, repeat with the remaining meringue. This is known as the macaronage and is the most critical part of macaron making. It is key that you achieve the right consistency and do NOT over mix. The consistency you are looking for is ribbon like. If the batter falls off your spatula like ribbons when you hold it up and takes 7-10 second to disappear back into the batter in the bowl then it is ready. This is the hardest part so it may need a little practice before you get it right.

Piping

Fill your piping bag with the mixture. Start piping your macarons onto your lined baking trays. When piping ensure your bag is held vertically to the paper so you achieve even flat macarons. To not have peaks on your macarons, stop applying pressure to your bag when you have achieved the desired size and flick the nozzle away in a circular motion.

Once piped, tap your tray on your kitchen surface to bring any large air bubbles to the surface, you may wish to pop them with a cocktail stick. Remember to carefully remove your templates.

Leave the macarons to dry or "form a skin" for around 30 minutes - you will know they are ready when you can gently touch the surface without your finger getting sticky.

While the macarons are forming their skin, heat your oven to 120°C. Place 2 trays into your oven. Turn the trays and swap their shelves halfway through baking time.

Bake for 20 mins - if they are firm on top and no longer "wriggle" at the feet (the frills that form at the bottom of the macaron while baking) they are ready, otherwise give them a little longer.

Remove from the oven, leave to cool on the trays then slide them off the trays while still attached to the parchment paper. Leave the macarons to cool completely on the parchment paper before trying to remove. Once cooled, match pairs of shells that are closest in size then sandwich them with your vanilla ganache filling.

If you want to paint your macarons you can do this before filling them. Use a very fine paintbrush and edible paint with some alcohol (vodka is fine) – be careful not to make it too wet or the macaron will dissolve.

Vanilla ganache filling

Split the vanilla pods and scrape out the seeds.

Stir the vanilla pods and seeds into the whipping cream and bring to the boil. Cover and leave to infuse for 30 minutes.

Slowly melt the chocolate in the microwave (do it in 10-20 seconds bursts so as not to burn the chocolate).

Once it is all melted, strain the infused whipping cream through a chinois and into the mixture. Mix until well combined.

To cool, transfer to a dish covering the ganache with cling film, the cling film needs to be touching the ganache.

Once cooled, place in a piping bag and pipe onto half the shells, then sandwich with the remaining shells.

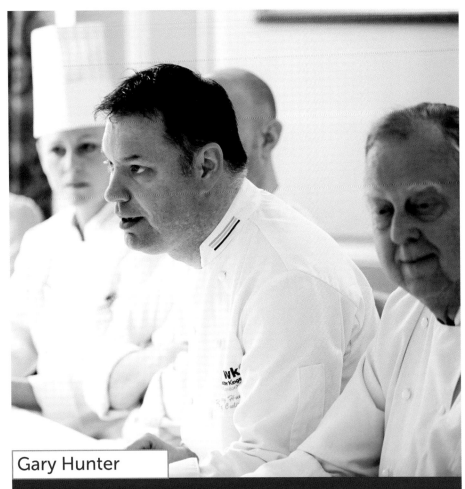

Gary Hunter

Gary is a qualified educator with over 24 years' practice from levels 1 to degree within further, higher and private culinary education. He is an experienced and award winning Deputy Principal at Westminster Kingsway College – the UK's oldest and most prestigious hotel school. As a UK Chocolate Ambassador for Callebaut UK Ltd, Gary delivers seminars, demonstrations and workshops in his specialism of chocolate work. Currently a Director for the PM Trust charity and for the International Hospitality Council Gary is also an internationally published author of seven Professional Cookery books with Delmar Cengage Learning and a further book published in 2014 titled 'In A Class of Its Own' by RMC.

Stuff you'll need

Almond sponge
150g icing sugar
5 tablespoons soft flour
150g ground almonds
6 eggs
30g unsalted butter, melted and cooled
6 egg whites
2 tablespoons caster sugar

Ganache
200g 70% dark chocolate, finely chopped
Finely grated zest of 1 orange
120ml fresh milk
110ml whipping cream
30g unsalted butter, softened
15g Invert Sugar

Coffee syrup
2 tablespoons caster sugar
2 tablespoons Instant coffee
130ml water

Butter cream
120g caster sugar
1 egg white
2 tablespoons instant coffee
200g unsalted butter, softened

Sorbet
275ml water
175g caster sugar
30g liquid glucose
25ml cointreau
Juice of 6 blood oranges, 425ml
Juice of 1 lemon

Get stuck in

Almond sponge

Preheat the oven to 220°C. Line a 20 x 30 cm baking pan with parchment paper. In a large bowl, sift together the flour and icing sugar, then add the powdered almonds. Mix well. Add the eggs, and beat until a pale colour has been achieved. Stir in the melted butter.
Beat the egg whites until stiff, and gradually add the sugar whilst continuing to beat until stiff peaks are obtained.
Add one-third of the aerated egg whites to the batter mix, mixing well, then incorporate the remainder, one-third at a time, folding in until consistency is obtained.

Opéra cake with blood orange and cointreau sorbet

just combined. Pour onto the baking tray and spread evenly.
Bake for 6 to 8 minutes, or until light golden and springy when touched.
Loosen the edges with a knife and carefully turn out onto a wire rack
covered with a sheet of parchment paper. Allow to cool.

Ganache

Place the chopped chocolate into a heatproof bowl and set aside. Bring the
milk, invert sugar, orange zest and 30ml of the cream to the boil. Pour the
hot liquid onto the chocolate. Wait 30 seconds, then add the butter and
blend with a whisk until smooth. Leave to cool until a spreadable

Preparation

Using a sharp knife, divide the sponge into
five equal sections and carefully peel off the
parchment paper from the sections. Each section
should be a rectangle of the same size. Soak the
first section in one-third of the coffee syrup, then
spread over a quarter of the ganache. Repeat
this two more times to create three layers of
sponge and ganache.

Place the fourth section of sponge on top, and

soak with coffee syrup
and spread with the
buttercream, but leave a
little set aside in a piping
bag for the final decoration.
Place the last section on top,
soak with remaining syrup
and carefully press down to
create a level surface. Chill
in a refrigerator until the
buttercream is firmly set.
Melt the remaining ganache
over a pan of very hot
water. Bring the remaining
cream from the ganache
recipe to the point of boiling
and incorporate into the
ganache. Allow to cool
until a smooth, spreadable
consistency is obtained and
spread over the top of cake.

Sorbet

Bring the water and sugar
to the boil in a saucepan.
Once the sugar has
dissolved, bring to the boil
and add the liquid glucose.

Coffee syrup

Place the sugar and 90ml of water in a pan and stir until dissolved. Bring to
a boil and add coffee.

Butter cream

Place the sugar and 3 teaspoons of water in a heavy based pan and make
a sugar syrup, i.e. stir until sugar is completely dissolved, then boil, without
stirring, until syrup reaches soft-ball stage, between 116 and 118°C.
Beat the egg white until soft peaks are obtained. Continue beating while
incorporating the hot syrup. Beat until mixture is cold.
Dissolve instant coffee in 1 teaspoon of boiling water, cool and add to the
butter whilst beating to a creamy texture. Add one half of the egg white
mixture and mix well, then gently fold in the remainder until well combined.

Continue to boil for 4 minutes to produce a stock
syrup.
Remove from the heat and allow to cool, then
add the orange juice, Cointreau and the lemon
juice. Chill the mixture, then churn in an ice
cream machine and place in the freezer for
service.

To serve

Cut the Opéra into suitable portions and pipe
three bulbs of buttercream on top of each
portion. Carefully place a fine nougatine wafer
on top and serve with the sorbet.

Graham Hornigold

Graham's career has spanned 28 years, with positions held as executive pastry chef at the Lanesborough hotel, the Mandarin Oriental hotel, Hyde Park, and later taking the position of group executive pastry chef of Hakkasan Group, overseeing 47 restaurants globally. He was recently named the UK judge for 2020's World Chocolate Masters Final. He is a previous UK Pastry Chef of the Year, and UK Group Chef of the Year.

Stuff you'll need

Sweet paste
200g unsalted butter, soft
160g icing sugar, sifted
80g whole eggs
400g plain flour
2g fine sea salt

Vanilla genoise sponge
100g whole eggs
50g caster sugar
50g cake flour
2g baking powder

Citrus pastry cream
240g milk
½ orange, zest
½ lemon, zest
15g cornflour
15g flour
30g sugar
50g egg yolks
175g butter, softened

Strawberry compote
1 punnet strawberries
20g icing sugar
1 orange, juice and zest

Garnishes
Strawberries
Raspberries
Lemon verbena

Strawberry citrus tart

Get stuck in

Sweet paste

Lightly cream together the butter and sugar.

Slowly add the eggs to combine. Scrape down well. Add the flour and salt - mix to combine. Roll the dough to 3mm, and then chill. Line tart shells, and blind bake at 160°C.

Vanilla genoise sponge

Sift together the flour and baking powder.

Place the eggs and sugar in the bowl of a stand mixer. Whisk on high speed for 10 minutes, until a thick sabayon is formed.

Lightly fold in the dry ingredients by hand, until just mixed.

Gently spread the sponge into a lined baking tray, 5mm high.

Bake at 160°C, for 5-8minutes, or until lightly-coloured.

Citrus pastry cream

Bring the milk to a boil. Add the zest and allow to infuse for 15 minutes.

Return the milk to a boil. Whisk together the egg yolks, sugar, flour and cornflour.

Pour the boiling milk over the egg mixture, whisk, return to the pot.

Cook, stirring, until it comes to the boil.

Boil for one minute, and taste to ensure the starches have cooked out.

Add the butter, whisking well until fully emulsified. Pour into a shallow tray, then cover with clingfilm to touch and refrigerate until set. When ready to build the tart, blend the crème patisserie lightly until smooth. Don't over mix or it will become runny.

Strawberry compote

Hull and halve the strawberries. Toss with the icing sugar, orange zest and juice. Allow to macerate for one hour.

To assemble

Place a disc of the sponge in the base of the cooked tart shell.

Spread the strawberry compote on top.

Pipe the pastry cream and use a palette knife to level off.

Garnish the tart with fresh-cut strawberries, raspberries and lemon verbena.

Ian McNaught

Ian has been cooking for 25 years and has held his position as head chef at The Roman Camp hotel for 20 of them. His restaurant has been recommended by the AA as one of the top 20 eateries in Scotland and has been awarded the Three AA Rosette Award for its restaurant dining.

Stuff you'll need

Cone

200g of dark Chocolate 70%

White chocolate mousse

425 ml double cream semi whipped

250g white chocolate

150ml water

50g caster sugar

2 gelatine leaves, soaked

Stuff you'll need

Panacotta

250ml coconut milk

250ml double cream

3 gelatine leaves, soaked in water

70g caster sugar

Fruit salad

Half a pineapple

1 mango

50ml water

250g caster sugar

Cinnamon stick

1 sprig of thyme

2 peppercorns

Mint leaves to garnish

50g pine nuts

Chocolate cone, white chocolate mousse and raspberries

Get stuck in

Cone

Make a cone shape using acetate.
Pour melted chocolate inside the cone and chill, allowing excess chocolate to run out the bottom of the cone and then place in the fridge to set.

White chocolate mousse

Bring sugar and water to boil and add chocolate. Stir until smooth and add the soaked gelatine leaves and a pinch of salt. Allow to cool and fold in semi-whipped cream. Chill until set. Transfer to a piping bag.

To serve

Paint a brush over the dish using melted chocolate. Place six raspberries around the plate with small sprig of mint and fill each cone with mousse and remove the acetate.

Coconut panacotta with fruit salad

Get stuck in

Panacotta

Mix the coconut milk and double cream together and bring to the boil.
Add sugar and the soaked gelatine leaves and put in moulds, put clingfilm in the moulds before you add the mixture in so you can get the set mixture out easier. Leave to cool and then place in the fridge for four hours to set.

Fruit salad

Chop the mango and the pineapple into bite-sized chunks and set aside.
Put the water, sugar, cinnamon stick, thyme and peppercorns in a pan and bring the mixture to the boil, then pour over the fruits while still hot. Put clingfilm over and put in the fridge while still hot. Leave until cool.
Toast the pine nuts in oven at 180°C for 5 minutes and allow to cool.

To serve

Remove from the mould and place on the plate. Place the fruit salad around the edge along with mint leaves, some little cress leaves and some pine nuts to garnish.

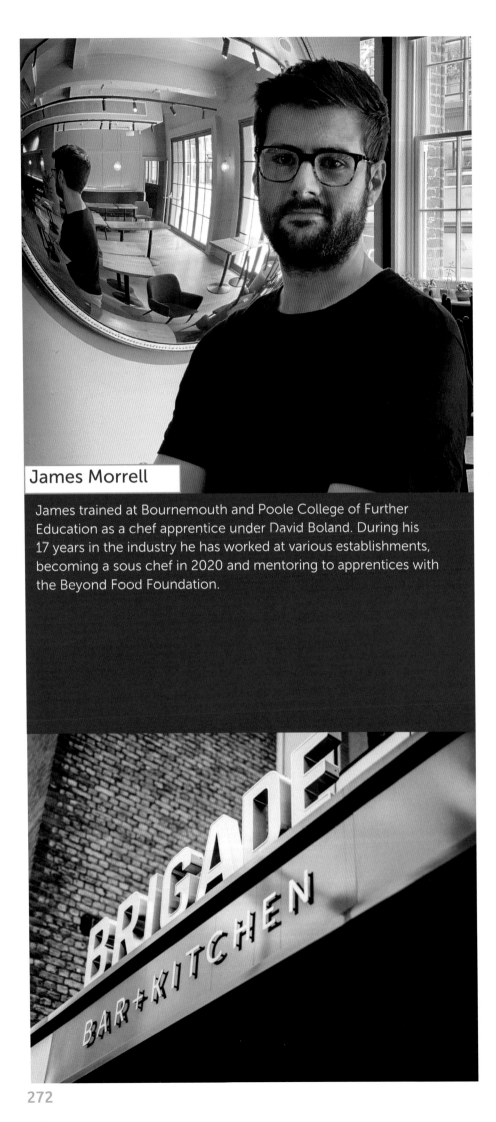

James Morrell

James trained at Bournemouth and Poole College of Further Education as a chef apprentice under David Boland. During his 17 years in the industry he has worked at various establishments, becoming a sous chef in 2020 and mentoring to apprentices with the Beyond Food Foundation.

Stuff you'll need

Chocolate mousse

125g 70% dark chocolate
125ml whole milk
125ml double cream
50g egg yolk
25g caster sugar

Hazelnut crumble

25g butter
25g hazelnuts
25g light brown sugar
45g flour

Red wine poached pears

1 pear
1 cinnamon stick
1 star anise
500ml red wine
225g caster sugar
1 orange

Vanilla cream

250g cream cheese
50g caster sugar
50ml double cream
1 leaf gelatine
1 drop vanilla extract

Dark chocolate mousse, red wine poached pear, vanilla cream and hazelnut crumble

Get stuck in

Chocolate mousse

Heat milk and cream in a pan to blood temperature. In a separate bowl, whisk egg yolk and sugar till fluffy. Pour half the milk mix into the egg mix and whisk. Add all the mix back into the pan and heat until the mix has thickened. Add in the chocolate and whisk until melted. Pour mix into a clingfilm-lined tray and chill.

Hazelnut crumble

Mix all ingredients together in a bowl and then bake at 200°C for 10 mins on a greaseproof tray. Leave to cool and then break up.

Red wine poached pears

In a pan, warm wine, sugar, cinnamon, star anise, zest and juice of an orange. Peel the pear and drop into pan and cover with parchment paper. Simmer for 20 minutes. Leave to cool in the stock. Take three tablespoons of stock and reduce to a syrup to serve on the plate.

Vanilla cream

Soak gelatine in cold water. Heat cream together with sugar, dissolve soaked gelatine in the cream mix. Add vanilla extract. Mix together with cream cheese. Leave to set and put in a piping bag.

To serve

Cut a bar of the chocolate mousse, place in the middle of the plate and top with the hazelnut crumble. Slice the pear in half and remove the core, place at an angle against the mousse. Finally, pipe three equal amounts of the vanilla cream around the dish and dress with some red wine syrup.

Jasmine Hemsley

Jasmine Hemsley is a cook, wellness expert and the founder of Hemsley + Hemsley and East by West. This recipe, taken from Jasmine's cookbook 'East by West', is a twist on the usual banana bread. A simple batter of buckwheat flour and ripe bananas is spiced with cinnamon and vanilla and peppered with crunchy walnuts and chewy raisins. It's naturally gluten-free, sugar-free and vegan too.

Stuff you'll need

290g buckwheat flour
2 teaspoons baking powder
1 teaspoon baking soda
½ tablespoon ground cinnamon
1⁄4 teaspoon sea salt
4 ripe bananas , mashed
(about 400g)
1 ripe banana,sliced (about 90g)
120ml water
11 teaspoons vanilla extract
60g raisins
30g walnuts

Get stuck in

Pre-heat the oven to 180°C.
Mix the buckwheat flour, baking powder, baking soda, cinnamon and sea salt together in a large bowl.
Mix the mashed bananas, water and vanilla together, then add to the bowl. Mix in the raisins, walnuts and remaining banana slices.
Transfer the mixture to a 750g loaf tin lined with baking parchment. Bake for 25 minutes, then turn the tin around and bake for another 15 minutes until the bread is firm-ish to the touch.
Allow to cool before slicing, then serve with butter.

Buckwheat banana bread with salty butter

Jean Marie Muzamunzi

Jean Marie is head chef at Bisate Lodge, Rwanda's first genuinely luxurious and eco-sensitive safari lodge. As a boy he was tempted to join the military, but fate stepped in and he was awarded a scholarship that allowed him to finish school and get a job as a chef in Kigali. The turning point in his life was when Wilderness Safaris sent him to Botswana and Zambia for training. He had never left Rwanda, let alone flown on an aircraft, and suddenly his horizons were being broadened. 2017 was a momentous year, marking the beginning of his career as head chef at Bisate.

Serves 4

Stuff you'll need

2 eggs

2 egg yolks

1 tablespoon vanilla extract

450g tinned caramel dulce de leche

125ml strong Rwandan coffee

35g plain flour, sifted

Get stuck in

Preheat oven to 220°C. Place the eggs, yolks and vanilla in the bowl of an electric mixer and whisk for 4 to 5 minutes or until very thick and pale.

Add caramel and coffee and whisk on low speed until just combined.

Add the flour and carefully fold through the mixture.

Divide the mixture between 4 cup metal dariole moulds.

Place the moulds on a small baking tray and cook for 10 minutes or until golden brown but still slightly soft in the middle.

Allow to stand in the moulds for one minute.

Using a small knife, carefully loosen the edges of the mould and invert the puddings onto the plates.

Serve immediately with ice cream.

Lava pudding

John Campbell

John achieved his first Michelin star in 1998, in his first year at Lords of the Manor Hotel and Restaurant in Gloucestershire. In 2002 he moved to The Vineyard at Stockcross as executive head chef. In 2007 it was awarded its second Michelin star. Three years later John opened Coworth Park with the Dorchester Collection, earning the restaurant a Michelin star in the first year of trading. John left the Dorchester group to create his own restaurant and cookery school, Woodspeen, near Newbury.

Stuff you'll need

Chocolate crumb
210g pastry flour
35g cocoa powder
160g unsalted butter
85g caster sugar
25g dried quinoa

Chocolate sponge
188g caster sugar
300g whole egg
150g pastry flour
25g cocoa powder
100g butter, melted

Chocolate spray
300g milk chocolate, lightly chopped
300g cocoa butter

Chocolate sauce
240g caster sugar
240g water
80g cocoa powder
250g whipping cream

Anglaise base
500g whole milk
120g egg yolks
80g caster sugar

Chocolate mousse
550g hay chocolate, finely chopped
300g anglaise base
450g semi-whipped cream

Malt purée
370g water
30g caster sugar
30g malt extract
5g agar agar

Saffron bubble
400g whole milk
10g caster sugar
¼g saffron strands
4g lecithin powder

Saffron gel
200g water
3 large pinches Spanish saffron
80g caster sugar
30g glucose syrup
10g caster sugar
8g pectin
10g lime juice

Sour sop sorbet
750g sour sop purée
30g sugar syrup
20g lemon juice

Get stuck in

Chocolate crumb

Place all the ingredients into a mixer and mix until a dough is formed. Refrigerate for 20 minutes.
Break up lightly and bake at 175°C for approximately 15 minutes or until cooked. Keep to one side.

Chocolate sponge

Warm sugar in an oven. Add to eggs, whisk in a mixer until it makes a heavy ribbon. Sieve the flour and cocoa powder together through a drum sieve and gently fold by hand into the sabayon, using a spatula.
Add approximately 150g mixture into melted butter and whisk until smooth, then fold gently back into sabayon mix. Spread with a palate knife until 2mm thick onto a silpat mat. Bake at 200°C for approximately 8 minutes or until cooked. Remove from oven and remove from the tray to chill.

Chocolate spray

Melt both the ingredients, until smooth up to 40°C. Use in the spray gun, as required.

Chocolate sauce

Place the sugar, water and the cocoa into a heavy-bottomed pan. Melt together, on a medium heat and bring to the boil. Add the whipping cream, and re-boil until the correct consistency is reached.
Strain through a chinois and cool quickly. Use as required.

Hay chocolate mousse, sour sop sorbet with saffron

Anglaise base

Place the milk in a saucepan and whisk in the yolks with the sugar. Cook to 86°C as an anglaise and pass through a chinois and cool.

Chocolate mousse

Weigh out 300g anglaise and emulsify with the chocolate to form a smooth elastic ganache. When the ganache reaches 35-40°C add one quarter of the whipped cream and fold in. When smooth, fold in the rest of the cream. Place the mousse in the mould, until just under the top lip and cover with a piece of chocolate biscuit. Cut to size to fit 2mm smaller than the aperture.

Malt purée

Soak the water and the sugar with the agar agar for 20 minutes. Boil for 2 minutes with the malt extract, until the agar has dissolved.
Remove and pass through a chinois. Then place in a small bowl and set in the fridge for 2 hours.

Place in a mixer and blend until smooth. Use a little water to aid blending if required.

Saffron bubble

Infuse the saffron with the milk and the sugar in a pan and heat to 70°C. Remove from the heat and add the lecithin and blend.
Pass through a chinois and then place into a tall container with a diameter of 8cm. Warm lightly and blend to make foam and use as required.

Saffron gel

Bring to the boil the water, saffron, sugar, glucose. Add the sugar and pectin mix and whisk continuously.
Boil for 2-3 minutes and then remove from the heat and add the lime juice.
Pass through a chinois and lightly cool. Roll out between two pieces of plastic until nearly see through. Freeze and cut to correct size.

Sour sop sorbet

Melt the sour sop pureé overnight or on the stove over a low heat.
Add the syrup and mix well followed by the lemon juice and mix well.
Churn in an ice cream machine.

Judy Joo

Judy pursued a career on Wall Street until realising her passion for cooking. Judy moved to London in 2007, and joined Restaurant Gordon Ramsay as a pastry chef. For the following few years, she also worked throughout other Gordon Ramsay restaurants including Maze, Claridge's, Pétrus, and Boxwood Café. Judy also staged around the world at restaurants including The French Laundry in California, The Fat Duck in Bray and Bangkok's Nahm restaurant. In 2011, Judy became the executive chef for The Playboy Club London, and in the same year became a regular face on TV. Her expertise in Korean cooking led to her own shows, 'Judy Joo's Return to Korea' and two seasons of 'Korean Food Made Simple'. London was the obvious choice for Judy's first restaurant as chef patron, and she opened the doors to her modern Korean restaurant Jinjuu in 2014.

Stuff you'll need

50g sugar
8g dry active yeast
200ml cup warm water (49°C)
1 tablespoon pure vanilla extract
1 large egg, lightly beaten
640g bread flour
4 tablespoons salted butter, softened
½ tablespoon salt
Garnish seeds as desired - sesame, poppy, etc.
Eggwash (one beaten egg with a splash of water)
NB. You can substitute equal amounts of honey or syrup for the sugar.

Walt's wonder bread

Get stuck in

Pre-heat oven to 180°C.
Dissolve sugar and yeast in the warm water. Stir in the vanilla and 30g of the flour. Stir in the egg, and set aside. Place in the remaining flour, butter, and salt in a food processor and mix. Add in the yeast mixture and process until a dough forms, about 30 seconds. Place the dough in a warm and buttered bowl. Cover with a buttered piece of plastic wrap, and set in a warm place until it doubles in size, about 1 hour.

Remove the plastic wrap (save it) and punch the dough down. Braid as desired and place on a lined tray. Cover with buttered plastic wrap, place in a warm area and allow to rise for 45 minutes.

Brush with egg wash and sprinkle with seeds of your choice.

Bake in oven for 35 minutes, or until the internal temperature is 91°C.

Justine Murphy

Justine is CEO and founder of the Mymuybueno Cookery School. Murphy launched Mymuybueno – now an international food business including an award-winning deli and chef agency – in Mallorca in 2011. Having survived a traumatic and food-deprived childhood, she fled Britain to chef on super-yachts and healed herself through the joy of cooking - and, just as importantly, of eating.

Serves 8

Stuff you'll need

Base

70g macadamias

70g almonds

70g pecans

100g brown rice syrup or maple syrup

40g desiccated coconut

80g Medjool dates, pitted

¼ tablespoon vanilla powder

¼ tablespoon Himalayan salt

Filling

400g cashews, soaked in water overnight

120g brown rice syrup or maple syrup

6 tablespoons carton coconut milk

¼ tablespoon vanilla powder

Pinch of Himalayan salt

100g cacao butter

Dulce de leche

200g Medjool dates, pitted

3 tablespoons brown rice/maple syrup

2 tablespoons almond butter

2 tablespoons water

¼ tablespoon vanilla powder

Pinch of Himalayan salt

Dulce de leche cheesecake

Get stuck in

Base

Line a 20cm cake tin with parchment paper. Place the macadamias, almonds and pecans into the food processor and whizz until they have broken down into small pieces. Add all the other ingredients and process until well blended and sticky. Press the base firmly and evenly into the prepared cake tin to ensure it's well compacted, then freeze.

Filling

Drain and rinse the cashews, discarding the soaking water, then blitz them in the processor with the syrup, coconut milk, vanilla and salt.
In a saucepan, melt your cacao butter until it becomes liquid. Add this to the processor last and continue to blend until the mixture is smooth and creamy.
Pour half of your vanilla cheesecake mixture over the set base in the tin, then tap the whole tin on a flat surface to remove any air bubbles and settle the mixture evenly.

Dulce de leche

Put all of your ingredients into the food processor and blitz well until thick, creamy and smooth.

With a teaspoon, dollop blobs of the dulce de leche all over the filling, ensuring you also get some blobs right to the very edge. Run a toothpick through the blobs in S movements to distribute the caramel. You want to create a marble effect, but as the caramel is thick you also want good size blobs left, so that when you cut the cheesecake it will look great and you'll get a good bite of caramel when eating it.
Repeat this process with a second layer of the cheesecake filling and caramel until you have used them both up.
Place the cheesecake back into the freezer and leave overnight to completely firm up. Remove the cheesecake from the freezer at least 10 minutes before you wish to serve, allowing it ample time to thaw and become easy to cut.

Kelvin Mullins

Kelvin Mullins (centre) is group pastry chef at Home Grown Hotels. He worked with James Golding as group chef director for over a decade, having ticked off postings in hotels in Zouz and Davos, Switzerland, Le Caprice, The Dorchester, Ninety Park Lane at the Grosvenor House Hotel, Nico Landis and Bruno Loubet. He is now based in Bournemouth, working for a chain of four, four star, two rosette hotels.

Recipe will make one large rabbit mould

Stuff you'll need

Blancmange

250g buttermilk
150g double cream
125g strawberries
75g icing sugar
2 gelatine leaves

Champagne and elderflower jelly

Half bottle of Champagne or Prosecco
10g elderflower syrup
22g water
35g sugar
3 gelatine leaves

Get stuck in

Blancmange

Purée the strawberries, pass through a sieve to remove the pips and add the icing sugar, whisking to incorporate.
Soften the gelatine in cold water
Heat the cream, but do not boil.
Remove from the heat and add the softened gelatine.
Now add the strawberry purée, followed by the buttermilk.
Whisk to incorporate all ingredients.
Pour into your rabbit mould, or into individual moulds, or even teacups.
Allow to set in the fridge, preferably overnight, before turning out.

Champagne and elderflower jelly

Open the fizz, and add to the elderflower syrup, taste and add more if desired.
Add the gelatine to the fizz to soften.
Gently heat the water and sugar.
Add the softened gelatine to the hot water and sugar mix. Once the gelatine has completely dissolved, add the sugar mix back to the fizz.
Gently stir, then pour onto a flat tray and allow to set in the fridge.

To serve

De-mould the blancmange onto a suitable plate, then surround with the jelly (you can chop this with a blunt knife or even a whisk). Finish with more fresh strawberry, herbs or flower petals.

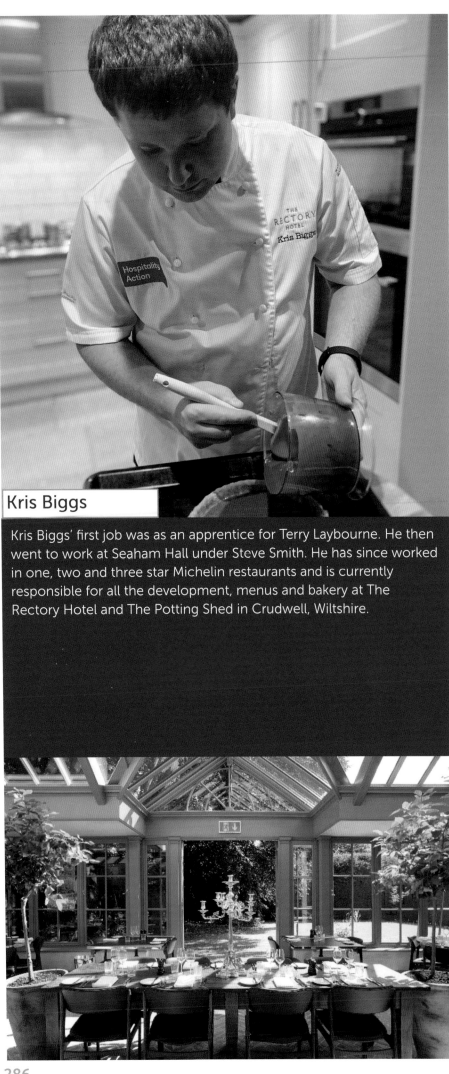

Kris Biggs

Kris Biggs' first job was as an apprentice for Terry Laybourne. He then went to work at Seaham Hall under Steve Smith. He has since worked in one, two and three star Michelin restaurants and is currently responsible for all the development, menus and bakery at The Rectory Hotel and The Potting Shed in Crudwell, Wiltshire.

Stuff you'll need

Sweet pastry
375g plain flour
180g unsalted butter
95g caster sugar
45g water

Salted caramel
65g caster sugar
250g whipping cream
20g soft brown sugar
70g egg yolk
Salt to taste

Banana crémeux
90g milk chocolate
45g 70% chocolate
100g banana chopped
50g whipping cream
25g caster sugar
½ gelatine leaf soaked

Salted caramel banana, and milk chocolate tart

Get stuck in

Sweet pastry

Bring together the flour, butter and sugar until a crumble texture. Add the water, bring together and allow to rest before rolling.
Roll the pastry tart and blind bake at 160°C.

Salted caramel

Place the sugar in a pan with some warm water, boil to a dark caramel.
Bring the cream to the boil, carefully add to the caramel mixture.

Whisk the egg and sugar together until pale, add the salt, whisk together, whisk in the caramel mixture and pass through a sieve, pour into the pre-baked tart case and cook at 115°C until set.

Banana crémeux

Melt the chocolates together over a baine-marie. Add the chopped banana.
In a seperate pan bring the cream and sugar to the boil then add the soaked gelatine add the chocolateand banana mixture and blitz.
Pour this over the set caramel tart and allow to set in the fridge.
Serve with raspberries and crème fraiche.

Liam Tomlin

Liam was born in Dublin, Ireland, where his career as a chef began at the age of 14. He went on to gain experience in some of Ireland and Europe's finest kitchens, eventually moving to Australia in 1991. For the next six years Liam worked with Dietmar Sawyer of Restaurant Forty One as chef de cuisine.

Stuff you'll need

2 lemons
425ml double cream
125g caster sugar

Get stuck in

Finely grate the zest from the lemons.
Halve the lemons and squeeze out the juice.
Strain the juice and measure out 115ml.
Mix the cream, lemon zest and sugar in a heavy-based saucepan and bring to the boil, stirring occasionally until the sugar has dissolved.
Reduce the heat and simmer for three minutes.
Remove the pan from the heat and whisk in the lemon juice. Strain the cream into a jug, pressing the zest in the sieve to extract as much flavour as possible. Discard the zest.
Allow the mix to settle for five minutes before skimming the froth off the surface.
Pour equal amounts of the lemon posset into glasses and leave to cool.
Cover the glasses with clingfilm and refrigerate for 24 hours to set.

Lemon posset

Lisa Steele

There's a wide selection of herbs and vegetables grown in the gardens of the Culloden Estate & Spa. General manager Lisa Steele has been working hard harvesting some of the fresh rhubarb. Although the hotel cannot share it with you in person this year, here's the recipe so you can try Hastings Hotels' rhubarb crumble and rosemary ice cream at home.

Stuff you'll need

Rhubarb
500g fresh rhubarb
75g caster sugar
2 cinnamon sticks
3 whole star anise
Zest of one lemon
50ml pomegranate or cranberry juice

Crumble topping
50g ground almonds
50g brown sugar
50g soft butter
50g plain flour
50g sugar
75g rolled oats
30g desiccated coconut
1 tablespoon ground cinnamon
1 tablespoon ground nutmeg

Rosemary ice cream
500ml milk
500ml pure cream
12 medium egg yolks
250g caster sugar
2 vanilla pods
1 stem rosemary

Rhubarb crumble and rosemary ice cream

Get stuck in

Rhubarb

Wash the rhubarb and remove the leaves, cut into 1.5cm pieces.
Place the rhubarb, cinnamon, star anise, juice and sugar into a saucepan and put onto the stove on a low heat with the zest of the lemon.
Continue to cook the rhubarb for a further 10-12mins until a soft and sauce-like consistency is achieved. Place into a heat resistant serving dish.

Crumble topping

Heat oven to 180°C. Place the soft butter, plain flour, ground almonds into a mixing bowl. Using your fingertips work the butter into the mixture until it looks like fine breadcrumbs.
Add the sugar, cinnamon and nutmeg and mix. Add the remainder of the ingredients, rolled oats and coconut, mix together.
Place the mixture onto a baking tray and roast in the oven until golden brown. Crumble topping is now ready to be placed onto the rhubarb.

Rosemary ice cream

Remove the rosemary leaves from the stem.
Split the vanilla pods in half and scrape out the beans. In a saucepan put the rosemary, milk, cream and the split pods and beans and bring to the boil.
Meanwhile put the egg yolks and sugar in a large bowl and mix well. Gradually pour the boiled milk and cream over the egg mixture, stirring constantly.
Return the mixture to a clean saucepan and cook over a low heat, stirring constantly.
Allow the mixture to come up to 86°C (thick enough to coat the back of the spoon).
Pass the custard immediately through a fine sieve into a bowl over an ice bath. Once cooled, churn the custard in the ice cream churner.

Marcel Ravin

Marcel is from one of the most glamorous hotels, Lâ Hotel de Paris Monte-Carlo, and he shares his signature chocolate soufflé. It's the perfect sweet treat to nibble on as you star spot and gaze at the panoramic views of Monaco from the hotel's iconic Le Grill restaurant, or, of course, to enjoy as the stars of your own dining room.

Serves 4

Stuff you'll need

Pastry cream

5 egg yolks

500ml whole milk

100g caster sugar

65g all purpose flour

Souffle

400g egg whites

200g caster sugar

20g butter

85g cocoa powder

400g pastry cream

10g icing sugar & cocoa powder, to dust on top

Chocolate soufflé

Get stuck in

Pastry cream

Bring the whole milk to boil in a pan.
Mix the egg yolks, caster sugar and the flour in a separate pan, then pour the boiling milk into
this mixture and place it over a low heat.

Souffle

Whisk the egg whites until they form stiff peaks. At the last moment, add caster sugar to
strengthen the egg whites.
Carefully incorporate the cocoa powder, and then the egg whites, into the pastry cream.
Butter and sugar two souffle moulds.
Pour the mixture into cake moulds and bake for 13 minutes at 200°C.
As soon as you remove the soufflés from the oven, sprinkle with icing sugar
and cocoa powder and serve.

Mariana Chaves

Mariana is a Brazilian/Portuguese pastry chef, with a background in Business Management, chocolate and wine. Her love for cooking was inspired by her Dad's restaurant in Brazil.

She moved to England in 2008 to attend the culinary school Le Cordon Bleu in London.

After graduating, she started working with chef Nuno Mendes at The Loft Project, Viajante Restaurant and Chiltern Fire House.

From to 2014 to 2018, Mariana was Head Pastry Chef at Fifteen playing an important role creating the menus and teaching the apprentices the art of Pastry ,eventually to become head Pastry Chef at Fifteen Cornwall.

Stuff you'll need

Chocolate mousse

1375g 55% chocolate
(Femme de Virunga – original bean)
600 g whipping cream
900g whole milk
450g egg yolk
20g sugar

Puffed barley

100g barley
300g water
Pinch of salt
Rapeseed oil to fry the barley

Barley crispy

200g barley
500g water
Rapeseed oil to fry the crispies.

Malt sugar

200g toasted malt crystal
100g sugar
2g salt
3g citric acid

Whey caramel

300g whey
120g sugar

Crystallised Piura Porcelana 75% Dark chocolate

150g sugar
120g chocolate
150g water

Femme de Virunga chocolate mousse, puffed barley, whey caramel

Get stuck in

Chocolate mousse

Bring the cream and milk to the boil. Whisk the eggs and sugar until smooth. Pour 1/3rd of the liquid over the egg mix and whisk to combine. Pour this back over the remaining cream and milk, return to the heat, and cook whilst constantly stirring with a spatula, until 80°C is reached. Remove from the heat and pass through a chinois.

Puffed barley

Toast the barley at 160°C for 15 minutes. Cook pearl barley until very tender. Drain and dehydrate for around 4-6 hours on a medium high setting. When almost completely dry remove from the dehydrator. Prepare a pan with rapeseed oil and pre heat to 220°C. Deep fry th barley until lightly puffed. Add some of the malt sugar.

Malt sugar

Roast the malt crystal at 160°C for 10 min, cool and blitz with the sugar, salt and citric acid.

Barley crispy

Roast the barley at 160°C for 15 minutes. Cook the barley until overcooked, blitz and spread on a silicone mat. Dehydrate at 75°C until dry. Deep fry at 180°C, season malt sugar.

Whey caramel

Make a dry caramel, deglaze with whey and reduce until a thicker syrup.

Crystallised Piura Porcelana

Make a syrup with the water, and sugar and cook until 135°C. The syrup will start getting some golden colour
Remove from the heat and add the chocolate. Whisk until the liquid completely crystallizes.

Michael Notman-Watt

We are The Syndicate Kitchen. We believe that the location and style of cooking is irrelevant. The focus is not what one person is doing, but what we (producer, collaborator, chef and diner) can achieve together. We celebrate the bonds people can create around food. This all starts with a simple idea, a bespoke private-dining and supper club experience created by award-winning, Sussex-based chef, Michael Notman-Watt From the planting of the seed through to the last mouthful of a dish, the process of growing and cooking is just as important as the act of eating and drinking. We want to celebrate that process and put a spotlight on all the hands that have made it possible.

Stuff you'll need

Meringue

2 egg whites

130g caster sugar

1/2 tsp white wine vinegar

1/2 teaspoon cornflour

10 large, ripe, green fig leaves with the stems cut off

Rose cream

300g double cream

40g icing sugar

2 teaspoons rose water

100g crème fraîche

Strawberries

500g hulled strawberries

30g caster sugar

Juice of half a lemon

Pinch of Maldon sea salt

To serve

3 large roses taken down into petals

Get stuck in

For the meringue

Pre-heat oven to 100°C and place the fig leaves in to dry. This can take anywhere between 1 - 10 hours depending on how well your oven vents. You will know they are ready when they snap and crumble in your hands, but are still green. Allow to cool out of the oven for 10 minutes then blend in dry, high-powered blender to a fine powder. Preheat your oven to 140°C. Whisk the egg whites with an electric hand mixer or stand mixer until they form stiff peaks, then whisk in 130g caster sugar, one third at a time, until the meringue looks glossy, finally whisk in the white wine vinegar, cornflour and 1 heaped tbsp of fig leaf powder until fully incorporated. Spread the meringue onto a greaseproof lined baking sheet in a layer which is half an inch thick (secure the baking paper in place with a tiny dollop of meringue in each corner). Bake for 1 hour for a slightly chewy centre or 1.5 hours for

Strawberry, rose and fig leaf Eton mess

a completely crisp meringue. Turn the oven off and allow the meringue to cool completely in the oven. Once cooled, the meringue can be stored in an airtight container.

Rose cream

Combine the cream, rose water and icing sugar and whip to very stiff peaks. Whip in the crème fraîche. Store in a sealed container in the fridge until needed.

Strawberries

Reserve 3 or 4 of the nicest strawberries to garnish the top. Roughly chop about a third of the remaining hulled strawberries and blend with the lemon juice, add salt and sugar, then blend until smooth.
With the remaining hulled strawberries, cut them into roughly the size of large peas and stir through the strawberry sauce.
Store in a sealed container in the fridge until needed.

To serve

We are going to layer the mess in a large family style serving bowl, or if you'd rather individual portions just repeat this layering in large sundae glasses.

Add about half of the strawberry mix to the rose cream along with about half the meringue (crushed into large bite sized pieces) and ripple the mix together. If you over mix, it isn't the end of the world, you will just have pink cream instead of a red ripple cream.

In the bottom of a large glass serving bowl, spoon about 1/2 of the remaining strawberry mix and crush over about 1/2 the remaining meringue (once again crushed into large bite sized pieces). Spoon over the rippled cream.

Spoon over the remaining strawberry mix, then the remaining fig leaf meringue in slightly larger pieces than before.

Slice the reserved strawberries, then add as a penultimate layer. Finally finish with a liberal sprinkling of rose petals.

Michel Roux Jr.

Michel Roux Jr. is the chef/owner of Michelin two-starred Le Gavroche in Mayfair, London, which he took over from his father, Albert Roux, in 1991. Michel also operates London restaurants including Roux at Parliament Square, as well as Roux at The Landau, the Palm Court and The Wigmore, all at The Langham Hotel. His TV career has included MasterChef: The Professionals', Food and Drink, Michel Roux's Service: First Class Chefs', Hidden Kitchens' and Remarkable Places to Eat. He's written seven cookbooks, the latest of which are 'Les Abats', dedicated entirely to offal, and 'The French Revolution', revisiting classic dishes from his traditional French upbringing.

Serves 4

Stuff you'll need

2 ripe pears, peeled and cored
1 tablespoon butter, melted
200g nougat

Chocolate sauce

2 tablespoons maple syrup
2 tablespoons cocoa powder
100g dark chocolate,
70% cocoa solids, broken into pieces

Poires rotis aux nougat et sauce chocolat

Get stuck in

Pre-heat the oven to 200°C.
Cut the pears in half, put them in a baking dish and brush them with a little melted butter. Cut the nougat into chunks and scatter them over the pears.
Roast the pears in the oven for about 12 minutes or until golden and tender.

Chocolate sauce

For the sauce, put the syrup and cocoa powder in a pan and add 100ml water. Bring to the boil, while whisking.
Add the chocolate and stir until it melts.
Serve the sauce with the pears.

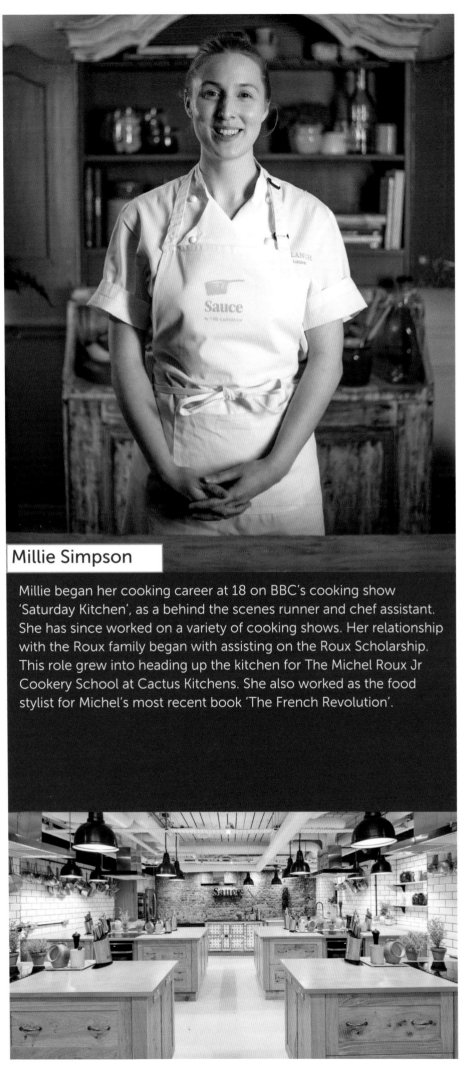

Millie Simpson

Millie began her cooking career at 18 on BBC's cooking show 'Saturday Kitchen', as a behind the scenes runner and chef assistant. She has since worked on a variety of cooking shows. Her relationship with the Roux family began with assisting on the Roux Scholarship. This role grew into heading up the kitchen for The Michel Roux Jr Cookery School at Cactus Kitchens. She also worked as the food stylist for Michel's most recent book 'The French Revolution'.

Stuff you'll need

The base

125g raspberry purée
30g caster sugar
10g cornflour
10g water

The meringue

160g egg whites
60g caster sugar

To serve

Finely-grated chocolate
Fresh raspberry compote
Icing sugar to dust

Get stuck in

The base

Bring the raspberry purée and sugar to the boil. Mix the cornflour with the water and add to the purée, whisking and return to the boil. Cook for a few minutes then remove from the heat and cool. Pre-heat the oven to 190°C.

The meringue

Whisk the egg whites until frothy, gradually add the caster sugar and then whisk until firm. Mix in a third of the egg whites with 100g of the raspberry purée until smooth.
Fold in the rest of the egg whites gently. Butter the moulds and fill each of them with a quarter of the mix.
Smooth the surface out using a pallet knife. Run your thumb around the inside of the ramekins to help the soufflés rise evenly. Place the ramekins in the oven and after 4 minutes give them a quick turn so the front ones are at the back.
Continue to cook for 4-5 minutes and remove - they should be well risen and soft and creamy in the middle.
Add fresh raspberry compote to the top, dust with icing sugar and serve immediately.

Raspberry soufflé

Nick Smith

Nick, a National Chef of the Year finalist, currently oversees the fine dining and hospitality for city law firm Ashurst. His varied career started in London working at a number of high profile establishments: notably Le Pont de la Tour, The Arts Club in Mayfair, and Chinon in Shepherd's Bush.

Serves 6-8

Stuff you'll need

Pudding
450g whole wheat bread
500ml milk
100g unsalted butter
170g soft brown sugar
2 free range eggs
2 pinches of cinnamon
1 grated zest of lemon

Candied lemon
1 lemon
10g icing sugar
10ml water

Creme chantilly
250ml double cream
15g caster sugar

To serve
9 blueberries
18 mint sprigs

Nelson's pudding

Get stuck in

Pudding

Break bread into small pieces and soak in milk. Pre-heat oven to 160°C. Line a 20cm square cake tin with greaseproof paper. Mix soaked bread until smooth. Stir in all other ingredients and spoon into prepared cake tin. Bake for 1 hour or until golden brown. Leave to cool in tin when baked.

Candied lemon

Peel the zest and finely julienne. Blanch zest in boiling water for 10 seconds, refresh in cold water. Place the lemon juice, lemon zest, water and sugar into a pan, and slowly reduce to candy the lemon zest. When transparent remove and leave to cool.

Creme chantilly

Whip double cream and sugar together to create a soft ribbon stage.
Remove the cooled pudding from the tin, trim the four edges, and cut into 6-8 equal bars.

To serve

Cut blueberries in half, pipe chantilly and finish with mint sprigs and candied lemon. Quenelle the creme chantilly next to the pudding.

René Cahane

René Cahane has been executive head chef at Windjammer Landing Beach Villa Resort since 2016. With more than 25 years of professional culinary experience working in five-star hotels, restaurants, and private members' clubs around the world, Cahane, who grew up in East London, is classically French trained and skilled in modern European, Caribbean and traditional British cuisines. He believes in using locally-sourced seasonal produce, using his unique skills to ensure the best flavours and qualities of a dish are delivered.

Stuff you'll need

Carpaccio

1kg pineapple fresh thinly sliced
50g sugar
90ml water

Raspberry jelly

100ml raspberry puree
50ml water
30g white sugar
3g gelatin powder

Coconut sorbet

300g white sugar
40ml water
20g liquid glucose
260ml coconut milk
260ml coconut cream

Get stuck in

Carpaccio

Boil water and sugar.
Remove from stove and add sliced pineapple, cover with clingfilm and allow to cool in the refrigerator overnight.

Raspberry jelly

Boil all the ingredients together.
Pour into a baking tray.
When mixture is cool, store in the refrigerator until set.
Cut into 2cm x 2cm size cubes.

Coconut sorbet

Bring sugar, water and liquid glucose to boiling point, then add coconut cream and coconut milk.
Allow to cool at room temperature and transfer to the refrigerator overnight.
Add liquid mixture to the sorbet mixing machine to make sorbet.

Saiful Huda

Indonesian born Saiful is executive pastry chef at the Intercontinental Bangkok. He has enjoyed a vibrant 20-year long career working for some of the world's biggest hotel chains. He prides himself on his strong knowledge of pastry, sugar work, cake making and chocolate decorating.

Stuff you'll need

Cheesecake

200g cream cheese
50g softened butter
20g sugar
80g milk
150g egg yolk
65g corn flour

Meringue

250g egg white
80g sugar

Cherry filling

220g cherry morello, frozen
20g invert sugar
30g caster sugar
3g pectin

Micro sponge

220g 50% almond praline
180g egg white
30g cake flour
2g salt

Baked cotton cheesecake

Get stuck in

Cheesecake

Mix cream cheese and butter in a bowl on top of a double boiler until mixed well. Boil the milk and sugar and add the mixture of egg yolks and corn flour. Keep stirring until it thickens.

Meringue

Whisk the egg whites until light and fluffy, add the sugar little by little until the meringue has a slight sheen to it. Fold the meringue into the cheesecake mixture.

Pour into a mould or baking tray and bake in a bain-marie tray filled with water at 140°C for 45 minutes.

Cherry filling

Put the cherries in the inverted sugar in a pan and cook on low heat for 20 minutes stirring constantly. Combine the pectin and the sugar together and stir into the compote. Bring to the boil, take off the heat and leave to cool, or put into a small sphere shape mould and freeze.

Micro sponge

Mix all the the ingredients then strain. Then put into a syphon bottle with two gasket cartridges and shake vigorously.

Pierce the bottom of a plastic cup and fill the cup with half of the mixture, using the syphon. Cook in the microwave at 900 watts for approximately 45 seconds.

To serve

Cut cheesecake into 9cm x 4cm or you can choose any shape as desired. Place the cherry filling on top put the chocolate sheets 1 centimetre higher than the rest of the sides of the cake. Decorate with glazed cherry ball/ sphere and pieces of the micro sponge.

Add some edible flowers or microgreens to decorate.

Simon Boyle

Having experience many things in life to take him towards being a social entrepreneur, from volunteering in the aftermath of the 2004 Tsunami to now working with over 3500 homeless people in London. Setting up and running social enterprise restaurant Brigade Bar + Kitchen in London, alongside PwC and BaxlerStorey has enabled Simon to channel his experiences to help others that are vulnerable and in need of inspirational change.

Stuff you'll need

Sweet pastry

240g butter
480g flour
120g caster sugar
2 eggs
Milk
Pinch of salt

Rhubarb jelly

1kg rhubarb, chopped
500ml water
2 limes juice and zest
1 orange juice and zest
5 mint leaves
1 vanilla pod

3 slices fresh ginger
300g caster sugar
4 leaves of gold gelatine

Custard filling

500ml double cream
5 egg yolks
100g caster sugar
Vanilla extract

Rhubarb topping

8 rhubarb stems
100g sugar

Rhubarb custard tart

Get stuck in

Sweet pastry

Crumb together by hand the butter into the flour. Add the sugar. Mix in the eggs and enough milk to form a soft dough.

Roll out and place into a 10inch ring, making sure you right angle the inside corners.

Blind bake the pastry until completely cooked.

Rhubarb jelly

Gather all the ingredients together in a pan and bring to the boil. Leave to simmer until the rhubarb is fully cooked. Remove from the heat and leave to infuse overnight.

Place into a muslin bag and hang to strain off all the liquid. Measure one pint and add 4 leaves of soaked gelatine.

Custard filling

Whisk yolks, sugar and vanilla together.

Bring the cream to the boil then pour a little over the yolk mixture to temper, followed by the remaining cream.

Skim off any bubbles and pour into the tart case and bake at 150°C for 10 minutes until it has set with a slight wobble. Leave to completely cool.

Rhubarb topping

Slice the washed and trimmed rhubarb into 1.5cm thick slices and sprinkle with 100g of caster sugar.

To finish

Layer the custard over the base, then place the rhubarb topping on top in one layer. Bake at 180°C until cooked but still very firm. This should take approximately five minutes. The rhubarb should be cooked through but still firm and hold their shape. Chill immediately.

Steve Groves

Steve was crowned MasterChef: The Professionals winner in 2009. In 2010, having held posts at Launceston Place, and The Inn at Perry Cabin, in the United States, he joined Roux at Parliament Square and became head chef in 2013. In 2019 Steve won The Craft Guild of Chefs' National Chef of the Year award.

Stuff you'll need

Base

500g banana purée

100g caster sugar

30g cornflour slaked with a little water

Soufflé

80g egg whites

30g caster sugar

140g base

Salted caramel sauce

150g caster sugar

50g salted butter

450g double cream

Peanut butter ice cream

300g frozen over-ripe bananas, peeled and cut into chunks

150g smooth peanut butter

20g icing sugar

Caramalised banana soufflé, salted caramel sauce and peanut butter ice cream

Get stuck in

Base

Make a dark caramel from the sugar.
De-glaze with the banana purée
Ensure caramel is fully dissolved in the purée.
Add cornflour mixture and cook out thoroughly.
Pass through a fine sieve

Soufflé

Pre-heat oven to 170°C.
Butter a ramekin and place in the fridge to set.
Whip the egg whites and gradually incorporate
the sugar to make a meringue.
Beat a third of the meringue into the base then
fold in the rest gently.
Fill the mould then smooth off the top. Run the
tip of your thumb around the edge.
Bake for 8 minutes, turning halfway through,
until well risen but still slightly soft in the centre.

Salted caramel sauce

Make a direct caramel with the caster
sugar in a saucepan.
Add the butter and whisk in.
Add the double cream and allow to simmer
until all the sugar is dissolved and the sauce is
homogenous.

Peanut butter ice cream

Blend everything together in food processor until
smooth.

To serve

Pour the caramel sauce directly over the soufflé.
Place a scoop of penut butter icecream on top.

Stuff you'll need

Parfait
500g coconut purée
5g dried meadowsweet
50g sugar
4g agar agar
1 vanilla pod

Meringue
200ml aquafaba (chickpea water)
50g sugar

Blood orange concentrate
1kg frozen blood orange purée
1 lime

Blood orange sorbet
1kg blood orange purée
½ leaf of bronze gelatine
100g sugar
75g trimoline
75ml water

Marigold oil
Small handful Marigold leaves,
200ml olive oil

To serve
Oxalis leaves

Tom Simmons

Tom's earliest memories are of roaming farmers' markets, foraging in the countryside, and harvesting his mother's vegetable garden. His and his partner Lois' love and respect for ingredients and nature is the foundation of their restaurant Tom Simmons, in London. Influenced by both British and French cuisine with an emphasis on his Welsh heritage, Tom has a personal relationship with each of his restaurant's hand selected suppliers and farmers, ensuring the best possible produce on the plate.

At 21, Tom was the youngest competitior to reach the quarter-finals of MasterChef: The Professionals 2011. Tom became head chef at Wolfscastle Country Hotel - where he was awarded two AA Rosettes, before opening his restaurant in London Bridge.

Meadowsweet and coconut parfait, blood orange, marigold and lime

Get stuck In

Parfait

Bring coconut purée to the boil with the sugar and meadowsweet.
Infuse for 15 minutes, strain through a chinois and add the vanilla and agar.
Cook out in a pan to activate agar, then chill.
Once cooled blend till smooth.

Meringue

Mix the aquafaba and sugar and incorporate with the coconut purée.
Freeze in moulds.

Blood orange concentrate

To extract the blood orange concentrate de-frost the blood orange purée through muslin, until the water is all that's left and still frozen but all the red orange has come through the muslin. You'll be left with an intense juice. Discard the frozen water. Season with the juice of one lime.

Blood orange sorbet

Heat the blood orange, sugar, water and trimoline in a pan until the sugar has dissolved. Add the soaked gelatine and pass through a chinois. Freeze in pacojet containers for 24 hours. Alternatively churn in an ice cream machine.

For the marigold oil

Heat the oil to 85°C and blend on full power with the picked marigold leaves. Pass through muslin and cool.

To assemble

Remove the parfait from the freezer and allow to thaw slightly so it's served semi-frozen. Roll in toasted and chopped almonds.
Finish the blood orange concentrate with a few drops of marigold oil and stir a couple of times to get a split effect.
Place the churned sorbet on top of the parfait and place oxalis leaves around and finish with the blood orange juice.

Veronika Kirchmair and Claus Haslaue

Veronika Kirchmair and Claus Haslaue are hosts of St. Peter Stiftskulinarium, Salzburg, the oldest restaurant in Europe. For the last 27 years, they have carefully lead the business into the 21st century, creating a symbiosis of tradition and modernity. Surrounding themselves with a savvy and passionate team of restaurant, service and event professionals, everything they do comes from the heart and soul.

Salzburger nockerl

Stuff you'll need

7 egg whites
2 egg yolks
80g granulated sugar
1 tablespoon vanilla sugar
30g plain flour
Butter to grease a baking dish
Optional: pureed fruit in base of dish
and icing sugar to dust

Get stuck in

Whisk egg whites until stiff, slowly work in the sugar.
Mix egg yolks with vanilla sugar and fold into egg white mix.
Gently stir in flour.
Spoon into mountain shapes in greased baking dish
(on top of pureed fruit if included).
Bake in pre-heated oven at 200°C for 10 minutes or until golden brown.
Dust with icing sugar if desired. Serve hot or cold.

Chef Finder

Crowdfunder Donors

The people below are awesome!
They saw the good in this book before it was even created. I would like to high-light that because of their generosity and trust that 100% of all sales will go towards inspiring people less fortunate

Agathe Delannoy
Aimee Gouk
Alan Watson
Alastair Creamer
Alastair Storey
Alessandro Mazza
Alexandra Ghinea
Amanda Callis
Andrew Pond
Anna Creed
Anthony Blades
Anton Edelmann
Anya Fearn
Becki Lovelady
Ben Purton
Bini Ludlow
Bob Pearson
Carol and Eddie Boyle
Carol Ingham
Caroline Talboys
Cecilia Judge
Charles Coldrey-Mobbs
Chris Maidment
Claire Webber
Clare Gillbanks
Claudia Nazer
Colin Brown
Daniel Wade
Darren Brittle
David Boyle
David Rodgett
David Smail

Diane Lyne
Duncan/Extract Coffee Roasters
Duncan Buxton
Elena Sharp
Fiona Rose
Fiona Statham
Gemma Waugh
Grant Strydom
Helen Mary Birtill
Hope Boyle
Ian & Mary Somerville
Jade Purewal
Jane Totten
Jeni Edwards
Jo Pisani
Jo Richardson
Joachim Mason
Joseph Boyle
Kate Gerrard
Kathryn Haworth
Katie Allen/Creme Conferences
Kieron Tarling
Linda Friend
Linda Jenkins
Lucy and Alex Thiel
Lucy Crofts
Marie Broad
Marion Sutherland
Mark Rachovides
Matthew Timmons
Melanie Pay
Michael Driscoll

Michele Cole
Michele Lynch
Michelle Pattison
Mike Stringer
Millie Street Allen
Monica Or
Nathan Sawyer
Nick Boyle
Nick Cromwell
Oliver Hatch
Patrick Brooks
Paul Carter
Paul Drummond
Paul Mason
Paul Preston
Peter Barcham
Phillippa Rose
Rebecca Morjaria
Richard Oldfield
Rosalyn Sharp
Sean Good
Sean Malone
Sharlene Sebo
Simon Houston
Steve Cox
Susan Osborne
Susan Richards
Tomas Sharp
Vicky Williams
Vitacress Limited
Wendy Bartlett
WSH Foundation

Acknowledgements

Firstly, I want to take this opportunity to thank my team. They're a group of exceptional individuals who have been relentless with their resolve to support challenged individuals during these challenging times.

To the chefs, without which we could not have prepared such an elaborate book, and so quickly – you have been incredible to jump in and support at such short notice and supply us with such great recipes.

To our collaborators and networkers, thank you for connecting furiously via social media, email and phone calls.

Thanks also to our apprentices – for your socially-distanced recipe shoots – and to the photographers for giving up their time.

Here are the names of just some of those who helped bring it all about (with apologies to any I may have missed – you know who you are):

Aviva Community Fund	Madeleine Bevan
Alastair Storey	Maddy Edwards
Amanda Hill	Marcilio Silva
Audrey Michel	Martin Miles
Bernice Saltzer	Matt Austin
Cara Hobday	Millie Street Allen
Caroline Green	Nic Crilly Hargrave
Cat Levins	Neil Stephens
Flo MacCool	Nick Boyle
James Morrell	Noel Mahony
Jan Seymour	Peter Marshall
Jon Cannon	Olly Hatch
Jodi Hinds	Rebecca Dixon
Joseph Boyle	Simon Esner
Josh Sims	Sharon MacCool
Katie Allen	Sue Thompson
Leon Seraphin	Tom Lindsey
Lesya Marshall	

Simon Boyle
July 2020

Chef Media

First published in 2020 by Chef Media
Produced by Chef Media
www.chef-magazine.com
ISBN: 9781908202987
Publisher: Peter Marshall
Author: Simon Boyle
Editor: Flo MacCool
Designer: Lesia Hrebeniuk
Public Relations: Salted PR